DINKYTOWN

· FOUR BLOCKS OF HISTORY ·

BILL HUNTZICKER

Introduction by Steven Bergerson

THE History PRESS

Published by The History Press
Charleston, SC
www.historypress.net

Front cover, top: Demonstrators spent a month occupying the buildings vacated by a developer proposing Red Barn, a fast-food restaurant, in 1970. *Photo by Cheryl Walsh Bellville*; *bottom*: Varsity Theater is one of the iconic Dinkytown buildings, opened as University Theater in 1915 and expanded and remodeled with its current Art Deco façade in 1938. On the distant right is the modern Southeast Library. *Photo by Bill Huntzicker.*

First published 2016

Manufactured in the United States

ISBN 978.1.46711.963.4

Library of Congress Control Number: 2016941435

To Linda Huntzicker, the love of my life.

To my daughter, Rachel L. Huntzicker, and son, James W. Huntzicker, whose kindness and encouragement make life worth living.

To my Southeast Minneapolis neighbors, who make this city an interesting and pleasant place to live.

CONTENTS

PREFACE

Dinkytown, a four-block business district across the street from the University of Minnesota in Southeast Minneapolis, has become a Rorschach test through which people reveal their politics, their religious faiths, their team loyalties, their dining preferences, their social lives, their college memories, their transportation choices and their attitudes toward history and historic preservation.

Your Dinkytown is what you make it.

The idea of a Rorschach test came from Swiss psychiatrist Hermann Rorschach, who, as a medical student, discovered that different people reacted very differently to the inkblot art he had created as a child. Following Rorschach's death in 1922, his single scientific achievement has grown ever more valuable as a means of analyzing a subject's personality by considering what the person sees in the unstructured inkblots.

Like the inkblot test, Dinkytown also took shape in the 1920s as a distinctive business district, even though it also had a history reaching back into the nineteenth century. But questions about the value of Dinkytown's history have become the center of public debate in recent years as city officials decide whether it warrants preservation as a historic district.

Both historic preservationists and those who want to replace aging buildings with new mixed-use apartment structures say they are working to save Dinkytown.

In 2015, the Minneapolis City Council approved the intersection where Dinkytown's four square blocks meet—Fourteenth Avenue Southeast and

Fourth Street Southeast—as a small historic district. The action was both the beginning and the end of a long conflict over what historic designation actually means, what Dinkytown is and what's so important about it.

Strangely, both sides of the preservation debate declared victory after the council's vote. Both property owners seeking change and preservationists headed into a more concrete discussion of historic district guidelines to delineate how the area could change with each side working for change in its favor.

This book explores the historical context of the Dinkytown debates and, relying on both historical research and personal interviews, tries to figure out what Dinkytown means.

Historical designation focuses on buildings or districts—what to save, what to demolish, what to rebuild. In Minnesota, historical designation requires a "period of significance," such as the era of sawmills and flour mills around St. Anthony Falls where two towns—Minneapolis and St. Anthony, each with its own side of the Mississippi River—were founded. Dinkytown's history lacks a single period of significance. Its buildings, several of which date back to the nineteenth century, have been recycled, reused and sometimes rebuilt over the 150 years since the University of Minnesota's rebirth in 1867. Of course, their meaning has changed as the people and culture changed within them.

For some recent residents who have moved on after college graduation, Dinkytown represents a district they have outgrown—a place where college students partied and once or twice even got carried away after Gopher sporting events at the nearby TCF Bank Stadium (built in 2009).

A few quality restaurants continue to harken back to the days when Dinkytown was a destination for a quiet evening out.

For earlier generations, it represented a district of coffee shops and bookstores that spawned beat poets, folk music and antiwar and civil rights movements. The Minnesota Eight planned their break-ins of draft offices around the state in a nearby church.

Sometimes, the politics was more than protest movements. Hubert Humphrey planned his initial run for Minneapolis mayor in a nearby apartment. Former vice president Walter Mondale continued in 2016 to meet colleagues at local restaurants to discuss law and politics.

Bob Dylan slept here in his transition from being Bobby Zimmerman from the Iron Range in northern Minnesota to becoming major icon in the national folk scene. Dinkytown's folk and blues music scene, though, was probably fully formed when he arrived.

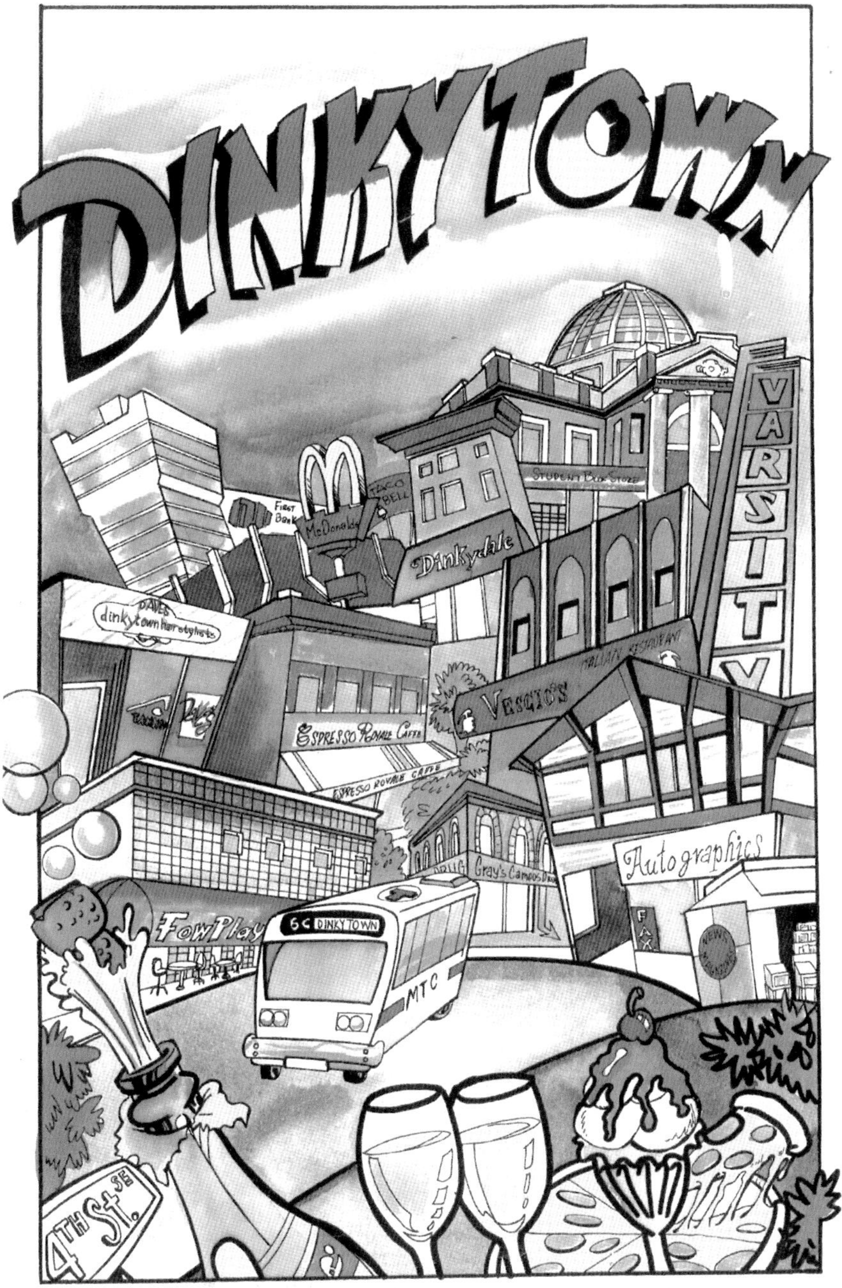

This Dinkytown poster was created by Shawn Van Briesen in the early 1990s for Autographics and the Dinkytown Business Association. *Courtesy Skott Johnson, former Autographics owner and former DBA president.*

Actor Lea Thompson attended Marshall University High School and danced with the Minnesota Dance Theatre of Dinkytown before moving on to forty-five performances with the American Ballet Theatre on her way to becoming star of the *Back to the Future* movies, the television series *Caroline in the City* and other notable accomplishments.

John (Woz) Keith Wozniak lived with his parents a block from Dinkytown when he attended nearby Marcy Open School, whose playground inspired the name (Marcy Playground) of his grunge alternative rock group whose single "Sex and Candy" broke records on some pop charts in 1997.

Returning World War II veterans and other students met with their professors over coffee here in the 1950s. High school students from the suburbs hung out with beat wannabes in the days when caffeine outsold alcohol. Students went elsewhere to imbibe because Minneapolis liquor control laws severely restricted the sale of booze. During the transition, though, pizza parlors, including Rocky Rococo and Pizza Hut, had electronic game rooms that attracted students from high schools.

People from around the nation, including many university graduates, appeared during the debates over historic preservation to demonstrate that Dinkytown has a strong character, but what the character has been remains open to debate. And this lack of consensus became an argument against historic preservation.

Nonetheless, local researchers sought to demonstrate that these four blocks made significant contributions to the city's history. Dinkytown hosted returning veterans in the 1940s and 1950s, stimulated a major folk culture in the 1960s and spawned civil rights and antiwar leaders in the 1970s. City officials were less interested in these findings than in an earlier period that saw the construction of buildings along major streetcar lines because the state's historic district designation required identifying a period of significance. Like politicians in other cities, the city council members, who have the last word on historic designation and design issues, designated buildings that looked historical to them. Activities within people's memories seemed more like nostalgia than history.

I have lived in the Marcy-Holmes Neighborhood almost continuously since 1968, when I moved here after graduating from Montana State University in my home state at the time. In the beginning, I wasn't thinking about Dinkytown's history, but I've seen many changes over the decades, participated in writing the neighborhood's long-range comprehensive plan and reported on the recent debates on historic preservation.

ACKNOWLEDGEMENTS

The author seeks forgiveness from the people I'm about to mention for any errors, slights, oversights or mistakes in fact or judgment and from those willing people I didn't get to interview in the time allowed.

I owe a huge debt to my wife, Linda Huntzicker, without whom I would not have the time to do this project.

The people at the Special Collections department at the Minneapolis Central branch of the Hennepin County Library were essential to getting this project completed. They have wonderful files, and they were amazingly helpful and patient with my naïve questions.

Susan Hoffman and her staff at the University of Minnesota Archives have also been incredibly patient and helpful. She has helped me locate many obscure photos and bits of information.

Susan Larson-Fleming and the other staff members at the Hennepin History Museum have collected material that some traditional librarians overlooked. They were also generous in sharing their material and their time with me. The staff of the John R. Borchert Map Library, University of Minnesota Libraries, brought maps and delightful historical documents and taught me how much you can learn just from looking at maps. They have many maps linked from their website.

It would be impossible to overstate the value of Penny A. Petersen and Ted Tucker to our neighborhood and to my work. They are a valuable source of encouragement and they conduct important work for the neighborhood—Ted with his many years managing and editing the *Southeast* newspaper and, later on, the city's planning commission working for livable neighborhoods and

Penny with her important histories and historical research. Both Penny and Ted provided much help and needed encouragement.

Steven Bergerson could have written this book. Some of his work from the 1970s was published in the *Southeast* newspaper and the *Minnesota Daily*. His manuscript and additional notes and photographs in the University of Minnesota Archives in the Elmer L. Andersen Library are readable and entertaining. If the sample of Dinkytown history in this book whets your appetite, try out Bergerson's box of materials at the archives. He generously shared his photographs taken in the 1970s and the aerial photo from 2016.

Melissa Bean, who left her position as executive director of the Marcy-Holmes Neighborhood Association after twenty-seven years of service to the neighborhood, has been patient and helpful with my varied inquiries. And thanks to photographer Cheryl Walsh Bellville for sharing her photos of the Red Barn protests.

Tom H. Swain generously shared his old family photos and stories with me. He has the oldest photos of Dinkytown I've ever seen. Thanks also to Miriam, David and Joseph Butwin for trying to help me understand the challenges their parents faced in translation of classic Yiddish works.

I'm grateful to Kristen Eide-Tollefson, Barbara Camm, Ossian Or, Britt Aamodt and others who have worked so hard to collect Dinkytown stories and artifacts, to preserve Dinkytown's history and to encourage me personally. And to principal city planner Haila Maze, who exhibits extraordinary patience in balancing the many interests in planning and answering questions along the way. Al Milgrom has also shared photographs and patiently answered questions from someone who is clueless about film.

The *Twin Cities Daily Planet* (tcdailyplanet.net) provided me the opportunity to write and publish about the Dinkytown debates. I was a volunteer reporter for the *Daily Planet* when I began some of the reporting that appears here.

And to all the people I have interviewed and named in this project and to those I have interviewed and didn't get worked into the manuscript and to those I have not yet interviewed, I have the best of intentions. Much is yet to be done on Dinkytown's quirky history. The city and the neighborhood will continue to write its history as we decide which physical portions of it are worth preserving and in what ways.

On a personal and spiritual level, I must thank my teachers Professor David W. Noble, now emeritus from the University of Minnesota American studies program, and Professor and Rabbi Joseph A. Edelheit, now emeritus from St. Cloud State University. The regular discussions I have with these two intellectual and spiritual giants help me stay somewhat sane in this insane world.

Introduction

RECOLLECTIONS OF THE HISTORY OF SOUTHEAST MINNEAPOLIS

When we were students at the University of Minnesota in the 1970s, I told Pat Flood that Bob Dylan had lived in Dinkytown. She said, "Wow, Bob Dylan lived here?" At the time, most of what I knew about Dinkytown came from Al Bergstrom over the counter of Al's Breakfast. We continued the conversation, and our mutual interest in the history of Dinkytown blossomed. Soon Pat and I were peeling back the layers of the onion that is Dinkytown. We found that the roots of Dinkytown extended to the university, into the neighborhood and ultimately back to the birth of the city.

The roots of Dinkytown were the roots of our city. The Falls of St. Anthony where sawmills turned logs into lumber became the engine of the industry. The falls hummed with sawmills that could cut two-by-fours precisely. The lumber was used for building stores and houses and ultimately hauled away by trains and sold to bring wealth to the area. The falls milled the lumber, the trains hauled it away, money came back, more track was laid, flour mills were built, trains brought in wheat and the whole lumber/flour industry blossomed. The "barons" ran the mills and sold the lumber and flour, and the industries blossomed. But in this blossoming there were stories that today we can hardly imagine.

Imagine the wonderful experience of sitting on a pile of slab wood on a clear winter night, looking up at myriad stars and listening to the roar of the falls. This was before the bright lights of the city and twenty-four-hour traffic.

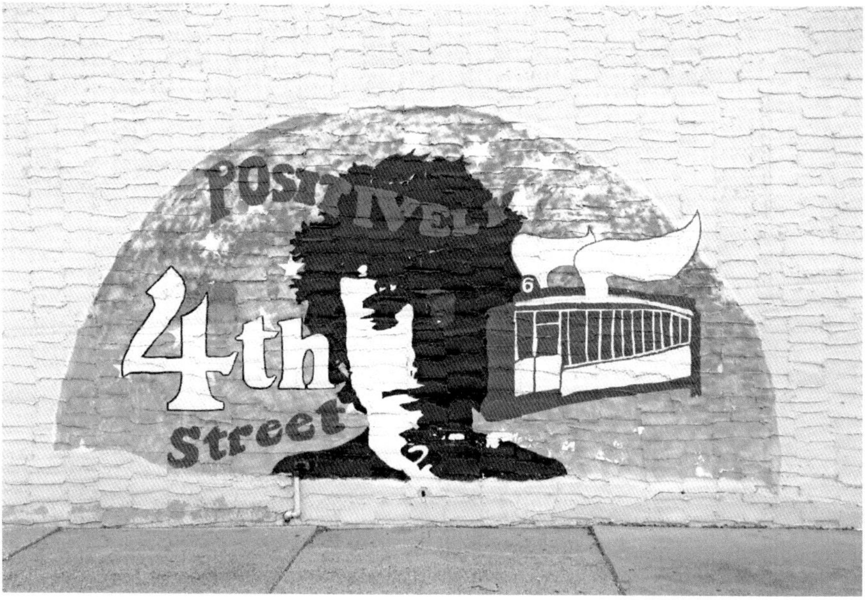

Student Serge Trobotsky painted this mural on the building at 1300 Fourth Street Southeast to represent Dinkytown icons Bob Dylan and the streetcars. *Photo by Bill Huntzicker.*

Imagine the men who pulled up stakes in the East and came to start a new life. Isaac Atwater became editor of the *St. Anthony Express*, a Supreme Court judge and a regent to the newly formed university. John S. Pillsbury started out selling hardware, but he eventually became an alderman, a legislator, a regent to the university and, ultimately, "Father of the University." They all have their stories; Pat and I fell in love with these stories.

But this story is about the university and the streetcars and the stores that sprang up at a corner in Southeast Minneapolis. It was a corner where you could buy coal or drugs or groceries and eventually school supplies and bicycles; it was an intersection where you could rent a horse and buggy for a day. By the 1890s, you could board a train at Fourteenth and University Avenues and go to New York or Seattle, and there was a boardinghouse at Thirteenth Avenue and Fourth Street that served six hundred meals a day. The real story is the people. It is the spirit of these people that brought together so many disparate forces from so many directions to create one of the great educational institutions of our country. They brought educational ideas from Europe, financial support from the industry of the falls and an attitude that encouraged students to think and explore.

William Watts Folwell brought ideas about education that germinated under Napoleon during the French Revolution and grew in German universities. Ideas Folwell presented at his first address in 1869 still fit perfectly in our twenty-first century. In the 1880s, Cyrus Northrop brought exciting ideas about education and politics from the East Coast. Pillsbury shepherded the wealth of the industries into education. His own children helped form the first fraternity and the first sorority. Professor Maria Sanford championed women's rights and supported the education of blacks long before it was popular to do so. These people and others came together in the community and at the university to create an environment where ideas flourished.

There was a special spirit shared by these people who together took a deserted campus with one empty building in the 1860s and turned it into one of the largest universities in our country with the largest student newspaper in the world barely fifty years later. These were the people who passed through what would become Dinkytown, walking from their homes or getting off the streetcar and crossing the footbridge to the campus. The bridge over the five tracks of the Great Northern Railway between Fourth Street Southeast and University Avenue was pedestrian only until 1901–2, when the Pillsbury Gates were built and the Fourteenth Avenue Bridge was widened to allow vehicle traffic. Dinkytown became the entrance to the university, but it also became the place where students gathered, shopped and spent casual time. This spirit became the spirit of Dinkytown through the entire twentieth century.

At the beginning of the twentieth century, there was a strong university with an established Greek system, and students enjoyed football at a new stadium. During the '20s and '30s, Dinkytown was a center for students, with bonfires at homecoming, snake dances and local characters like "Stiffey" selling overpriced malts and sodas during the Depression. Then came World War II, when University Avenue was closed so soldiers could practice marching, and Nicholson Hall was dubbed "USS Minnesota" as Minnesota did not have a battleship in the U.S. fleet. When the GI Bill brought soldiers who had traveled the corners of the world back to the U, the soldiers brought thoughts and ideas, forming the foundation of the writer/poet/intellectual movement that coalesced after the war. Then there were the coffeehouses and bookstores. There were readings and poetry and music. Dinkytown was the perfect place for Dylan, a place where he could think, learn, create and grow—an environment where he could flourish, and flourish he did.

It is now 160-plus years since Fourth Street and C Street (Fourteenth Avenue Southeast) were charted and surveyed on the north side of Tuttle

Creek and a block away from what would become one of the great universities of our country. How this corner developed and grew into Dinkytown is a rich and fascinating story that needs to be told—one that I have always wanted to tell but that needed more research than I felt I had time to do. I am proud that Bill has incorporated the research Pat and I did over 40 years ago and expanded it with even more historical research. I hope the work that Bill has done gives you an understanding of the germinating, budding and blossoming of Dinkytown. It is a fascinating story.

STEVEN BERGERSON

1
A HISTORIC NEIGHBORHOOD

Clearly, Dinkytown will not be an ordinary historic district.

For starters, it became the fourth historic district—three previously designated—in the same Marcy-Holmes Neighborhood in Southeast Minneapolis. The oldest, of course, is the St. Anthony Falls Historic District that straddles the Mississippi River where the first lumber and flour mills were built as early as the 1820s. This district comprises eight thousand acres, thirty-nine buildings and fourteen other structures that preserve, recall and re-create elements of the world's largest flour-milling industry from 1880 to 1930 around the falls.

The Fifth Street Southeast Historic District, from about Fourth Avenue Southeast east to I-35W, seeks to preserve some of the oldest homes in Minneapolis, where many of the city's founders lived. They built their homes along Fifth Street in what was then a pioneer village called St. Anthony. The merchant families, mostly from New England, built architecturally distinguished and aesthetically exciting homes that were near their businesses along the riverfront in St. Anthony.

One of those founders, John Sargent Pillsbury, built a mansion at Tenth Avenue Southeast and Fifth Street Southeast that later became home to presidents of the University of Minnesota and a center of social life of the campus five blocks away. Getting to the president's house from the campus required travel through the blocks that were later known as Dinkytown.

In the first three decades of the twentieth century, large homes for Greek organizations were built throughout the neighborhood but concentrated

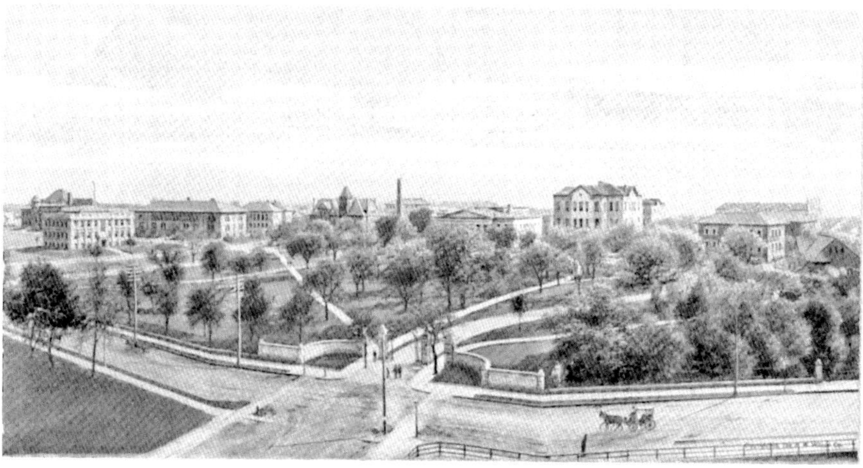

H.W. Wilson company shows the campus after Pillsbury Gate in 1902 and before Old Main burned in 1904. *Courtesy University Archives, University of Minnesota, Twin Cities.*

in a "Fraternity and Sorority Row," the third historic district between Fifteenth and Nineteenth Avenues Southeast across University Avenue from the campus. This University of Minnesota Greek Letter Chapter House Historic District was designated in 2003. Rapid growth of the university from 212 students in 1870 to 17,500 by 1930 stimulated the growth of Greek-letter chapters.

The first was founded in 1874, and the growth of Greek societies led to a demand for new houses, with twenty-two fraternity and eleven sorority houses built in the area between 1907 and 1930. Many of them retain their original façades and interiors symbolic of their desired permanence.

Thus, Dinkytown was only one part of an eclectic neighborhood, even though it defines the neighborhood for many of the students and others who pass through. On its website, the Marcy-Holmes Neighborhood Association also lists the "different urban character" of each area of the neighborhood.

They are the Riverfront, where the city began and became a behemoth of industrial agriculture; the West Side of I-35W, a quiet residential area with diverse housing styles, including Fifth Street Southeast; and the Ninth Street Southeast Industrial area, a favorite walking and biking destination that was once industrial and may soon see new businesses and more midrise mixed-use development like those buildings which have recently divided Dinkytown.

The East Side of I-35W "relates closely to the University of Minnesota—most of the housing, retail, and services within this area cater to students, faculty, staff and others associated with university life," and of course, "the Dinkytown business district serves the neighborhood, campus area, and region with an eclectic mix of businesses—as it has for over 100 years."

Although a century makes a nice round number, Dinkytown as a business district has been around for a lot longer than that; on the other hand, the name Dinkytown appears to have been around for much less time.

2

WHAT'S IN A NAME?

Curious about the name Dinkytown, a reader wrote to the *Minneapolis Star* for an explanation in the 1970s. "We got as many explanations as persons we talked to on your query," a columnist responded on April 14, 1973. "We asked Melvin McCosh, a former long-time Dinkytown book dealer, who said the name comes from a man named Grodnik, who in 1902 owned the building where Gray's Drugstore is now. McCosh said that Grodnik is a Slavic name, a variation of which means tiny village, hence Dinkytown."

McCosh, who lived in a Victorian house at the corner of Fifth Street and Fourteenth Avenue Southeast, operated a long-standing bookstore that shared a building with Bridgeman's ice cream parlor and restaurant at the corner of Fourteenth and Fourth Streets. McCosh worked at being a nonconformist by posting anti-holiday and other rebellious posters in his window. Residents remember him posting a sign during university homecoming telling visitors to go home. Nonetheless, loyal customers showed up to support him when Bridgeman's landlord evicted him to expand the restaurant. Among the tenants in the rented rooms upstairs of McCosh's home a block away were bookseller Bill Breer and civil rights activist Marv Davidov.

Although the name Grodnik is carved above the door of the Loring Café, McCosh may have associated the name with eastern European and Russian cities that end in *K*, or he simply made up the idea as one of his many jokes. Local news media occasionally revisit the name's origins. Ruth Hammond consulted a language professor for the *Minneapolis Tribune* and reported on

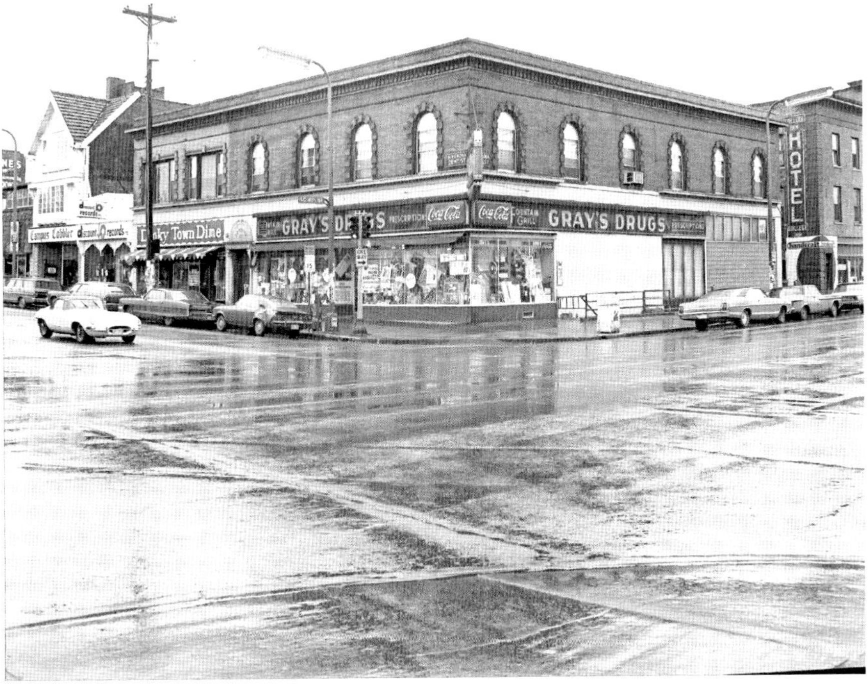

Streetcar tracks remained in the street when Steven Bergerson took this photo in the 1970s with Dinky Town Dime to the left of Gray's Drug and College Inn on the right. *Photo courtesy Bergerson, from his collection housed in the University Archives, Elmer L. Andersen Library, University of Minnesota.*

October 8, 1977, that the word *Grodnik* in Russian refers not to the small town but to a person who came from a town.

A Wikipedia entry for Dinkytown, however, elaborated on the Grodnik hypothesis:

> *"Grodnik," meaning a small (or dinky) town. The name of the early owner was Louis Grodnik. He owned a haberdashery at that location and built the building. His brother, Hela Grodnik, always claimed that he was the one who named the area when he said that "This is getting to be a real 'Dinky Town.'" Hela then went on to work for another brother, Jacob Grodnik, at Grodnik Jewelry at Seventh and Hennepin downtown. Louis also owned a haberdashery at Fourth and Hennepin known as "Grodnik and Fassbinder."*

Reflecting McCosh, this view sees *grod* meaning "town," as in Stalingrad and Leningrad, and *nik* is a diminutive, making the result a small or dinky town. The online encyclopedia also suggested that the name came from a popular Gopher football player Frank "Dinky" Rog, who had a large circle of friends in the area in the late 1940s and early 1950s.

But Wikipedia's first hypothesis is the most widely acknowledged and believed: "It's a small town-like area; everything is within walking distance." In forty-five years of asking people about Dinkytown, filmmaker Al Milgrom found many students, especially those from small towns, who found in Dinkytown a place to feel comfortable. It became a refuge from and contrast to the larger, more impersonal adjacent University of Minnesota campus—one of the two largest urban campus in the nation.

The *Minneapolis Star* writer also cited other prominent local sources:

> *The late Ed Perine, who owned Perine's Campus Book Center, once said the name came from two men who ran a dry-cleaning shop in Dinkytown. But John Fallon, one of the twins who owned the shop, said it was called Dinkytown when they got there. Then we talked to Al Bergstrom, owner of Al's Breakfast, and he believes the name came from a tiny railroad way-station in the area where workers got off to go to nearby grain elevators and flour mills years ago. He said the way station was called Dinkytown.*

Steven Bergerson, who has done as much Dinkytown research as anyone, subscribes to Al Bergstrom's theory about the railyard but relates it to switch engines called Dinkys, or Dinkeys.

The railroad trench through Dinkytown remains one of its defining characteristics, even though bicycles and pedestrians far outnumber trains there today. Al's diner still keeps prepaid books so customers can pay ahead for meals; employees say this practice goes back to a time when railroad workers constituted a large portion of the clientele.

Dinkytown folklore also applies the name to the small trolleys, particularly the ones on the line connecting the campuses in Minneapolis and St Paul. Those streetcars were sometimes called Dinkys.

A news item in the *St. Paul Sunday Globe* of July 7, 1895, reports weather damage and illustrates the importance of the area, the railroads and the dinkies.

> *An Interurban car was almost in the middle of a string of poles that went down, but escaped without damage, and was afterwards trundled down to the Milwaukee tracks and run down to the Minneapolis East side station.*

> *The ten Interurban cars which were cut off at the Minneapolis end were put on the east side lines, and a set of "dinkies" manned for the Interurban service, which had the advantage of being reversible. Passengers to St Paul had to walk from the Milwaukee tracks to Twenty-eighth avenue, where they took the Interurban cars again for the rest of the trip.*

The article also said there was undetermined amount of storm damage to the university's farm in St. Anthony Park.

The *Star* in 1973 also contacted Oscar Mohn, who had been a barber in Dinkytown for almost fifty years, and Maury Bernstein, a longtime Dinkytown resident and musician. "They think the name came from a movie theater called the Dinky which was there 50 years ago. Mohn said people used to say, 'Let's go down to the Dinky.' The word dinky also was a 'cool,' 'in' word at that time, like people use the term 'far out' today," Bernstein said. Then in about 1940, the Dinky Town Dime started and the name stuck. "'It wasn't until the Dinky Town Dime hung out its shingle that the name caught on,' Bernstein said."

"So, take your pick of the explanations," the *Star* concluded. "The Minnesota and Hennepin County Historical Societies couldn't come up with any different ones."

The *Minnesota Daily* once offered a more confident, definitive explanation. "The name did not come all at once according to Bob Hanson, who owns the House of Hanson grocery and claims to be 'the oldest living businessman in Dinkytown.'" World War II veterans returning in droves to complete both high school and college made the name popular. "Dinky" had become connected with the area a few years earlier, Hanson explained.

> *"Some people say other things, but I was around here long enough to remember. There used to be the University Theatre where the Varsity is now.*
>
> *"It was a small theatre with four or five rows on each side and an aisle down the middle. It was pretty small so everyone called it 'dinky.' So when people talked about going to the movies they talked about 'going to the dinky,'" Hanson said.*

In his manuscript in the University Archives, Steven Bergerson said another theater, called the Dinky, opened at 1417 Fourth Street in 1913 and remained there until 1918, "when it was converted to a repair shop for automobiles. This theatre was half the size of the original Varsity Theatre, then called the University Theatre, which opened in 1915. Oscar Mohn, who

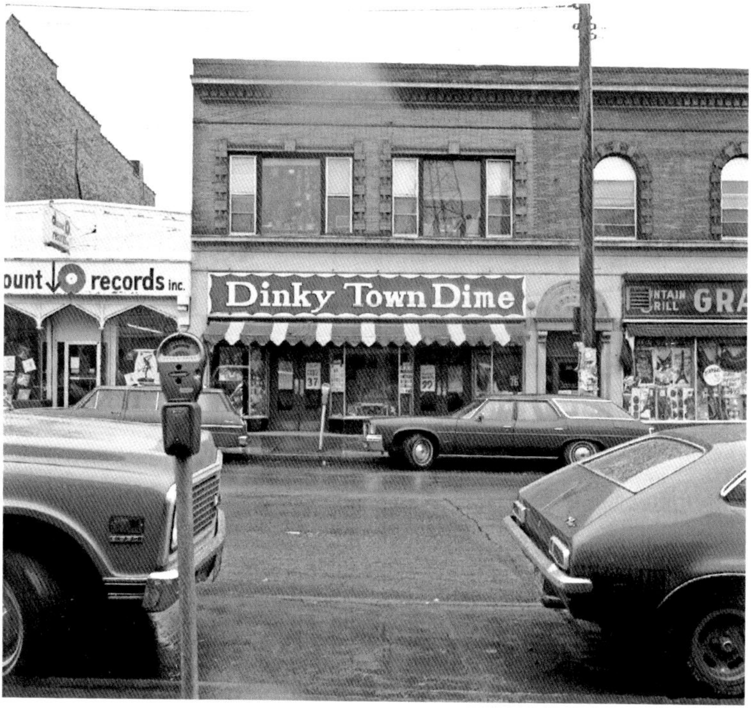

This page: Dinky Town Dime and Gray's Drug, prominent stores since the late 1940s. *Photos by Steven Bergerson housed in the University Archives, Elmer L. Andersen Library, University of Minnesota.*

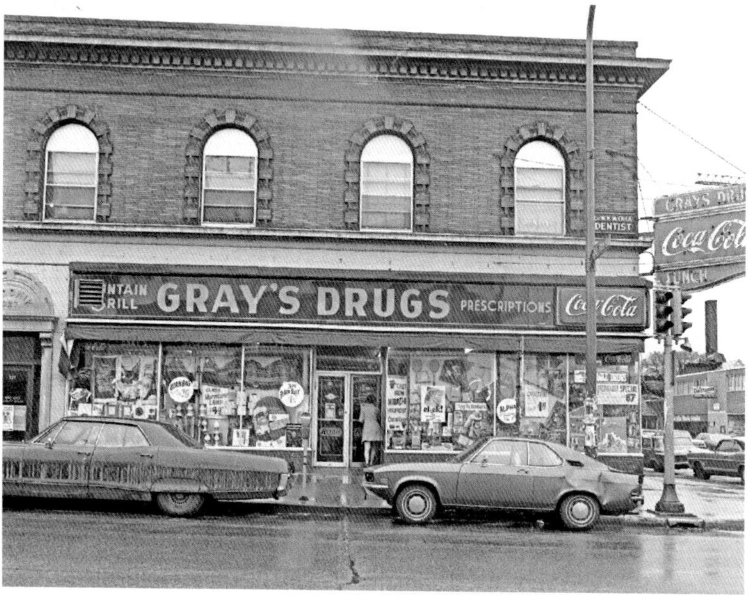

started barbering in 1919, said the theatre at 1417 was called the 'Dinky,' though Harvey Goldstein said the University-Varsity theatre was also called the 'Dinky' in the thirties."

"Al Johnson recalls some young men at his fraternity saying they were going to 'Dinkytown' in 1929 and no one knew where that was," Bergerson wrote. "Maybe the name came from the fraternities. Someone said that the name was actually shortened from Dinky Downtown, as Fourth and Fourteenth was the first shopping area outside of downtown."

Jennie Isabelle Hiscock should have known something about the name when *Minneapolis Tribune* reporter Dave Wood wrote about her on July 14, 1979, after she had lived in the same nearby house for ninety-three years. "And the name Dinkytown! Ugh! When a student who lived with me came home calling it Dinkytown—I forget just when—I was disgusted. But I guess it's an appropriate name—the stores certainly aren't very lovely." The names have changed, she said, but "the people around here are just as lovely as they ever were."

Wherever the name came from, each theory of the name's origin has its adherents, who are sometimes passionate about theirs being the correct view.

The first commercial use of the name, as listed in Minneapolis city directories, appeared in the directory of 1946 after the Dinky Town Dime variety store opened with Arch Fecht as manager. No business with Dinky, Dinkey or Dinkytown in the name appeared in previous Minneapolis city directories.

Dinkytown's long-standing anchor business, Gray's Drug, which was next door to the Dinky Town Dime, appeared in the directory in the same year. In 1944 and earlier, the directory listed Gray's Cut Rate Drug Store with Arnold M. Grais as manager at 1400 Franklin Avenue East. In 1946, the company added a Dinkytown branch: Gray's Cut Rate Drug Store with Worley W. Andrews, manager at 329 Fourteenth Avenue Southeast and 1413 Franklin Avenue East. In 1948, the Dinkytown store was listed as a branch of the drugstore on East Franklin. In 2016, the Loring Pasta Bar occupies the site that housed both Gray's Drug and the Dinky Town Dime.

3
GROWING WITH THE UNIVERSITY

The business district that became Dinkytown began soon after the University of Minnesota closed its original campus—then a single, barely used building—in the central business district of the small growing village of St. Anthony and moved to its current location. The towns of Minneapolis and St. Anthony grew up on the two sides of St. Anthony Falls where the two cities had competing milling industries. Franklin Steele had started his sawmill on Hennepin Island in 1848 and founded the town of St. Anthony a year later. He also provided the land for the university's first building when it was founded in 1851, but failing to turn over a clear title, he later decided he needed the land back as the town grew.

The first bridge across the Mississippi River anywhere connected the two settlements in early 1855, and the two towns merged in 1872.

The university's original site is called Richard Chute Square at 28 University Avenue Southeast in what was originally St. Anthony. The site now hosts the Ard Godfrey house, built by Godfrey for his family after they came from Maine to operate Steele's sawmill. The house has been moved several times from its original location closer to Main Street and the Mississippi River. The university's building had served mostly as a preparatory school that failed to attract many students during the hard times of the 1850s and the Civil War.

The new village near the falls appealed to visitors for both recreational and economic reasons. "In the fifties and sixties," historian Willliam Watts Folwell wrote, "Minnesota was widely advertised for its salubrious climate, exempting its citizens from malaria, pneumonia, typhoid fever, and tuberculosis. Among those who came to Minnesota seeking health was the naturalist Thoreau."

High expectations and disappointment accompanied the university's early decades. Enrollment varied, and the institution failed to attract many students, forcing the school to open with fits and starts.

The university's need to move a few blocks eastward coincided with a lack of students for higher education, the growing sectionalism of the emerging Civil War and an economic depression called the Panic of 1857. In a world devoid of other selling points, settlers in Minnesota looked to the uplifting value of scenery and the spiritual value of nature.

After several years of floundering and running up debts, the regents failed to create the Harvard on the plains that they had foreseen in their founding documents. It remained for John Sergeant Pillsbury—a prominent St. Anthony businessman who began a hardware store before joining other family members in creating a flour-milling industry that bears their name—to save the university. Taking advantage of the federal funds, Pillsbury began paying off debts, soliciting investments and cajoling legislators to finance the institution on the new site downstream from the falls. Pillsbury was both the state's governor and a member of the board of regents.

Continuing to claim that their university would put Harvard in the shade, the regents sought a site overlooking the Mississippi River near an early outlook called Cheever's Tower.

The extent to which the site had already become a tourist attraction is illustrated by the interest of prestigious visitors who stopped there on their carriage ride from St. Paul to St. Anthony after coming up the river by steamboat. As Steven J. Keillor wrote in *Grand Excursion:*

> *A mile or so from the falls they passed a ninety-foot-tall wooden observation platform, Cheever's Tower, built by the eccentric St Anthony hotel owner William A. Cheever. Some stopped to see it. The bottom was as wide as a house, some forty feet square, but higher up it partly lost in length and width what it gained in height, until it was only six feet by six feet at the top, where the Stars and Stripes waved. There was a fee of a dime to climb the stairs. Cheever placed mottos on his hotel doors and windows, and here he had painted in black letters, "Pay your dime and climb." From the top one could enjoy the "view of the country for forty miles around, embracing Fort Snelling, the Falls, the river, and a number of bright and sparkling lakes."*

The excursion celebrated the completion of the Chicago and Rock Island Railroad connecting the Atlantic Ocean and the Mississippi River in early 1854; it was cause for national celebration and an opportunity to stake a claim on the Mississippi River for antislavery forces in what was then the West. To celebrate the fact that the railroad allowed travelers to cover the entire width of the then United States in two days, two trains with nine cars each left Chicago for Rock Island, where passengers boarded seven steamboats for St. Anthony Falls to celebrate transportation and the expanding nation. Among the celebrities on the tour were New York political boss Thurlow Weed, historian Herbert Bancroft and former president Millard Fillmore with his son and daughter.

Local boosters had promoted the industrial power and potential of the falls, but many visitors were surely disappointed after the hype that had compared it to Niagara, which is ten times its height. Similarly, the view from Cheever's Tower must have disappointed any who believed claims about a forty-mile view. At the time of the excursion in 1854, St. Paul was the head of navigation, and the tower was not on the direct route between St. Paul and St. Anthony. Although most steamboat traffic could not get beyond Fort Snelling at the confluence of the Minnesota and Mississippi Rivers, there eventually was a Cheever's landing and a ferry across the river that competed with Steele whose ferry above the falls had begun as early as 1847 before the bridge was built on his site.

The excursion passengers, however, had to find their own way to St. Anthony, mostly by coach, from St. Paul. On the eve of Minnesota statehood in 1858, local residents perceived the West, which included Minnesota, as more stable than the East. "Never since Minnesota was discovered," wrote the *Falls Evening News*, "has money been so scarce as now. Almost everyone has a pile of bills but the banks which issued them have suspended or failed and the paper pictures no longer represent the 'tin.' The west was sound, Minnesota sounder and St. Anthony and Minneapolis soundest of all until the great banks of the east slammed their doors in the long faces of creditors." As a result, the newspaper continued, "Men chase each other up and down the streets to collect bills payable," in a situation the newspaper said would soon lessen the contrast between the beggar and the broker.

In the same year as the depression, 1857, the university started its new campus.

Strangely, the first building on the new site—selected because of the uplifting scenery and isolation from the growing city—faced not the river but the expanding city and a developing railroad. Industrial development

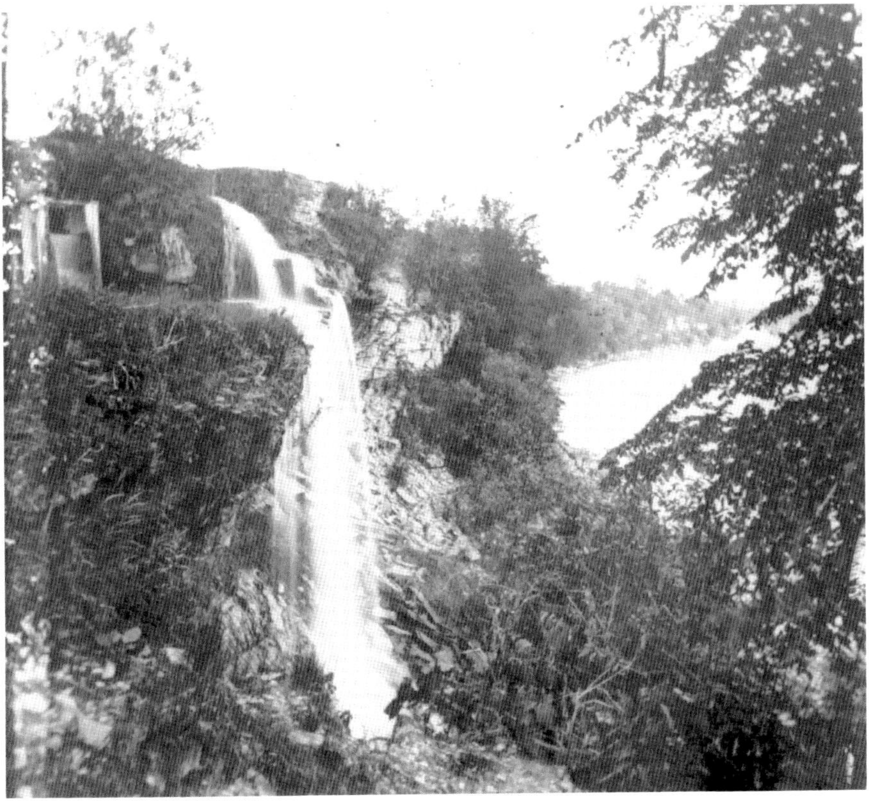

The Silver Cascade, where Tuttle's Creek (or Tuttle's Brook) emptied into the Mississippi River. *Photograph by William, H. Illingworth, 1868; courtesy special collections, Hennepin County Library.*

involved replacing a creek with a railroad and drying up a waterfall that ran into the river near where Bridge No. 9 stands today. As the campus expanded, the buildings faced the grass-covered Knoll between the "thoroughfare" in front of them and University Avenue.

Congress also granted Minnesota the authority to charter railroads, in part to meet the increasing pressure for a rail line from St. Paul to St. Anthony—two major centers of commerce in the new state. On June 28, 1862, the William Crooks locomotive traveled the ten miles between the two cities on the line operated by the St. Paul and Pacific Railroad Company. Regular service for passengers and freight began on July 2.

The William Crooks, the engine that pulled Minnesota's first railroad passengers from St. Paul to St. Anthony through the Dinkytown area, was built in New Jersey in 1861 and came up the river by steamboat for the Minnesota and Pacific Railroad that became the St. Paul and Pacific Railroad the next year. (The locomotive, named for the railroad's chief engineer, carried passengers until 1897. James J. Hill, president of the St. Paul and Pacific's successor, the Great Northern Railway, had the engine restored to pull his personal train. After later restorations, the engine, listed on the National Register of Historic Places as one of the few surviving locomotives of the Civil War era, is owned by the Minnesota Historical Society and displayed at the Lake Superior Railroad Museum in Duluth.)

In 1864, before the Civil War ended, the legislature appointed three men—Pillsbury, St. Anthony mayor Orlando Merriman and state senator John Nichols—to supersede the regents to fix the university's financial problems. As noted, Pillsbury pulled together funds from his personal fortune, the state legislative appropriations and federal land grants to pay off major university debts and to build the new campus. By 1867, the university was ready to begin anew in the fall semester with its second founding. Its first president, William Watts Folwell, was inaugurated in December 1869. Two students received the first bachelor of arts degrees in 1873, and the first doctor of philosophy degree was awarded in 1888.

When they arrived in Minnesota, Folwell and his wife boarded with a family at the corner of Second Avenue and Second Street Southeast, and the town was still known as St. Anthony. "A search for a suitable house resulted in a lease of what was known as the Fletcher House, at the corner of Fourth Street and Fourteenth Avenue. It was in part a railroad 'depot,' where the cars from St. Paul ran down onto Main Street. But it had some good rooms and was surrounded by a showy round picket fence. We remained there two, or was it three, years," Folwell recalled in the 1920s.

Folwell's memoir provides evidence that the intersection at the center of Dinkytown was an early station—some have called it a car barn—for the early horse-drawn streetcars. An 1885 plat map lists the site as Minneapolis Street Railway, the usual term for the horse-drawn system, and an 1892 Minneapolis map shows a State University Veterinary Hospital where barns once held horses for the city's streetcars. Gray's Drug Store later occupied the corner. Below the word "Northern" (above the railroad tracks in the map on page 31) is a rectangle that shows a "station" along the tracks near the university. Three railroad companies used the five tracks shown in Dinkytown. Several buildings line University Avenue Southeast between Fourteenth and Fifteenth Avenues where only one stands today. Olivet Baptist Church is on the corner of Fourth Street and Thirteenth Avenue Southeast where the Library Bar was in 2016. Housing and businesses appear to be filling in the four-block grid.

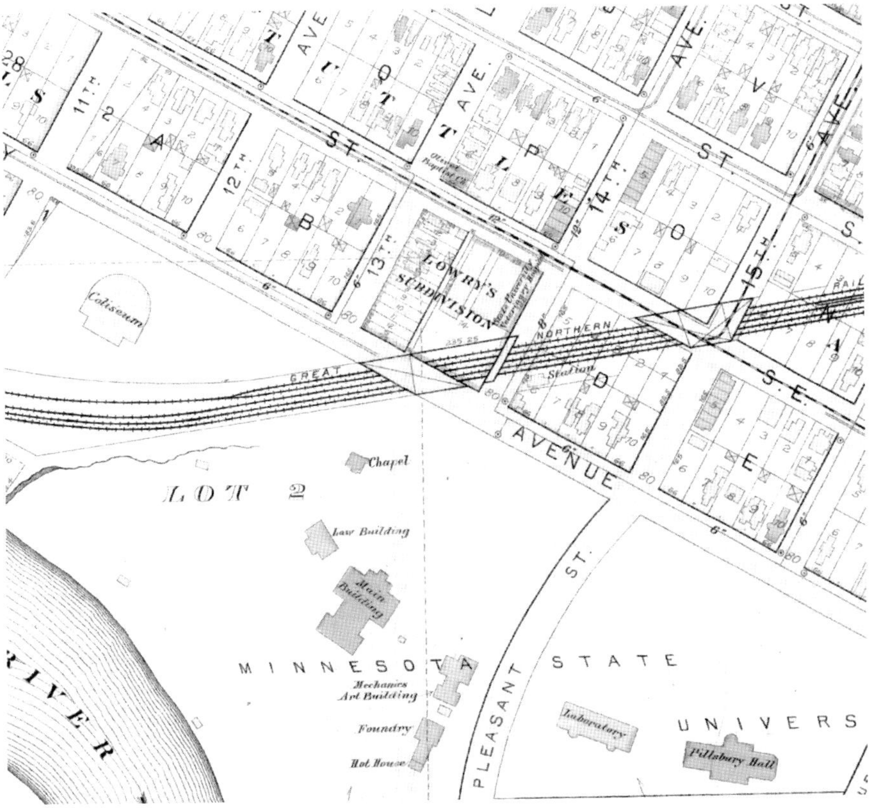

Campus buildings face Dinkytown, and a row of connected buildings appears on the 400 block of Fourteenth Avenue Southeast in this detail of an 1892 map. *Courtesy John R. Borchert Map Library, University of Minnesota Libraries.*

On campus in 1864, the sole building, Old Main, had fallen into neglect because of the economic hard times and war. A legislative committee found a family living in the building, supposedly to take care of it, with turkeys, hay and wood stored in separate rooms and the door of the basement ruined by wood splitting.

Thus, even the first building had been neglected by the time Pillsbury stepped in to rescue the campus. As University of Minnesota historian James Gray wrote:

> *The first of Pillsbury's many walks to the university must have been disheartening. He went with a committee of the legislature to see exactly what sort of untidy problem he had introduced deliberately into the neat design of his days. The news was very bad indeed. Old Main was in*

> *the quite illegal possession of a group of casual folk who became surly at having their privacy invaded. As the committee members entered one room turkeys flew at them in bewildered excitement; in another the squatters had improvised a barn loft; in the central hall the floor had been ruined by wood-splitting operations.*

Campus growth was further complicated by the railroad tracks that were later the main lines of the Northern Pacific and the Great Northern Railroads. In the early twentieth century, however, another railroad line also ran straight through university property where Morrill and Johnston Halls stand today.

The Morrill Land Grant Act allowed regents to access land for the creation of public state universities to educate the children of farmers and workers with education in "agriculture and the mechanic arts." The law was passed during the Civil War in 1862, the same year that Minnesota's leaders were distracted by the Dakota War that made travel unsafe in parts of the state.

Reflecting on Pillsbury's role, university historian Gray wrote that the former governor, state senator and business leader used his connections to make the new campus both the state's land grant college with an agricultural focus and its major higher education institution—a rare combination. And Pillsbury became protective of his investment. "For during his lifetime not a day passed that he did not walk from his home [now the official residence of the president of the university] to consult with the president of his day about matters of university policy," Gray wrote. "And often on pleasant evenings in the spring, or on nights in the coldest January, students saw him walking along the university paths almost as though he had come to see that everything was locked up properly."

At the time of these walks, the university was expanding both on campus and in its influence on surrounding neighborhoods, including Dinkytown. In the early years, though, university-related businesses grew up along University Avenue Southeast across the street and railroad from the campus, and the rest of the neighborhood became residential, mostly as St. Anthony expanded eastward. As noted earlier, a number of the founders of St. Anthony built large homes in the neighborhood, especially along what is now Fifth Street Southeast.

The aerial view photo displayed on page 33, taken in about 1924, shows the proximity of Dinkytown and the University of Minnesota to the industrial area of the Mississippi River. At the top of the scene is, at the time, the world's largest flour-milling district on both sides of St. Anthony

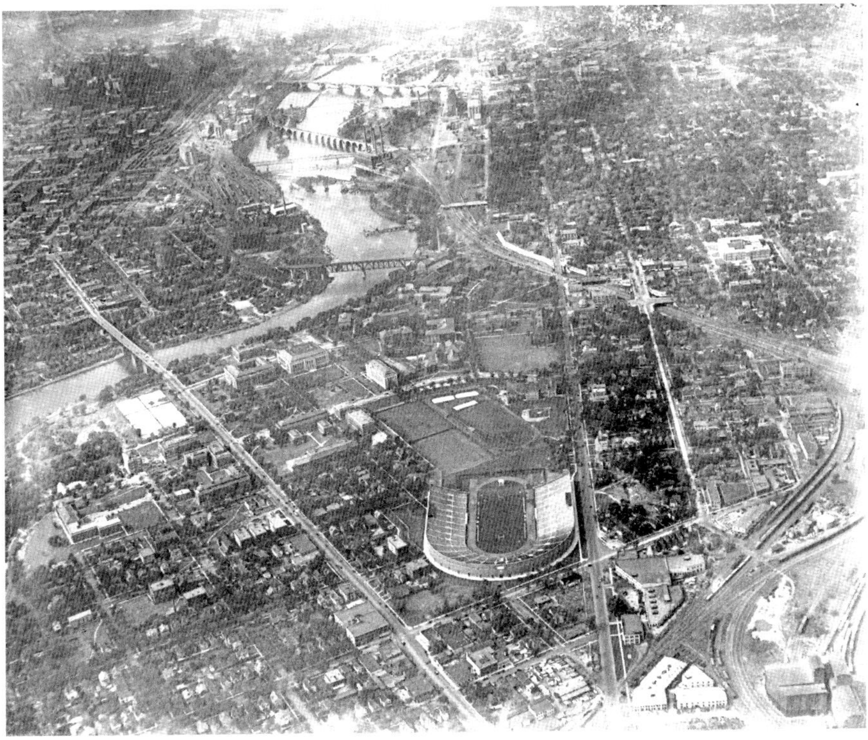

This 1924 photo (above) and detail (below) shows Dinkytown, the university, the riverfront with the bridges and St. Anthony Falls upstream in the industrial area of the Mississippi River. The detail shows a newly completed John Marshall High School on the right. *Photo courtesy University Archives, University of Minnesota, Twin Cities.*

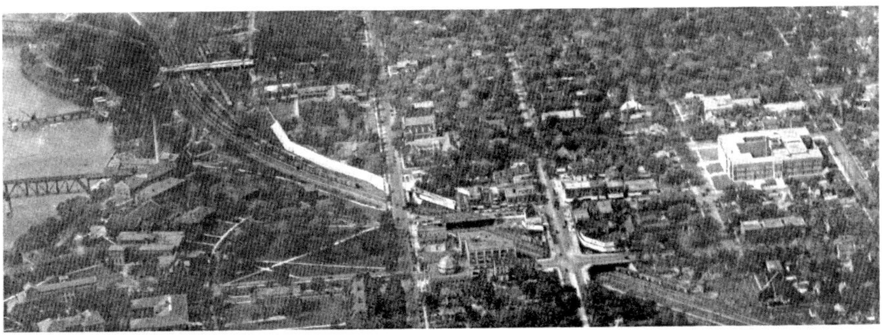

Falls. The Tenth Avenue Bridge had not yet been built, but an earlier Tenth Avenue Bridge connecting Sixth Avenue Southeast and Tenth Avenue South is shown. This bridge, which was torn down for scrap iron in World War II, still stands in this photo. Business buildings line University Avenue across from the campus where the main buildings still face the Knoll. The mall has only two or three buildings without Northrop Auditorium. In the detail, you can see the new John Marshall High School on the right, and the campus Knoll is the dark area on the left. The high school was closed in 1982 and demolished in 2013.

4
CAMPUS NEWS AND ADVERTISING

When the first student-run publication, *Ariel*, debuted in 1877, its writers reflected on "the tenth anniversary of the formal opening of the Minnesota State University," renewed the founders' optimism and advocated a student newspaper. The university's "progress during its first decade is almost unprecedented and it ranks now among the first of the American Colleges, with the exception of Harvard, Princeton, Yale and Cornell. The want of a college paper is now seriously felt by all interested in the growth and prosperity of our University."

Minnesotans needed a publication to remain informed about the university, their sons and daughters and the university's "opportunities for social culture and intellectual improvement." The writers also said they would help students, who "also need a paper which shall be an exponent of their interests." They said their noble goals surely would be worthy of support from every friend of the university. They sent out complimentary copies of the first issue with the hope of reaching subscribers and other patrons.

Like the university itself, the publication was conscious of the surrounding community and it sometimes moralized and lectured fellow students, often in one-liners. In a column criticizing people for writing in library books, the *Ariel* wrote: "A true lover of books will treat them with as much respect and regard as he will his sweetheart." Like other columns, this one reflects the dominance of men on campus.

Ariel columns mix similar short factual tidbits from both local observations and exchange publications, longer essays that could be excerpts from students' English papers, updates on employment of recent graduates, rumors, inside information and jokes, humor and attempts at humor.

Occasionally, it's hard to tell the difference between fact and opinion, seriousness and humor. One example of supposed humor is this excerpt from when a major pathway in the campus was being built: "The new walk is very promiscuous in its construction. Stones, gravel, rocks and dirt, hold equal sway on its varied surface. Probably the work is experimental, the object begun to find out which kind of material will make the best walk. From the general result we should judge they haven't found the right article yet."

And there's this comment, made as the university completed its library collection: "The University recently purchased about three hundred books for the library. They look old enough, dirty enough and dog-eared to be standard works, which they probably are." In a subsequent issue, *Ariel* clarified this item, saying the books were not dog-eared and dirty and that the library was clean.

The back page of the twelve-page paper is devoted to advertising, and it suggests that Dinkytown did not yet exist as a separate business district in 1877. None of the addresses for businesses on the advertising page is in Dinkytown. Instead, they are on Washington Avenue South across the river and on Nicollet and Hennepin Avenues in downtown Minneapolis. One advertisement runs across the top of the back page stating, "Buy your Groceries and Cigars of Wesley Neill: 38 Washington ave. S., Minneapolis: A large stock and complete assortment."

With the exception of the one-line ad across the top of the page, the entire second column—the middle of three columns—is a display advertisement for Gaslin, Wales & Chute's. A boldface heading tops the column targeting the campus, "University Headquarters," downtown on Nicollet Avenue is the "Largest and Finest Book and Stationery House in the City." The store claims to have a complete stock of textbooks always on hand, a full line of mathematical instruments and drawing tools, the lowest prices and guaranteed satisfaction. "Our Mr. Wales has been East several weeks, and has selected the largest, finest, cheapest and most varied assortment of HOLIDAY GOODS ever brought to Minneapolis. Our prices are the VERY LOWEST. Do not buy until you have visited us./Gaslin, Wales & Chute,/125 Nicollet ave., opposite Post Office."

The following ad also beckons students: "If you want a first class hair cut or a good shave, give C.F. Wilkins, under First National Bank, a call, and be satisfied. He makes a specialty of keeping First Class Workmen." Although this advertiser assumed the reader knew these buildings, subsequent advertisements on the page gave addresses, mostly downtown on Nicollet, Hennepin or Washington Avenues South.

After the cities of Minneapolis and St. Anthony merged in 1872, the St. Anthony side of the river became East Minneapolis, even though parts of it were actually north of downtown. Southeast Minneapolis includes the university and neighborhoods surrounding the campus—University District (later called Marcy-Holmes), Southeast Como and Prospect Park/ East River Road.

A dry goods ad for E. Parker (East Side) is the first *Ariel* reference to a business belonging to a neighborhood on the university's side of the river. The East Side is that part of Minneapolis east of the Mississippi River, and Northeast is north of East Hennepin Avenue.

Ariel reads like a small-town community newspaper blending the campus and community, as can be seen in an obituary in its second issue dated December 19, 1877:

> *Harry E. Young*
> *There is seldom a more painful office than to record the premature death of an acquaintance and friend, cut off suddenly in the midst of a strong and promising young life. Harry Young, the subject of this Memoir, died at his Uncle's residence, on University Avenue, on Monday December 3d. after an illness of but one hour caused by a fall from the framework covering the stone piers now in process of erection for the East Channel Bridge.*
>
> [He was a former university student and] *a youth of uncommon stability of character, manly, grave, trustworthy, even-tempered, mature in his manners and free from every vice. These qualities promised a serious and useful manhood, and the more so as they were united to a strong well-developed body, and a prepossessing presence. We must regret the rash courage with which he ventured into danger, but he has left a memory full of satisfaction for what he was. Having gone, we have laid him away to rest with the hope and belief that his young life will find its truest fruition and perfection in the world of the infinite.*

In its second issue, *Ariel* also celebrated its first issue as a success, apologized for numerous typographical errors in the first issue (some of which may remain in the quotes above) and listed details of its operation with John H. Lewis as managing editor.

"The editorial office of *Ariel* is in room 35, on the first floor, where we will be glad to see any of our friends on business; and where all contribution and offerings from the good people of Minneapolis and St. Paul in the form of tables, easy chairs, settees, writing desks, opera, lecture and concert tickets, cigars, etc., will be received with becoming editorial grace and modesty." This note seems to assume that readers all know that the office is in the single campus building, Old Main. "*Ariel* is published monthly during the college year, by the Senior and Junior Classes of the Minnesota University. Terms, $1.00, always in advance, per volume of ten numbers. Communications for publication should be addressed to M.D. Taylor, University, Minneapolis, Minnesota."

5

THE UNIVERSITY COMMUNITY

In the summer of 1878, I bought what was known as the Moulton House on the corner of Fifth Street and Tenth Avenue Southeast, which is still our home," Folwell wrote in his 1920s memoir. "The house had been built in three portions under different roofs—the front part in 1857, and that was simply known as 'the house.' There was a very showy fence on the street side of the property, but the gate had nothing but an iron rail suspended on a chain to keep it closed." The property, listed as 1020 Fifth Street Southeast in his memoir, is now part of the Delta Gamma sorority, on the corner of Fifth Street and Eleventh Avenue Southeast.

"The student body was always respectful and responded to the social invitations to our house, to find Mrs. Folwell a most gracious hostess," Folwell wrote, indicating a close relationship between students and staff. In fact, he occasionally personally checked out neighborhood rental housing to determine whether it was acceptable for students.

Toward the end of his presidential tenure, however, Folwell encountered opposition among faculty and students. He had been an officer in the Civil War, and he ran the university like the military, issuing demerits for infractions, such as missing the required daily chapel. Students eventually rebelled.

"The newspapers with but a few exceptions of little importance were favorable," Folwell recalled. "There was always some, but never violent, opposition. It was felt that I confined myself too closely to pedagogic duties and did not popularize the institution by appearances on public occasions with papers and addresses, and this was true. Friends of denominational colleges, mostly clerical, were naturally critical, and a few zealots denounced the state university as a 'godless concern.'" He consistently saw the many religious colleges in the state as competition for the university as it tried to grow its enrollment; students also complained of the slow growth. Folwell's critique of the disenchantment was both straightforward and apparently accurate:

> *By a friendly tip I learned that a small group had planned a riotous demonstration about my house. Two faculty friends and I were on the watch, and at my inquiry, "What are you doing here?" the students dispersed. One of my friends, who should never have owned a pistol or had it in his pocket, pulled one out and fired at nobody, but the bullet went through the leg of one of the young men. A grand jury investigation resulted in "no bill." All these influences had a cumulative effect on the regents. Certainly a majority had come to the conclusion that the time had come for my retirement.*

Nonetheless, the regents granted Folwell another year as president, ending his term in 1884. Afterward, he continued as a faculty member and librarian. Although Folwell retired from teaching in 1907, he continued his association with the University of Minnesota to write the definitive Minnesota history and other works in the campus library, now called Burton Hall, and in his home at 1020 Fifth Street Southeast, across Fifth Street from Pillsbury's mansion.

As early as 1881, Folwell told the regents that the size and shape of the campus was awkward, implicitly suggesting that the campus would expand into the surrounding neighborhoods.

Folwell predicted campus imperialistic expansion:

> *The campus is not merely too small, it is monstrously ill-shapen. It is a very scalene triangle with the obtuse angle and one of the acute angles sheared off. No person would willingly select such grounds for private uses. These grounds can only be added to and improved in shape at vast expense and by means of legal proceedings vexatious to citizens. The lands which can be so procured are utterly barren and must be fertilized a great cost before even grass will grow.*

Railroads over, around and through the campus created additional problems with five tracks in plain view only five hundred feet from the main building.

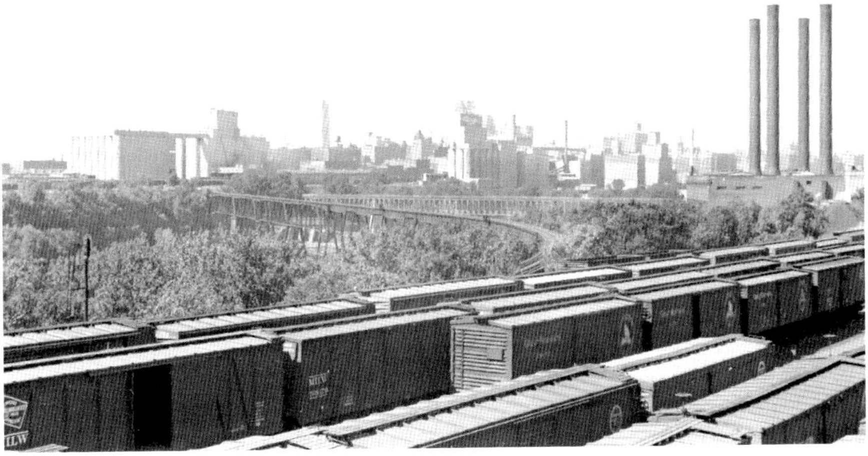

The Great Northern and other rail lines' heavily used tracks ran through Dinkytown and along the riverfront between the campus and Main Street. *Library of Congress.*

> *A hundred trains a day will soon be passing. Their noise, their dust and smoke will seriously disturb the quiet which should reign about a place of study. If the new library building shall be placed where the architect and landscape artist recommend, there will be but 350 feet between it and these railways, 720 feet directly in front of the front door of the main building are the large horse-car stables of the Minneapolis Street railway.*

In addition, Folwell said, "The railroads cross the campus at a most unfortunate angle cutting off a larger amount of frontage."

Besides the railroads, the expansion of the city's riverfront industries and increased urban traffic would also make campus expansion difficult and conflict with the sedate environment required for study. The location and orientation of the first building made it impossible to expand without crossing railroad tracks. Some tracks once crossed what is now the campus where Morrill Hall and Johnston Hall stood in the early twenty-first century. Growth of housing southeast of campus and the increased traffic on University Avenue Southeast, he said, will pinch the campus, making expansion very expensive. In addition, industry had expanded on Main Street downhill from the campus, and two grocery stores had opened nearby.

Of course, all of Folwell's predictions of university expansion came true. The university expanded to the east up University Avenue Southeast and took out acres of housing. In the mid-1960s, it expanded across the river to the West Bank. What was probably not anticipated, however, was that the

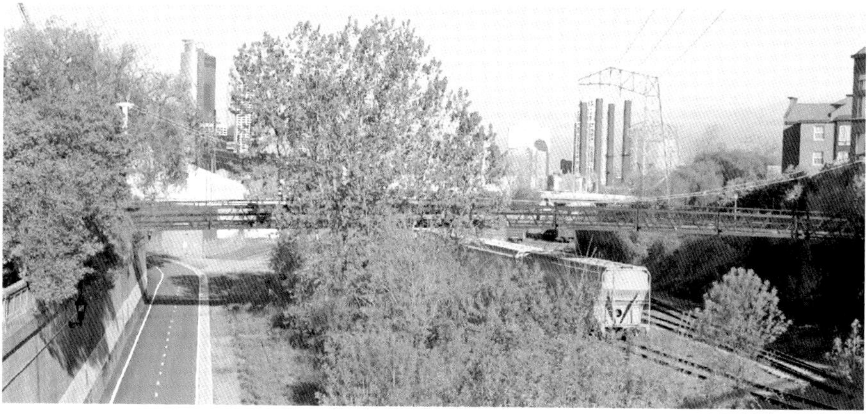

The paved Dinkytown Greenway shares the Granary Corridor with the few remaining railroad track in the trench through Dinkytown. *Photo by Bill Huntzicker.*

major railroad lines would eventually disappear. Expanding campus athletic facilities and commercial development displaced many of the massive granaries and railroad yards east of the campus, and a bicycle and walking path replaced mainline railways years after passenger trains stopped using the stations in downtown Minneapolis. Two major railroad bridges—Bridge No. 9, built for the Northern Pacific, and the iconic Stone Arch Bridge, built for the Great Northern—today support only pedestrians and bicycles.

The Dinkytown Greenway bicycle path begins east of the campus, follows the railroad trench through Dinkytown, crosses Bridge No. 9 and connects to Second Street South near the Guthrie Theatre and Mill City Museum. Bicyclists hope to eventually connect Dinkytown and the campus to the Stone Arch Bridge along what was in 2016 still a university and railroad service road.

6

UNIVERSITY ACTIVITIES SPILL INTO NEIGHBORHOODS

Pillsbury had built his mansion, as noted, at the intersection of Fifth Street and Tenth Avenue Southeast. Folwell lived in another large home across Fifth Street Southeast from the man considered the "father of the university" for his heroic professional, personal and political involvement in creating the institution. Folwell continued to live in his home after leaving the presidency while remaining at the university as a librarian, historian and political science professor. He lived there for most of the time he worked on his definitive four-volume history of Minnesota. Cyrus Northrop, his successor as university president, lived around the corner and across Tenth Avenue Southeast from Pillsbury.

Folwell's memoir suggests he got along well with his successor. "It was my good fortune to be succeeded as president by the wise, sagacious, magnanimous Cyrus Northrop, who remained my great friend to the end. Because of his generous tolerance my teaching and other college work were moderate during my twenty-three years under him as chief."

Northrop was inaugurated on June 11, 1885, in the Coliseum, the university's first building on Dinkytown's side of the tracks, about where Sanford and Wilkins dormitories stood in 2016. The structure was built in 1884 for $35,000 as a military drill hall and auditorium to seat 3,500 people. The wooden building, officially known as the Military Building, burned down on July 24, 1894.

Northrop, who came from Yale University, said he felt like a stranger in a strange land in Minnesota, where the campus had only about one hundred

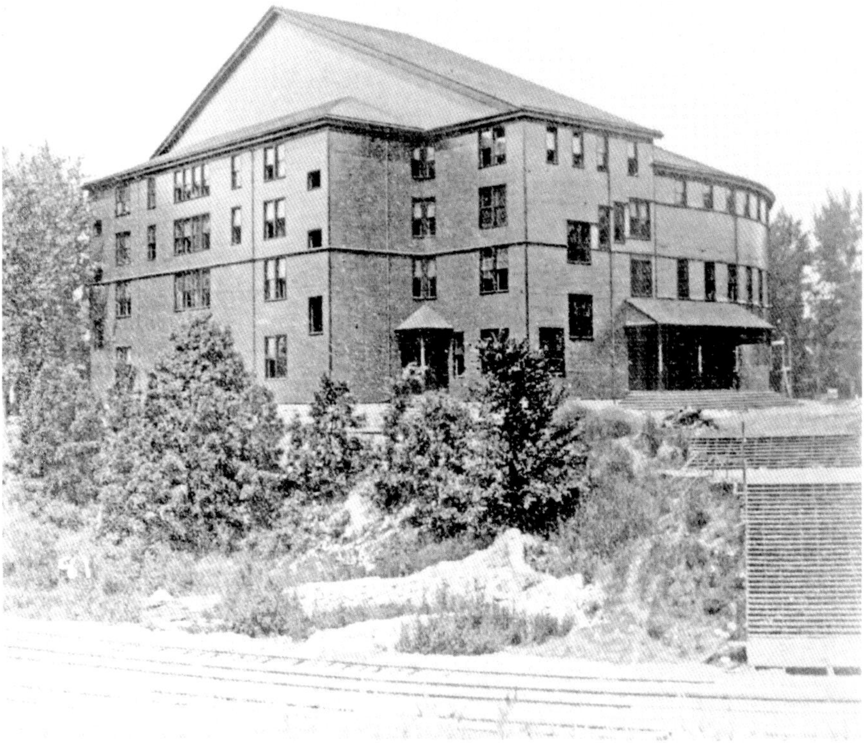

The university crossed the tracks to build this Coliseum. Dormitories Sanford and Wilkins Halls stand on this site in 2016. *Photo courtesy special collections, Hennepin County Public Library.*

students when he arrived. He wrote in a memoir quoted extensively by his biographer, Oscar Firkins:

> *The president had no secretary or typewriter during the first thirteen years of his service. There were no telephones. Professors did not have to travel very far to see the president inasmuch as nearly all of them worked in the same building and had to pass his door on the way to their own place of labor; and they could always go in and see the president whenever they chose to do so. His office was never shut or guarded during office hours. If the professor found the president free from other callers, he could tarry if he chose after his business was finished and be human for a while and talk about something besides shop.... The institution was not so large then as now and the number of things to be attended to each day was smaller.*

Even as the campus grew and the president acquired a staff, Northrop lived near campus—in fact, he built his home across Tenth Avenue Southeast from Pillsbury, who now had two university presidents as neighbors. "It was not the President's way to walk abroad much of what was the campus," Northrop's biographer Firkins wrote. "It was characteristic of his simple tasks that he should build a house within walking distance of the University, and that he should walk to and from his work with unpretentious regularity. But when he had once reached the Old Main or the Library building, his habit was to stay there and to stay pretty regularly in his office except when summoned thence by the imperious call of chapel."

Northrop's twenty-seven-year term made him the longest-serving president in the history of the University of Minnesota. After his retirement at the age of seventy-seven, residents could see him working in his yard.

Maria Sanford, described as the most beloved female faculty member and whom the regents voted matron of the university, lived a few blocks away at 1401 Sixth Street Southeast in 1890 and 1900, before moving to 1050 Thirteenth Avenue Southeast. Sanford, who taught rhetoric, a required course, came to know more students than other faculty members. She also became known as a lecturer on suffrage, women's rights, peace and temperance.

Surrounding them and throughout the neighborhood were increasing numbers of faculty members and industrialists looking after their

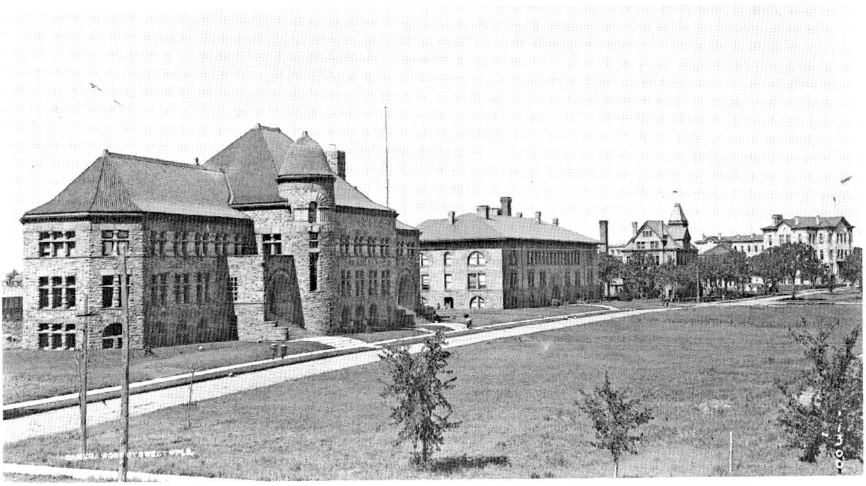

The earliest University of Minnesota buildings faced the campus Knoll and University Avenue Southeast. *Photo from University Archives, University of Minnesota, Twin Cities.*

investments on the riverfront. By the turn of the century, their community evolved around the Main Street and Hennepin Avenue businesses, a growing number of churches and the fledgling campus. Some of their large homes later became fraternity and sorority houses.

On campus, a university began taking shape with a row of new buildings lining the campus thoroughfare that began at Dinkytown on Fourteenth Avenue circling the Knoll and ending up in front of the Armory on Seventeenth Avenue Southeast. The second campus building, Eddy Hall, was built in 1886 and still stands in 2016. So do Pattee Hall (1889); Pillsbury Hall (1889); Nicholson Hall (1890); Wulling Hall (1892); Burton Hall (1894); the Armory (1896); Jones Hall (1901); Child Development building, originally a mines building (1903); Shevlin Hall (1906), built on the site of Old Main after it burned; and Folwell Hall (1907) on University and Fifteenth Avenues Southeast. Wesbrook Hall was built in 1898 and demolished in 2011. Pillsbury himself donated the $150,000 to build the then science building named for him. The Student Christian Association, later a music education building, was constructed in 1888 and torn down in 2010.

7

TWO KEY URBAN BUSINESSES

ACADEMIC AND SUPPORT

As the campus grew, so did Dinkytown. Some of its initial businesses, such as the H.W. Wilson Company, were intimately connected to the university, and others, such as the Swain Transfer & Fuel Co., met the needs of the growing city.

Halsey W. Wilson created a business that was in both the campus and Dinkytown. Wilson never knew his parents; both died before he was three years old, but his upbringing by a grandmother in rural Massachusetts and later an uncle in rural Iowa prepared him for an entrepreneurial life. At the age of twelve, he worked as a hired hand, often abandoning studies for farm work. His assignments included guarding twenty cows. John Lawler wrote in a company history:

> *This was not an easy assignment, for the shortage of fences in the area permitted cattle, if not carefully watched, to roam for miles about the countryside. Wilson frequently had to remain in the saddle for a whole day at a time, with only his dog, "Shep," as a companion on his lonely vigil. But he was much more than just a cowboy. He also drove wagons during the harvest season, weeded the vegetable garden, fed the chickens, cleaned out the barns, gathered wood for the kitchen stove, picked fruit in the orchard, delivered messages between the house and the fields, and even found time to sell subscriptions to a boys' magazine as a means of acquiring small prizes.*

Arriving at the University of Minnesota, he paid his expenses by taking on a variety of jobs, including a long paper route by horseback and

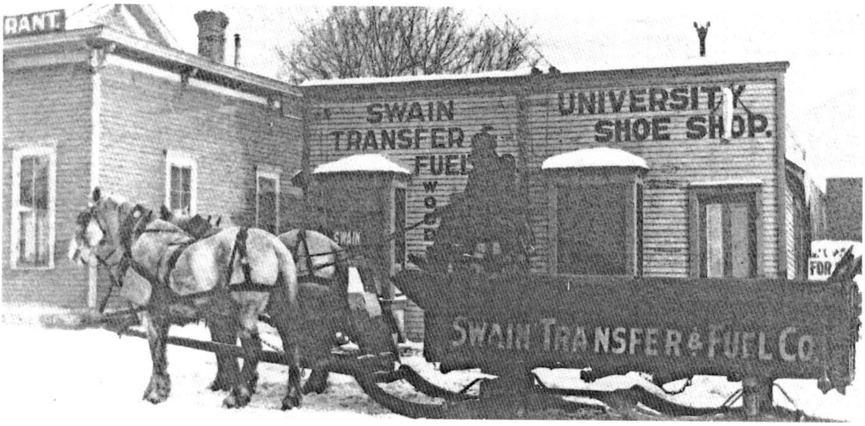

Swain Transfer & Fuel Co. was at 408 Fourteenth Avenue Southeast about 1904. *Photo courtesy Penny A. Petersen and Marcy-Holmes Neighborhood Association, from* Hiding in Plain Sight.

janitorial duties in a church. From the church, he acquired a printing press used to print programs and moved it home as another source of income. Fortunately, his roommate, Henry S. Morris, didn't mind the new furniture.

The two young men knew how to exploit a business opportunity: textbooks. "Many professors ordered textbooks in bulk from the publishers for their classes, but they, too resented the extra work," Lawler wrote. "This situation seemed to offer a splendid opportunity." The firm of Morris & Wilson was born on December 4, 1889, with the partners operating out of their bedroom, visiting classrooms, taking orders and delivering books in person. The university came to their rescue, offering them a twelve- by sixteen-foot room in the basement of Old Main, creating the university's first bookstore. After two years, Morris graduated, moved on and eventually sold his half of the business to Wilson. When Old Main burned, Wilson rescued books from both his store and the library also in the building.

As the business grew, the university provided an additional room and assigned post office duties to the bookstore as well, giving students and teachers reason to visit the store almost daily and providing the owner with an opportunity to add a new product: bicycles and instructions for using them. He also kept track of customers' interests and kept them informed about new books, reviews and magazine articles that would interest them.

Building a successful book business and getting into the business of helping customers find books led Wilson to consider creating a directory of books. In the same year that he bought out Morris, Wilson started the

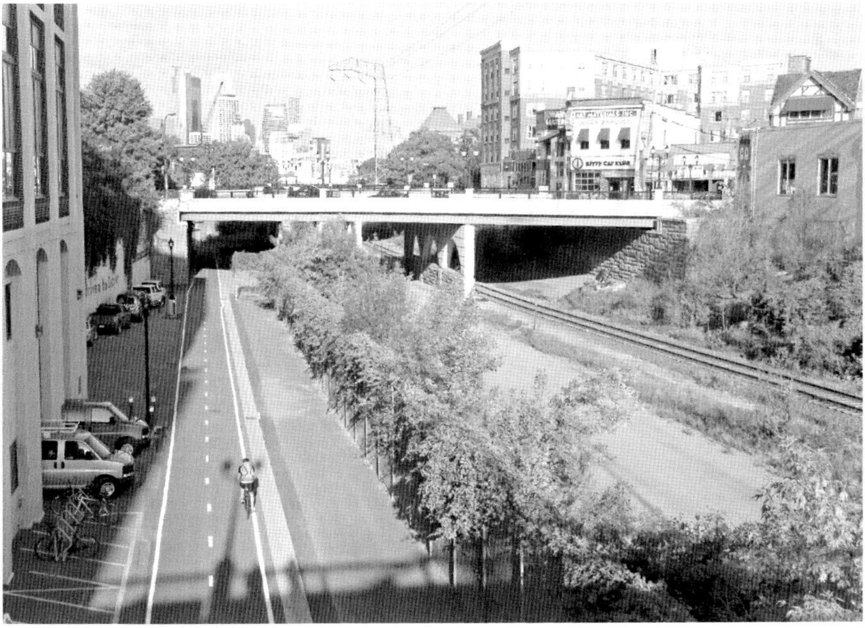

One lone railroad track and a bike path run through the trench where five railroad tracks of mainline railroads used to run. *Photo by Bill Huntzicker.*

Cumulative Book Index, which collected data about books, book reviews and other publishing information.

In response to requests from researchers and librarians, he began the *Readers' Guide to Periodical Literature* in 1901. Librarians had been collecting similar information, but Wilson designed an efficient indexing system and realized that publishing the index in book form would be cheaper than using library cards. And it cost little more to make one thousand copies than it did to make one. (The *Readers' Guide* was such a basic part of my research tools in elementary and high school in small-town Montana that it makes me goosebumpy to think it was invented in Dinkytown.)

Figuring that his business would be easier and publications distributed in a more timely manner if the company were closer to the publishing industry, Wilson sold his Minneapolis bookstore and moved to White Plains, New York, in 1913. He moved again, to the Bronx, in 1917. Wilson died in 1954, and his company introduced an electronic version of the *Readers' Guide* in 1984. The company went online with WilsonWeb in 1997, and in 2011, the H.W. Wilson Company merged with EBSCO to combine academic search engines with other library resources.

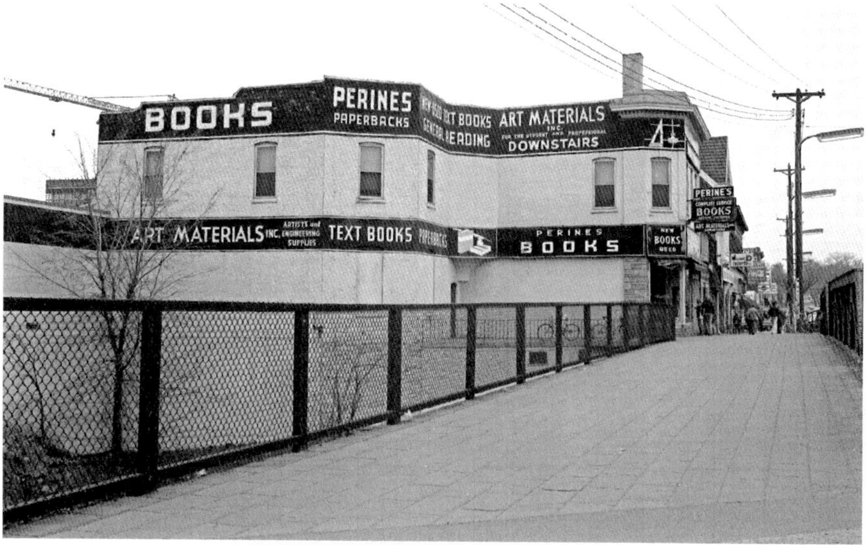

Perine's Bookstore was a long-running institution at this site, which previously and subsequently housed restaurants. *Photo by Steven Bergerson.*

Before moving from Minnesota, however, Wilson had to figure out how to sustain his reference and library aids in their own right because he was still using the bookstore to underwrite the publication of the library resources and collections of documents, such as primary materials for debate teams. Only about twenty core staff members agreed to move with him, but the furniture, books, papers and files filled fourteen freight cars leaving Minneapolis.

Even before moving his business off campus, Wilson had expanded into Dinkytown with services of obvious value to students and faculty. In the 1900 through 1904 city directories, the H.W. Wilson Company is listed under books and stationery at 315 Fourteenth Avenue Southeast in what was probably a new building. The building was a long-term address for Perine's bookstore in the 1950s and later the Kitty Cat Klub with Annie's Parlor upstairs. From 1906 through 1911, the company was listed as booksellers, stationers, printers and publishers at the corner of University and Fourteenth Avenues Southeast, across the street from the university's wrought-iron gate.

In the 1886–87 city directory, H.W. Wilson is listed as a student living at 928 Fifth Street Southeast. This address is a block away from those of university presidents Folwell and Northrop, both of whom he remembered when he was interviewed for Lawler's 1950 book.

A fledgling city in the nineteenth century needed hardware, coal and firewood. These needs were provided by Swain Transfer & Fuel Co.,

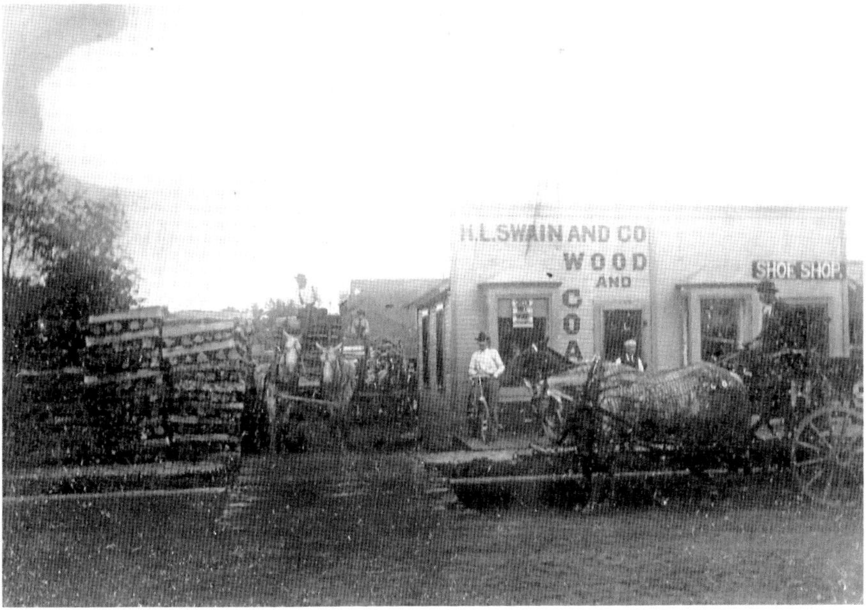

H.L. Swain sold wood and coal for fuel and did commercial hauling by horses and wagons before trucks. *Courtesy Tom H. Swain.*

formed when Howard Swain left farming in 1885 to go into business in Southeast Minneapolis. He opened a hardware store on East Hennepin and later moved to 413 Fourteenth Avenue Southeast in Dinkytown. Swain sold the hardware business to William Simms, who built a new building in 1904 that housed Simms Hardware for generations and still stands as the Caffé Espresso Royale coffee shop.

Swain's great-grandson is Tom H. Swain, retired insurance executive, former university vice-president and chief of staff for Minnesota governor Elmer L. Andersen. He recently wrote about his family's roots in Dinkytown as part of his autobiography, *Citizen Swain*:

> *My grandfather, Charles I. Swain, took over the business in 1898, moved it to 408 Fourteenth Avenue, acquired a partner named Farmer, and expanded by adding a hauling service. Among its specialties was hauling the trunks of arriving university students to their dorms and apartments, and back to the train station again at semester's end. The company's wagons and horses—and eventually trucks—were housed between Fourteenth and Fifteenth Avenues on the site now occupied by the Dinkytown McDonald's.*

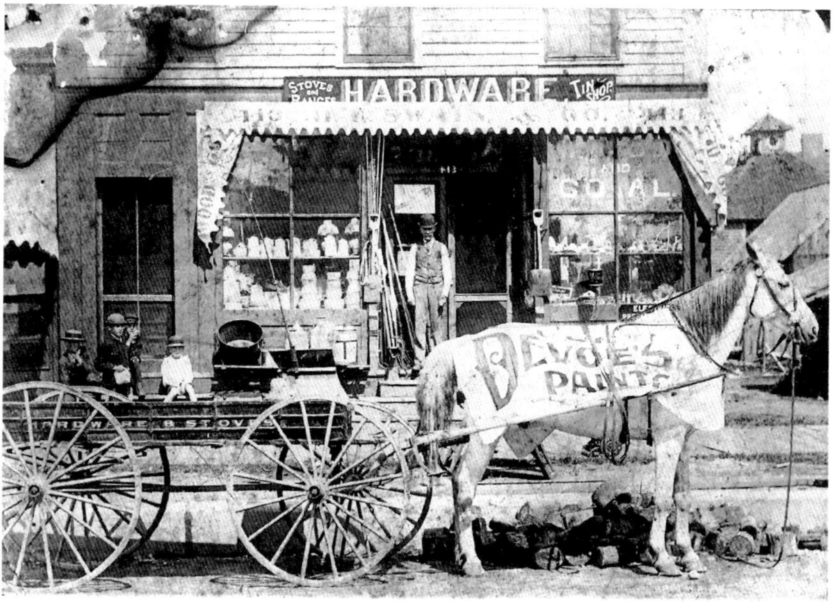

H.L. Swain and William Simms founded a hardware, coal and wood store. This photo is labeled 1891 at 413 Fourteenth Avenue Southeast. *Courtesy Tom H. Swain.*

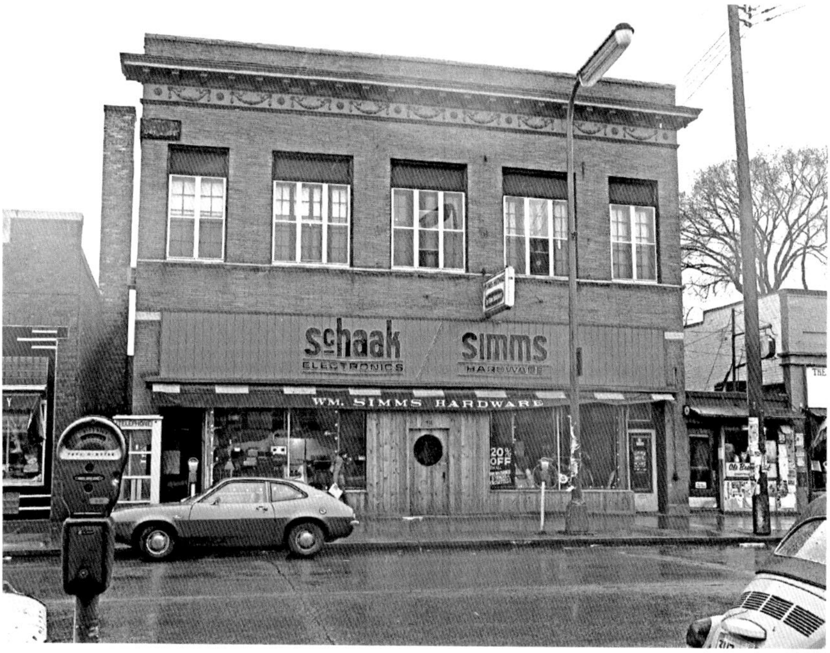

In the 1970s, Schaak Electronics and Simms Hardware shared this building, which had been a hardware store built by W.M. Simms in 1904. *Photo by Steven Bergerson.*

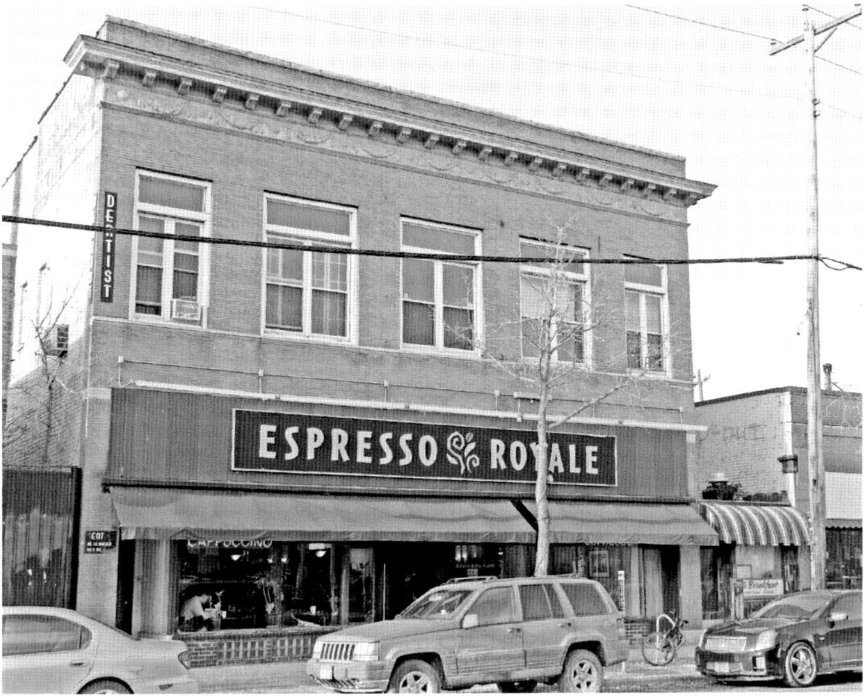

Espresso Royale occupies the building that was Simms Hardware Store. The iconic Al's Breakfast, with the blue-and-white striped awning, was built as a storage shed against the building. *Photo by Bill Huntzicker.*

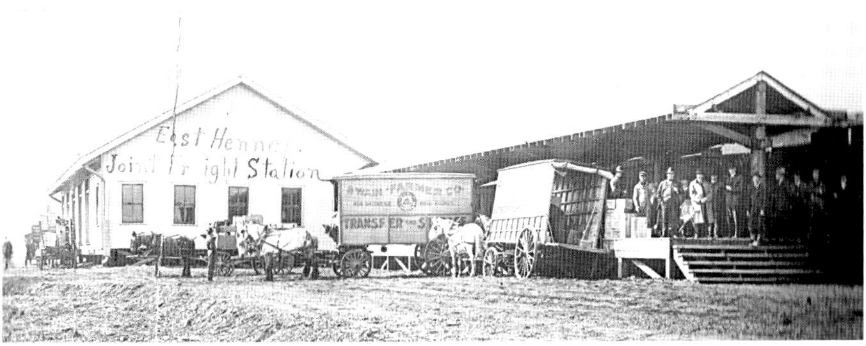

Swain's wagons display the store's address as 414 Fourteenth Avenue Southeast. They're at a freight depot on East Hennepin. *Courtesy Tom H. Swain.*

After having been gassed, sustaining a concussion and receiving a battlefield promotion, Earl Edmund Swain, Tom Swain's father, returned from World War I in to take over the family's Swain Transfer & Fuel Co.,

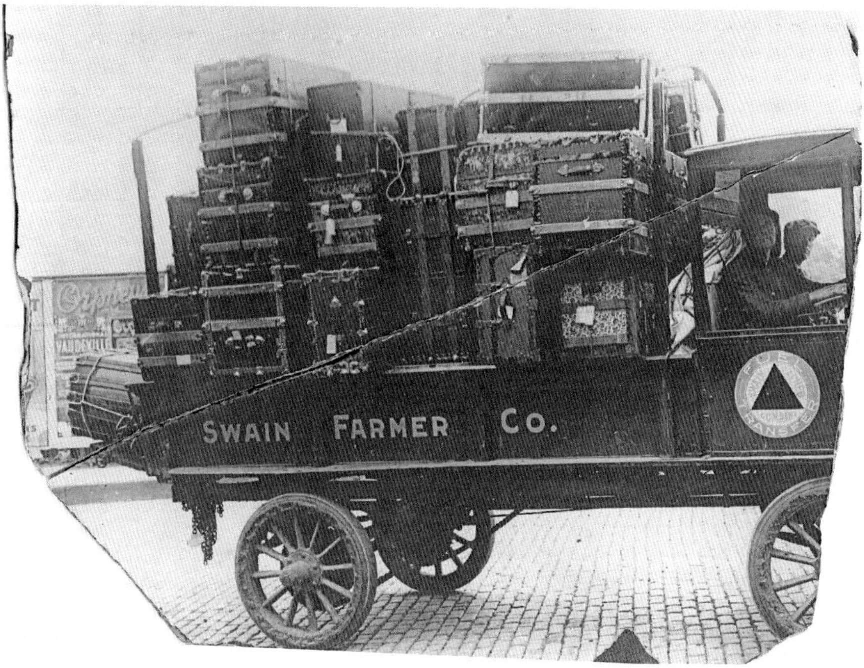

As the campus grew, Swain specialized in hauling trunks for students going to and from railroad stations. Photo about 1914. *Courtesy Tom H. Swain.*

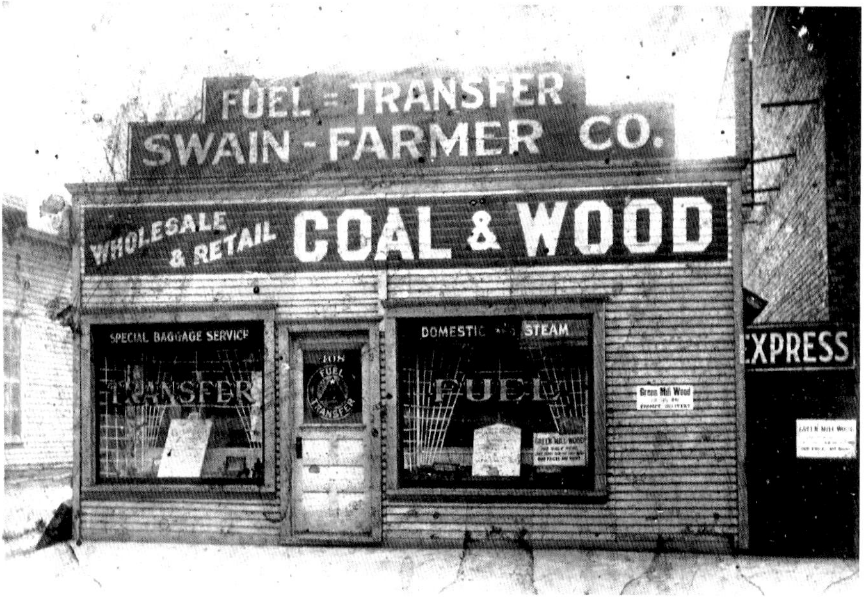

This Swain storefront is at 408 Fourteenth Avenue Southeast. *Courtesy Tom H. Swain.*

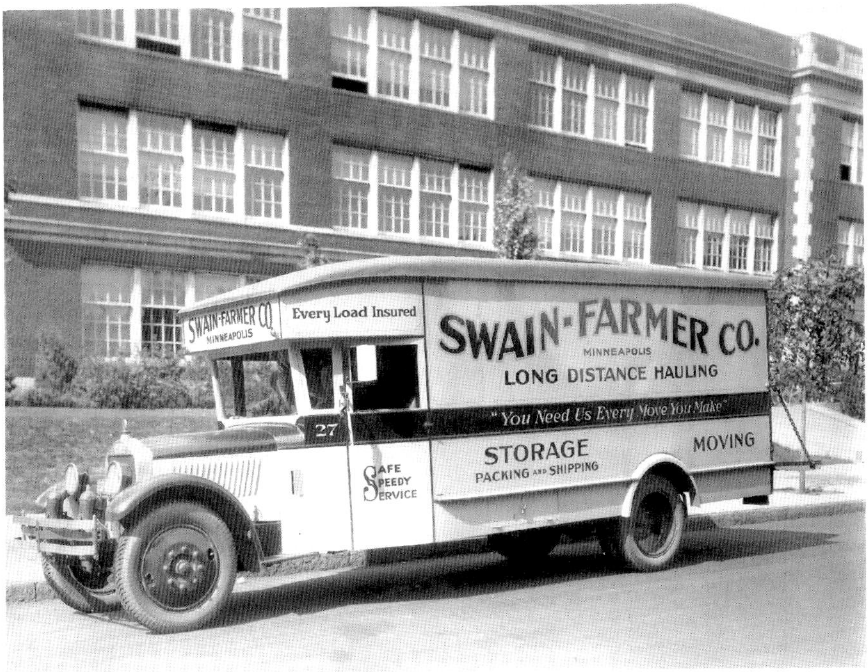

This truck was originally a city bus, but it had a van body installed for hauling furniture. In the photo, the truck appears to be in front of a new Marshall High School in the 1920s. *Courtesy Tom H. Swain.*

then at 423 Fourteenth Avenue Southeast. He was invited to represent small business owners among the mediators working to end the violent 1934 truckers strike that was crippling Minneapolis, but he also had many friends and relatives among Teamster Union leaders. Swain Transfer & Fuel Co. continued to have offices in Dinkytown into the 1940s and a coal yard north of Dinkytown against the railroad tracks across from Van Cleve Park.

Tom H. Swain began with the university as a student in 1938 working the athletic ticket office and became ticket manager and the first athletic scholastic adviser in the 1940s. His mother, Lucille Holliday Swain, also had created a position by leading many songfests in city parks. The *Minneapolis Tribune* said, "She had the whole town singing."

Tom drove his father to the Milwaukee depot one day to drop him off for a business trip to Madison, Wisconsin, and never saw him again. No one knows what happened to him.

Further development of Dinkytown can be seen by the opening of the University Drug Store, listed in the city directory in 1907 with Carl A.

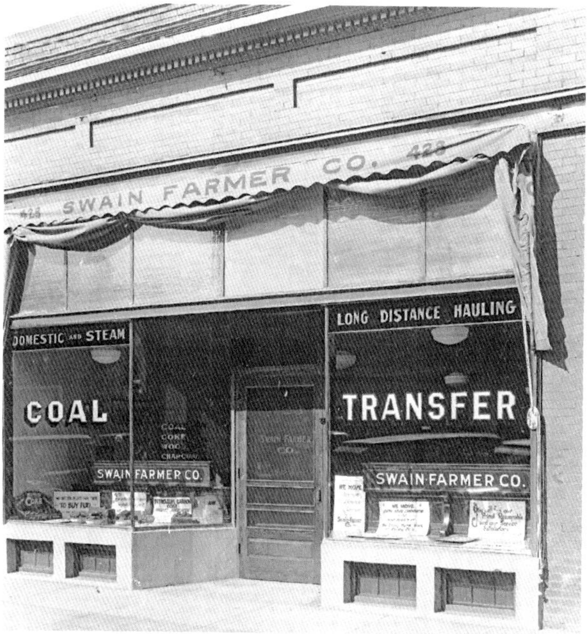

Left: After Swain started the hauling business, signs in his window at 423 Fourteenth Avenue Southeast read, among other things, "We move anything anywhere anytime" and "We enjoy hard work and plenty of it." *Courtesy Tom H. Swain.*

Below: An early Swain building later became home of Standard Heating, Tub Laundry and Wally's Falafel and Hummus. *Courtesy special collections, Minneapolis Central, Hennepin County Library.*

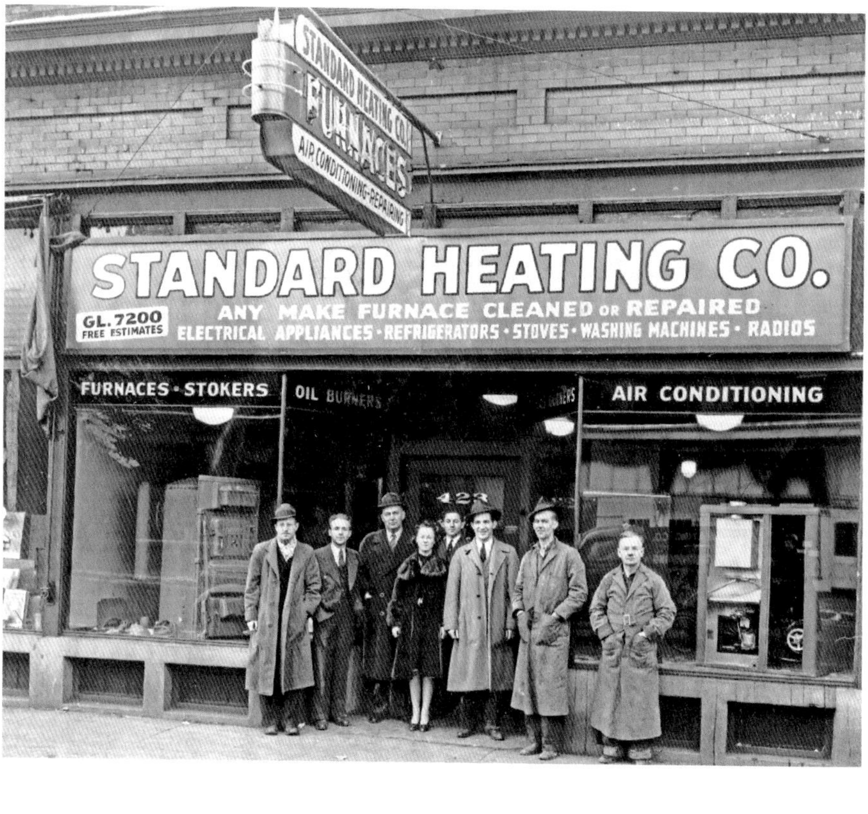

Schmid as proprietor and goods noted as "Drugs, Druggists, Sundries and Stationery," at 400 Fourteenth Avenue Southeast. This corner long housed a drugstore, even when Gray's was cater-corner across the street. The drugstore was followed by a gift shop; in 2016, it was Goldy's sports apparel.

One of the first Swain buildings was taken over by Standard Plumbing and Heating, which moved on to become a successful business in Minneapolis and St. Paul. In 1948, two young veterans who had attended the university set up the Tub Laundromat in the building, and Wally's Falafel and Hummus was there when this was written in 2016, though Wally's was moving into a larger storefront in the same building.

Like Standard Plumbing and Heating, a number of businesses operated in Dinkytown on their way to larger markets. Sound of Music, a stereo and hi-fi store started in St. Paul in 1966, opened one of its first stores in Dinkytown. By 1983, the company faced so much competition in the same field that it expanded its electronic offerings, moved to the suburbs and changed its name to Best Buy in 1983. By 2016, the company's website claimed $40 billion in annual revenue from more than 1,400 stores.

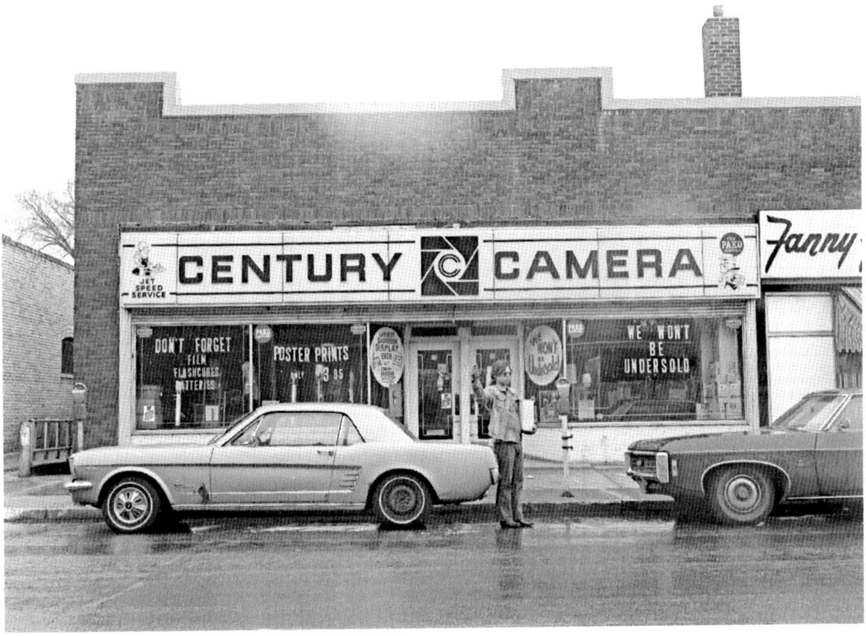

This Dinkytown Century Camera store building later became the Steak Knife restaurant. *Photo by Steven Bergerson.*

Some students also saw business opportunities in Dinkytown. Harvey Goldstein, who had been photographer for the *Daily* and other campus publications, opened his first camera store, Campus Camera, in 1936. The company opened a downtown store in 1945 and later became Century Camera. The Dinkytown store later became National Camera Exchange already in downtown Minneapolis and Twin Cities suburbs. The site was later taken over by the Steak Knife restaurant.

8
THE UNIVERSITY TURNS AWAY

When John S. Pillsbury died in 1901, his daughter donated a wrought-iron gate that provided, beginning in 1902, a decorative entrance to the campus from Dinkytown on Fourteenth Avenue Southeast. His widow, Mahala, lived in the Pillsbury mansion until her death in 1910, and her family donated it to the university as a home for university presidents and their families. It served this function until 1964, when the mansion was demolished to make room for a married student housing development. During its time as the president's home, the house became a social center at various times for students and faculty.

After rejecting Folwell's suggestion that the university relocate, the board began reconsidering an 1885 decision to sell a right of way to the St. Paul and Northern Pacific Railroad, later the Northern Pacific, through what is today the center of the campus. Historian James Gray said the railroad ran "violently along the edge of the old cluster of buildings, reducing to the tragedy of impotence the delicate operations of many departments." Scientists complained "that vibration ruined instruments, that smoke and cinders reduced to squalid comedy all the immaculate purposes of the laboratory, and that noise completed the ruin of academic seclusion."

At the same time, the university began to reconsider the layout of the campus. Turning its back on the original campus and Dinkytown, a new campus layout was first designed in 1907 by St. Paul architect Cass Gilbert, who had designed the state's new capitol, built in 1905, and several depots and other buildings for the railroads. Gilbert's original design allowed for the

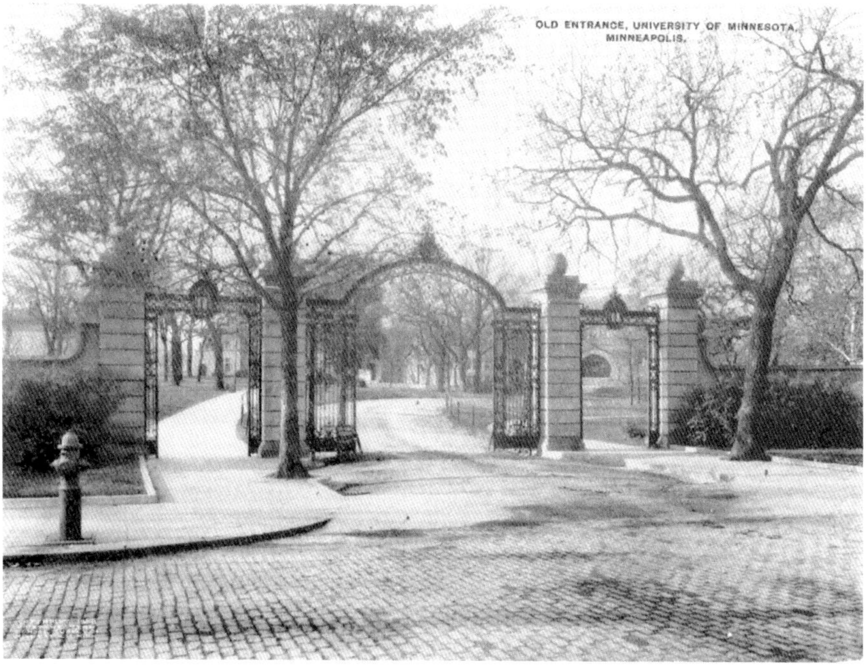

This page: The Pillsbury Gate was completed in 1902 to honor John S. Pillsbury. As cars grew and roads widened, the wrought iron and parts of the Pillsbury Gate of 1902 disappeared. *Photos from University Archives, University of Minnesota, Twin Cities.*

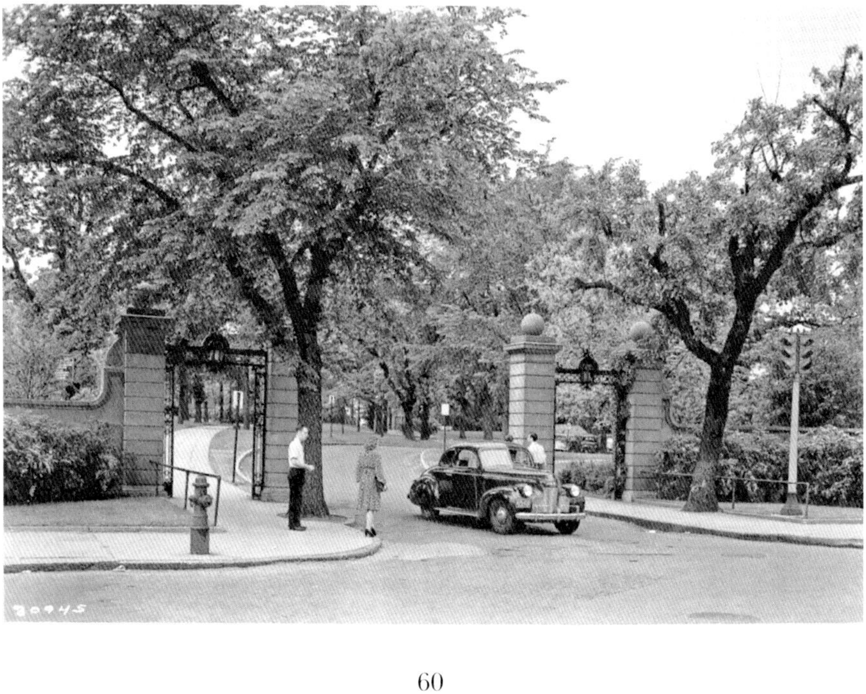

campus to face the river with a mall headed by Northrop Auditorium and lined by classical columned academic buildings.

Through much of the century's first decade, the regents struggled over the Gilbert plan and even over paying the architect for the design, wrote historian Gray. "They wrangled, too over the suitability of his design, over materials to be used in buildings, and over the total expense of the project. During the years of World War I, the blueprints and models were put away and all but forgotten. But in 1920 they were brought out again and it was evident at once that the scattered buildings already constructed had committed architects of the future inevitability to the Gilbert plan."

During the Vincent administration, the regents began multigenerational negotiations over the railroad tracks and found little support off campus to force the railroad to vacate the tracks. "A more conciliatory approach had to be found," Gray wrote, "and the university began to talk about elevating the tracks, about depressing the tracks, about putting a tunnel under the campus." But the railroad didn't budge, and President Lotus D. Coffman inherited "the old struggle" in 1920, even though the campus had grown around the tracks.

Finally, after years of negotiations, the rail line was rerouted. Gray wrote:

> *Rerouting took the trains over the nearby Great Northern tracks and left to the university its original broad surfaces on which to complete, in the future, its stadium, its set of athletic buildings, its new engineering group, its new library, and its new law school. Though the price of this face lifting was many times over what the university had gained in the first place by granting the right or way, no one thought of this irony as the face of the campus no longer frowned with tracks.*

What Gray called the "curious duel between commercial traffic and academic tranquility" was furthered because

> *a major line of the street railway system neatly bisects the campus, along Washington Avenue, and the severed parts of the Mall have been rejoined by* [foot]*bridges thrown across the highway. A second streetcar line edges into the campus from another side. But this is a less violent invasion for it is the friendly, tradition-encrusted intercampus line which links the main unit to that of the Department of Agriculture five miles away.*

Students somctimes knew the drivers of the intercampus car that went from the turnaround near Eddy Hall on campus along Fifteenth Avenue through Dinkytown to the St. Paul campus. By then, Dinkytown already had a long history with mass transit, beginning with the separate horsecar companies founded in Minneapolis and St. Paul. The St. Paul City Railway had begun in 1872. In 1875 the Minneapolis Street Railway ran from Dinkytown to downtown. By 1889, Minneapolis had sixty-seven miles, and St. Paul had fifty-three miles of the horse-drawn lines that extended from each city's downtown without reaching each other. Most people owned neither horses nor cars and depended on such public transportation.

According to the Minnesota Streetcar Museum, "Despite the advantage of steel wheel on rail, the cars were still horse powered, and horses were a problem. Up to seven were required to keep a single car in service all day. They produced epic quantities of manure. They were slow, couldn't handle steep hills and were subject to disease....By 1891, the entire Twin Cities system was electric except for the two cable lines, which converted a few years later."

In contrast to other cities, the Twin Cities' urban transit benefited from stable corporate ownership. Thomas B. Lowry, an officer in the Minneapolis firm, purchased a controlling interest in the transit system in 1877 and in the St. Paul railway in 1884 and merged them into the Twin City Rapid Transit, which Lowry used to promote his real estate interests. The company, whose ridership peaked in 1920 and revived during the gasoline and rubber rationing of World War II, phased out its streetcars, replacing the last with buses in 1954. A government agency, the Metropolitan Transit Commission, purchased the company in 1970.

The four-stacker coal-fired steam plant at the end of the Stone Arch Bridge a few blocks from Dinkytown had provided electricity for the streetcars. It was acquired by the university to heat and cool the Minneapolis campus through 2016. The smokestacks can be seen in the distance of photos that show the railroad tracks.

The Minnesota Streetcar Museum's Como-Harriet Streetcar Line continues to run restored streetcars on a mile of original right of way between Lakes Harriet and Calhoun in South Minneapolis. That stretch is all that remains of the route that once ran between the Twin Cities through Dinkytown.

The new campus expansion began to take shape in the 1920s following Gilbert's design although with different architects and variations on the original designs. Buildings around the Knoll faced Dinkytown, but the

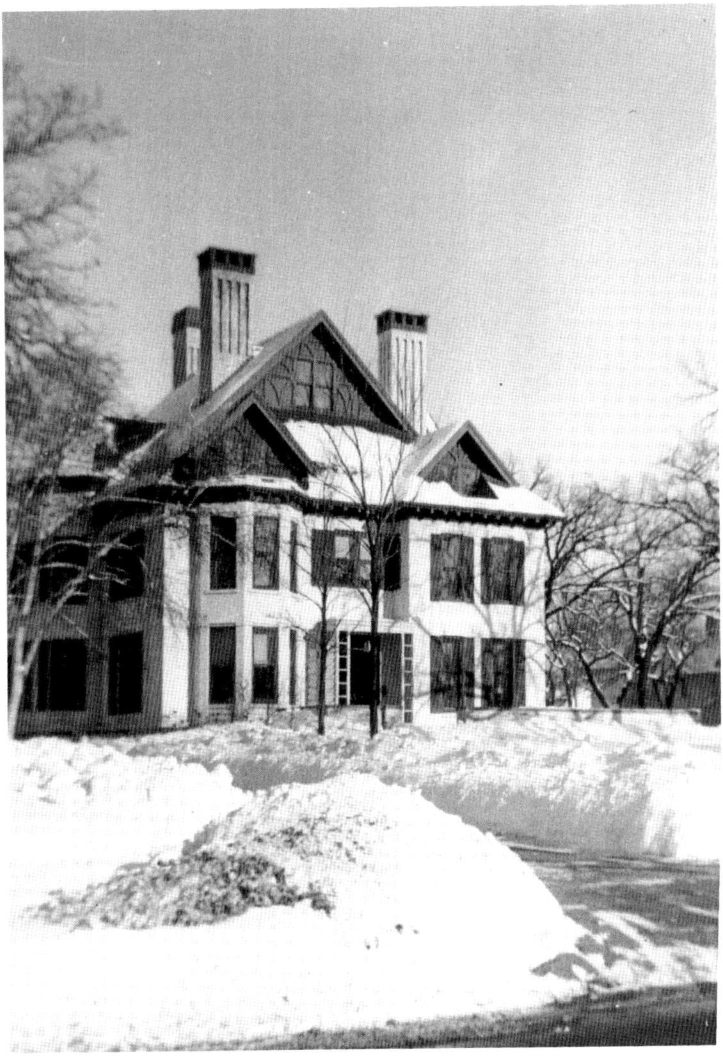

John S. Pillsbury's family donated his mansion to the university, for which it served as a president's home for much of the twentieth century. *Photo courtesy Hennepin History Museum.*

Gilbert plan created a mall that faced in the opposite direction toward the river after it turned east.

As the campus turned away, its social life increased in Dinkytown and the surrounding neighborhood. Vincent was the first president to live in the Pillsbury mansion. The place, Gray wrote,

> *became such a center of liveliness as the community of teachers and students never had seen before. Mrs. Vincent created a ballroom on the third floor and here undergraduates were turned free of official restraint to dance to the music of a player piano. At other times of the day the dance floor became a basketball court onto which stately, sometimes reluctant, faculty wives were driven by Mrs. Vincent's resolute devotion to exercise.*

Two high schools—John Marshall and University High—served as bookends for Dinkytown, making it a popular place for high school students to hang out, especially when the two schools were active. High school students often hung around the railroad tracks, the campus and parking lots and other open spaces. University High School, created in 1908 as a laboratory school for education students, merged with Marshall in 1968. In the years before the merger, University High was in Peik Hall just inside the university's gate on Fourteenth Avenue Southeast and Marshall was on the site of Marshall apartments. Marshall-University High School at 1313 Fifth Street Southeast closed in 1982; the building served as a technology center and business incubator until its demolition in 2013, which made way for the mixed-use apartment building. Peik Hall continues to house the university's teacher-preparation program.

9

RELIGION ON AND OFF CAMPUS

President Vincent advocated the university as a place for the free expression of creativity. "With his arrival the two campuses became scenes for an endless succession of plays, games, parties, fairs, and bouts of public speaking. Within its first year the new administration seemed to have sponsored more public events of a combined social and cultural character than the whole of the University's previous history could show," Gray wrote.

Vincent removed the routine of daily chapel that Northrop had continued without Folwell's required attendance. Many denominational groups took over religious activities as the campus and university community grew larger and more diversified.

A building for the Student Christian Association (SCA) was constructed on Fourteenth Avenue Southeast just inside the campus in 1888, and it rented space to the YMCA, which eventually took over the SCA's activities. The YMCA moved out of the building in 1914, when it was occupied by the music education department.

Two branches of the Minneapolis YMCA—the university branch and the Southeast branch—shared the same building when it opened in 1923 at 1425 University Avenue Southeast. The YMCA moved from the campus to the corner of Fifteenth and University Avenues Southeast—the southeast tip of Dinkytown's four-block core—and later to 1801 University Avenue Southeast. The original building, subsequently used by child welfare and music education departments, was demolished in 2010.

Organized Christianity, of course, had come to Minnesota with the original settlers, especially the New Englanders who founded St. Anthony. As their village expanded, many of the churches grew and moved into newer and larger monuments to their faiths. Pillsbury, Folwell and Northrop attended the First Congregational Church, which was founded in St. Anthony in 1851 and by 1897 resided in its current building at 500 Eighth Avenue Southeast, less than two blocks from Pillsbury's mansion. Northrop, a Yale professor at the time, said Pillsbury took him to church during his recruitment visit to Minnesota.

When a Baptist minister arrived in 1852, he said he found "all denominations worshipping in a rude school house" they shared by alternating hours and even weeks on University Avenue between Second and Third Avenues, according to a church history. The Baptists had built a twenty-five- by thirty-five-foot wood building that was plain, ugly and lacked a floor. "The society is already in debt for this pile of lumber, and its credit is very like the Minnesota atmosphere, when far below zero," he wrote. "To add to our tribulations, we have no title to the lots on which our house stands." The church history declared the founding years over by 1880. "They had been years of heartbreaking struggle, financially and spiritually. In the period from 1850 to 1880 there had been 14 ministers and 12 pastorless years. Thus the average pastorate was 1¼ years. The miracle is that a church continued to exist."

Nonetheless, the Baptists could be seen as a metaphor for several of the neighborhood churches. For a time, they rented a hall over a dry goods store near Main Street and Fourth Avenue Southeast. The congregation, known as the First Baptist Church of St. Anthony from 1850 through 1879, moved to six locations before settling in Dinkytown in 1878 as the Olivet Baptist Church at the corner of Fourth Street and Thirteenth Avenue Southeast. The Baptists acquired the building from Methodists in a complex trade. In 1922, the church sold that building to the Perine Book Company for $10,000 and moved into a new building at the corner of University and Thirteenth Avenues Southeast—its current location. One former Baptist Church building, between Fourth and Fifth Streets on Ninth Avenue Southeast, was taken out for the construction of I-35W in the 1960s.

The University Baptist Church—the name taken with the move in 1922—built a large structure with the expectation that the state convention would move its offices into the building. Church lore contends that state leaders differed with the university over a number of issues, such as evolution, and decided not to move to the campus. "As a result of not having the state

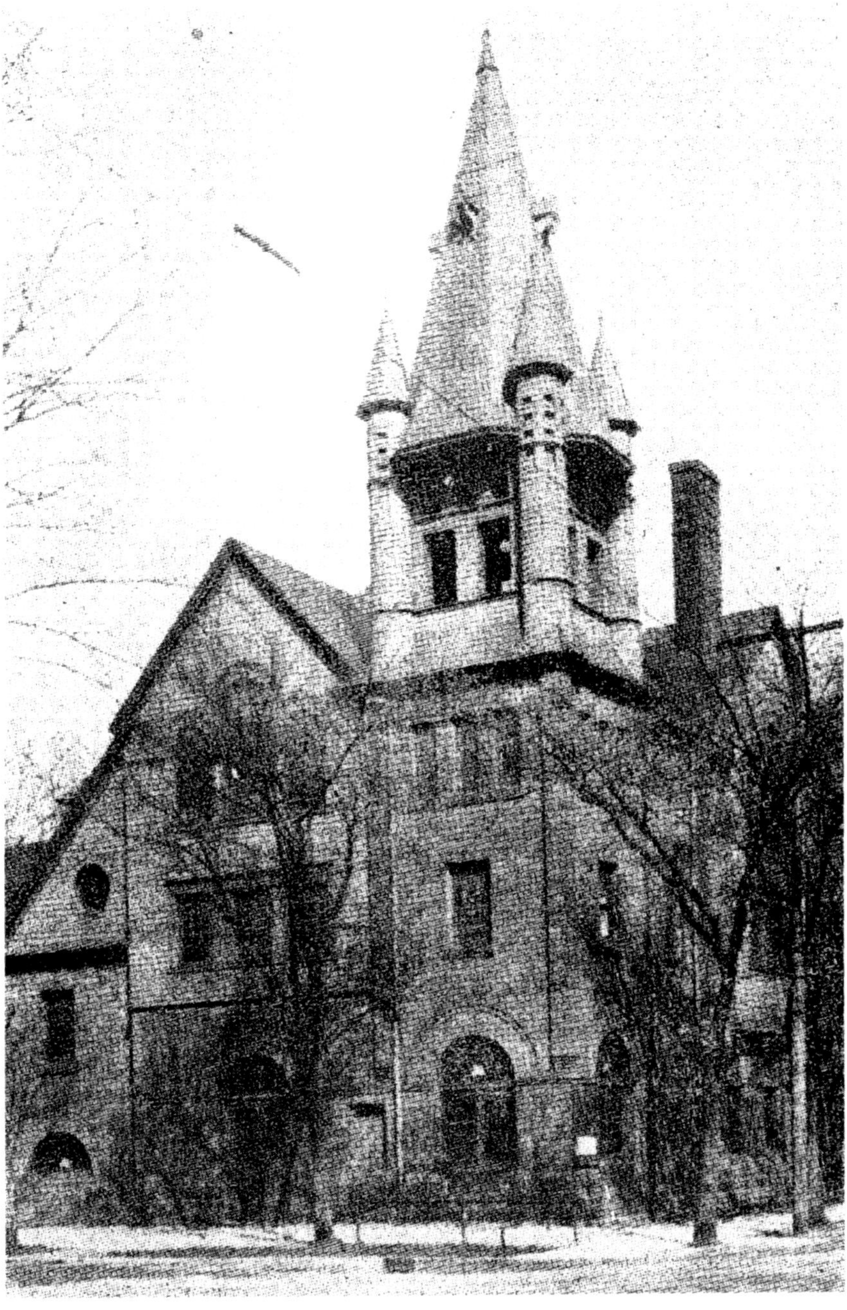

Olivet Baptist sold its building, which became a dance studio, restaurant and dry cleaning business before a fire destroyed it. *Photo courtesy University Baptist Church.*

convention here, we had to figure out different ways to pay for things," said Reverend Doug Donley, who was minister in 2016.

Like the earliest churches in St. Anthony, several congregations shared the same space in 2016. Donley said the church building hosted four congregations with services each week, down from five the previous year. Besides his congregation, the building hosted Episcopal Parish of the Holy Trinity and Saint Anskar led by Reverend Bill Teska, True Believers Fellowship–Pentecostal with Pastor Shalom Reed and the Wesley Foundation, a Methodist campus ministry with Reverend Cody Neilson as campus minister. The Grace Point Southern Baptist, which had also prayed in the building, moved in 2015 to the basement of Coffman Union on campus.

Although church records show that Perine Book Company bought the Olivet Baptist building, there's no indication Perine ever opened a bookstore there. Over the years, the corner building dominated the block with businesses ranging from dry cleaning to a relocated Sammy D's Italian restaurant.

In the early 1960s, the building became home to the Minnesota Dance Theatre, founded by Loyce Houlton. Born to Norwegian parents in Proctor, Minnesota, Houlton studied at Carleton College in Northfield before going to New York City in 1946 to study with renowned dancers, including Martha Graham, and to earn a master's degree in dance education at NYU. Returning to Minnesota in 1959, she married, raised four children and taught at the University of Minnesota.

In 1964, the MDT performed Houlton's original adaptation of the Nutcracker Fantasy for the first time and a year later teamed with the Minneapolis Symphony (later called the Minnesota Orchestra) for more than twenty years of holiday seasons of the ballet at the university's Northrop Auditorium. A *New York Times* critic in 1979 called Houlton's Nutcracker performance one of the nation's ten best.

Houlton blended classical ballet with modern dance and developed her own technique for teaching dance. Her company performed at prestigious venues around the world. Future actor Lea Thompson danced with the company in its premiere of Loyce Houlton's *Carmina Burana* in 1978, and Prince opened his film *Purple Rain* at First Avenue in downtown Minneapolis as a fundraiser for the MDT in 1983, the same year Houlton choreographed Joseph Papp's television movie *Swan Lake, Minnesota*. After Houlton died in 1995, her daughter, Lise Houlton, succeeded her as artistic director of the company, now housed in the Cowles Center in Minneapolis's theater district.

10

A RELIGIOUS REUNION IN 2014

Reverend Bill Teska, who leads a small Minneapolis Episcopalian congregation that meets in the University Baptist Church at 1219 University Avenue Southeast, and Don Olson, who spent twenty months in federal prison for disrupting draft offices in 1970, led a discussion one Saturday evening in November 2014 on the role of religion in the peace and civil rights movements of the 1960s. Their reunion was part of a series of discussions led by people working to preserve historic Dinkytown.

Many of their old meeting places near Dinkytown no longer exist. Olson, who did time in federal prison in Springfield, Illinois, for disrupting Selective Service offices in Winona, Minnesota, was among the Minnesota Eight—draft resisters who attacked draft records in several Minnesota cities in 1970.

Olson said churches played a role in the social change of the 1950s, '60s and '70s. One of the meeting places was the Wesley Foundation at Twelfth Avenue Southeast and Fourth Street Southeast with people who were "very much involved with the draft resistance movement," said Olson. "They served a couple of meals a day at the church, early in the antiwar movement in 1966. The early meetings of the Vietnam mobilization against the war began there in the basement. We planned the draft information center and smoked some dope there occasionally." The building became the Minneapolis Free School and later Little Red Schoolhouse. It has since been torn down and replaced by an apartment building.

"The Newman Center at Seventeenth and University was also important," Olson said. "The Newman Center was more student oriented than the St.

Lawrence Church on the other side of Dinkytown." The Newman Center building has also been demolished and replaced by a university residence hall. An activist priest was Father Harry Bury, who began preaching against the war as soon as he got to the Newman Center in 1965, Olson said. "Father Harry Bury was a much-beloved priest from 1965 to 1970," who celebrated Vatican II. After Vatican II, Olson said, Bury could encourage Catholics to become conscientious objectors under the church's definition of a just war. Bury once chained himself to the U.S. Embassy in Saigon to protest the war, and he put up the North Vietnamese flag on a courthouse. Teska said Father Bury got arrested for doing Mass in St. Peter's Square. "He was literally a prisoner of the Vatican."

"Newman Center was tied not just to the University but to Dinkytown," Olson said. "They brought the Catholic worker founder in 1963 for a week of talks on Christian anarchism, peace and service to the poor." They had a Catholic worker farm in southern Minnesota. Senator Eugene McCarthy was there, exploring his Catholic beliefs of the time. They also brought in community organizer Saul Alinsky, who taught people how to protest, and comedian and protestor Dick Gregory as speakers.

Others recalled that the Hillel House brought in people to discuss race and religion.

Author Nor Hall said she and Teska in 1972 engaged in "theological conversation about the role of communes in the United States at that time and what the church ought to be in conversation about." They worked with a commune that had a house in the city and a farm in the country. "The most exciting development is the need of a north country co-op that would be a real service to the community and would produce some income," she said. "I worked for the co-op; I learned to cut cheese and weigh nuts."

Hall wrote a dissertation on liturgy and its functions as the voice of the community with a spiritual and social core. "That was a big part of this social change," she said.

Teska noted:

> *My biggest claim to fame was that I had the idea for the New Riverside Café* [on West Bank]. *As soon as we opened the door, it was run by the people working there. It was a collective with workers' self-management based on examples in Israel. As part of our ministry, I felt we needed a place where people could perform in this hotbed of creative energy that wasn't a bar. It was so good, not a bar. It had good food at an affordable price. You could always get a free meal there if you needed it. They tried a*

> *"take what you need and pay what you could afford" policy, but this turned out to be not a sustainable business model.*
>
> *There were enough bars. Here you could hang out and talk. My sacred hope was that it would become a center of political organizing, community building. I wanted to be a street priest in a store front in the West Bank, but the church had no money.*

Some people from different denominations, including the Newman Center, the Episcopal Center and "both kinds of Lutherans," pooled their resources for Teska to live on the West Bank. "I learned over the summer the development plans which were about to destroy the neighborhood and turn it into what is now the Cedar Square West—except it was going to take out the whole thing," he said, explaining his activism in that process.

"It was really quite amazing," Teska said. "A hundred years ago, they were hanging people for organizing unions. And now the American tradition was to transform society in the direction of peace and justice. Those things kind of converged in the 1960s so at its best the church was at the civil rights movement and the antiwar movement."

Participants shared more laughter than solemnity as they recalled the spirit of the movement. Teska said he has been in recovery for twelve years, but some folks shared amusing stories of altered consciousness in the 1960s. "Liturgy is intended to alter consciousness, singing is to do that," he said.

The discussion was hosted by the University Baptist Church at 1219 University Avenue Southeast, which in 2015 began a series of monthly concerts to revive Dinkytown's folk music tradition.

11

BOOKSTORES PROLIFERATE

Edward G. Perine—who founded the Perine Book Company, also known as Perine's Bookstore—was listed in the *Minneapolis City Directory* of 1900 as a student boarding at 3389 Stevens Avenue, which is thirty blocks south of downtown. In 1901 and 1902, Perine was clerk for Nathaniel McCarthy, an editor and publisher for the *Journal of Religious Education* and the Religious Publishing Company at 622 Nicollet Avenue in downtown Minneapolis. From 1905 through 1913, he was a clerk for the H.W. Wilson Company, and in 1912, he was listed as a salesman. In 1914, the year before he opened his own book business, he was a clerk for North-Western School Supply Company.

The 1899 city directory lists the University Bookstore, with H.W. Wilson as manager, at the University of Minnesota campus.

The University Book Store was at 300 Fourteenth Avenue Southeast in the 1907, 1908 and 1909 city directory lists. In 1909, the 1401 University address was also listed as the H.W. Wilson Company, but it was probably the same corner building. Under the University of Minnesota entry with Cyrus Northrop as president, the list of campus offices includes two other off-campus facilities: University of Minnesota Hall, 519 Fourteenth Avenue Southeast, and University Press, 1401 University Avenue Southeast. A university elementary school is listed as being on campus in 1908 and 1909.

The 1914 and 1915 city directories have a business category called "UNIVERSITY BOOKS AND SUPPLIES," and among those listed are two within a block of each other: Minnesota Co-operative Company, 331 Fourteenth Avenue Southeast, and University Book Store, 1401–5 University

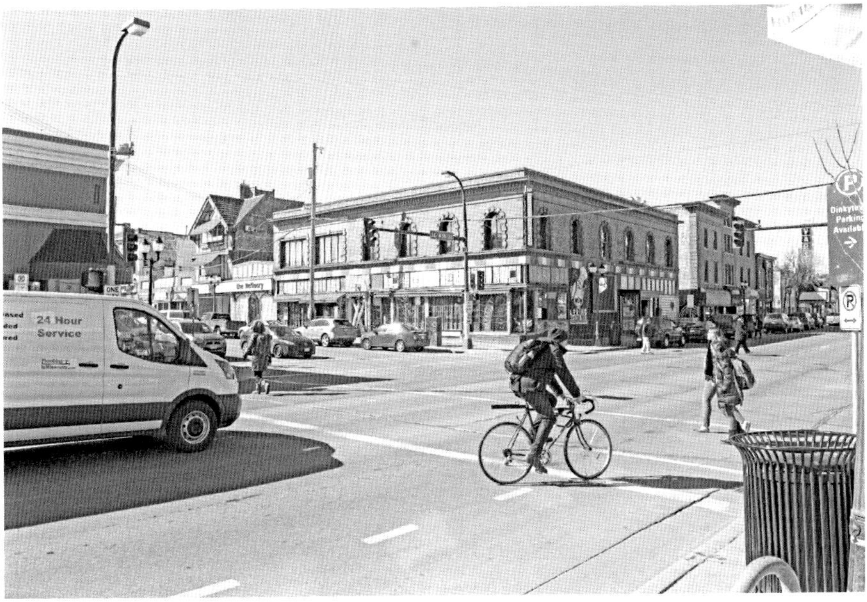

Loring Café has replaced the iconic Gray's Drug on the corner that was once the terminus for the first horse-drawn streetcar in Minneapolis. *Photo by Bill Huntzicker.*

Avenue Southeast. These addresses are a block apart, with the co-op on the site later occupied by Gray's Drug and Loring Café. Two addresses directly across the street from the university's Pillsbury gate were probably the same building: 300 Fourteenth Avenue Southeast and 1401–5 University Avenue Southeast. In 1914, the city directory lists University Book Store at the two addresses in different places in the book.

In the 1916 directory the University Book Store is listed at 300 Fourteenth Avenue Southeast, with both the Minnesota Co-operative Company and Northwestern School Supply listed at 1401–5 University Avenue Southeast. In the same edition, under "books and stationery," the University Book Store is also listed at 1401–5 University Avenue Southeast, probably the same building as the other address of 300 Fourteenth; both addresses are on the corner of Fourteenth and University Avenues. After listing university president George E. Vincent, the directory lists a University Printing Company, also at 1405 University Avenue Southeast. Another bookstore, Perrine Book Company, was added in the same block at 1413 University Avenue Southeast, an address just a couple of doors east of the other bookstores.

In 1920, 1921 and 1922, Minnesota Co-operative Company and the University Book Store are listed separately but at the same address at

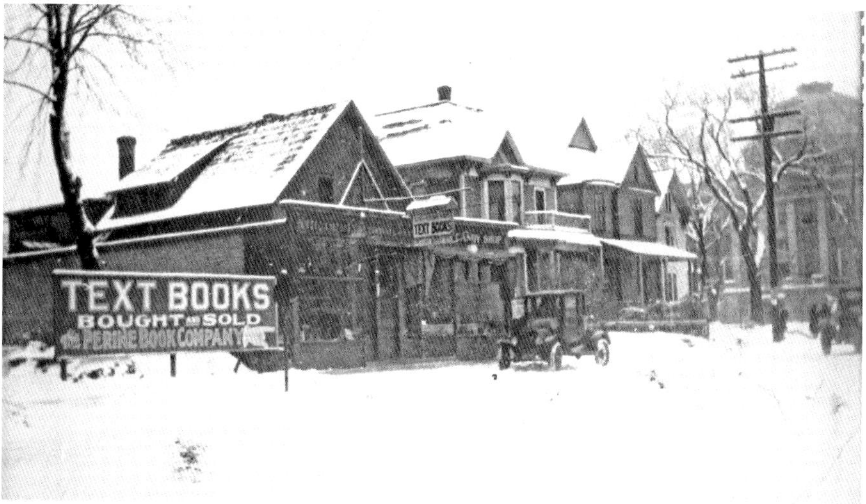
TEXT BOOKS
BOUGHT SOLD
PERINE BOOK COMPANY
TEXT BOOKS

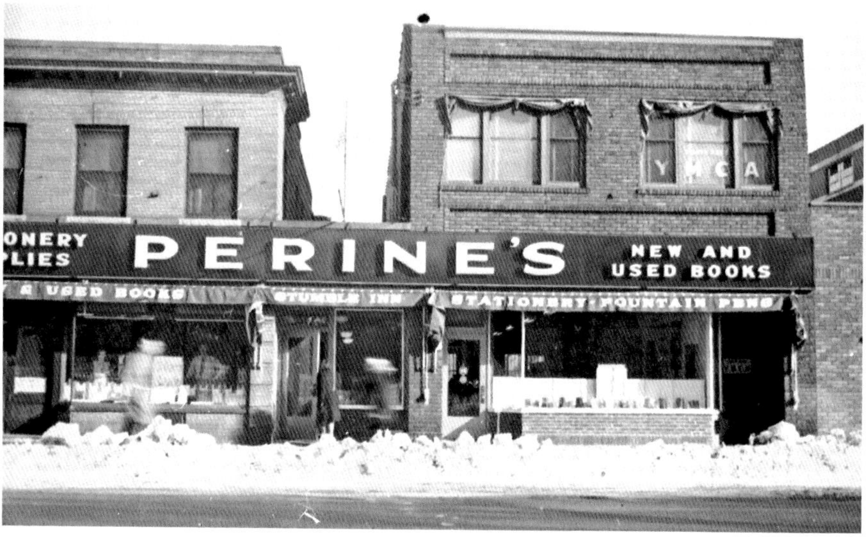
YMCA
PERINE'S
NEW AND
USED BOOKS
& USED BOOKS
STUMBLE INN
STATIONERY · FOUNTAIN PENS

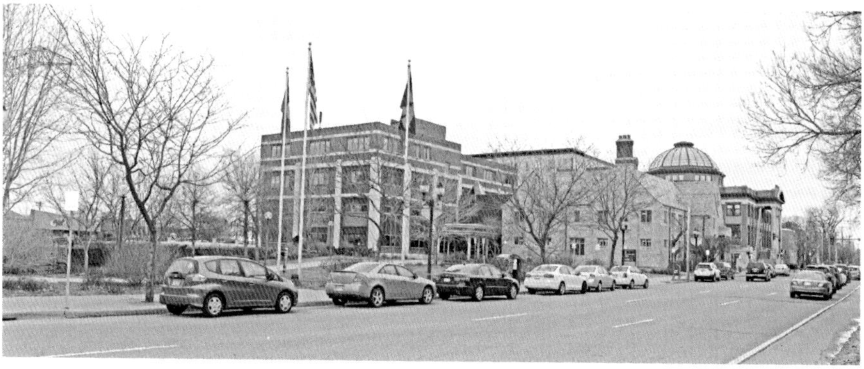

1401 University Avenue Southeast, the former home of the H.W. Wilson Company. Perine's remained to the east in the same block at 1411–13 University through the 1940s.

The point here is that it's hard to follow how many bookstores there were and how much they were corporately related to one another. But it appears that Perine's appeared along University Avenue while H.W. Wilson's store or its successor was still down the block on the corner of Fourteenth and University Avenues Southeast. At the same time, the co-op was still at the iconic corner of Fourth Street and Fourteenth Avenue Southeast.

In 1948, "PERINE BOOK COMPANY" had a premium listing in all caps with E.G. Perine as president and Fred S. Taylor as secretary-treasurer and featuring "College Text Books" at 1411 University Avenue Southeast. Perine's residence was 5617 Third Avenue South.

"The Twin Cities literary scene has some of its roots in the Dinkytown area," noted the city's 2015 draft report for historic designation. The report continued:

> *During the 1950s–1970s, it was a gathering place for writers and readers, with several new and used bookstores. The Loft Literary Center, now located in Downtown Minneapolis, was originally founded in Dinkytown in 1974 in a loft above Rusoff & Co. Book Dealers, 1302 Fourth Street SE. It originated as a venue for local writers, and went on to host readings by a number of prominent authors. It is now one of the nation's largest literary centers.*

The Loft also provided a support group for local authors to read and comment on one another's work.

The report listed other bookstores, including McCosh's Book Store, 1404 Fourth Street Southeast; Perine's Campus Book Store, 315 Fourteenth Avenue Southeast; the Paul Robeson Bookshop, Fifth Street and Thirteenth Avenue; Heddan's Book and Magazine Store, 430 Fourteenth Avenue Southeast; and Dinkytown News newsstand, corner of University and Fourteenth Avenues.

Opposite, top and middle: Some of Dinkytown's earliest businesses, such as Perine's Bookstore on University Avenue Southeast, began in Victorian houses. *Photos from Steven Bergerson collection, University Archives, University of Minnesota.*

Opposite, bottom: Buildings have been removed, and the sites of H.W. Wilson Co. and the original Perine's are a lawn and sidewalk leading to university offices today. *Photo by Bill Huntzicker.*

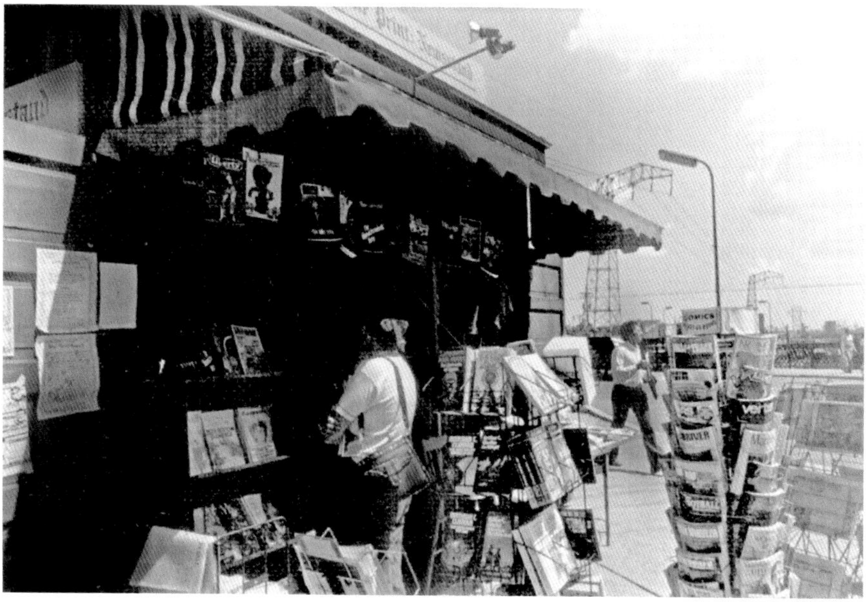

This newsstand at Fourteenth and University Avenues Southeast was on what has been empty sidewalk since the bridges were replaced. *Photo from Linda Gammell, 1974; courtesy special collections, Hennepin County Public Library.*

"There were several periodicals published in the area as well," the designation report noted. "The *Minnesota Review* was a journal of creative and critical writing distributed from Dinkytown in the 1960s. *Nickel and Dime Quarterly* was published in the 1960s by Lewis Hyde, an influential writer and critic. The *North Stone Review*, a literary journal, was published in Dinkytown in the 1970s." The report also mentions the *Little Sandy Review*, a nationally distributed publication that specialized in folk music, and the *Ivory Tower*, the literary section of the *Minnesota Daily*.

Student Garrison Keillor, who worked at the *Ivory Tower*, once said the literary types worked there while "real men" worked in the newsroom of the *Daily*. He also said he was grateful for the opportunities to try out his personas in the campus media. "I was an English major and hung out in Vincent Hall, and the basement of Walter, in a cloud of cigarette smoke. I spent a few years in the basement of Murphy, at the Ivory Tower, imitating E.B. White, and in Eddy Hall, imitating Edward R. Murrow." In those days, the *Daily* was in Murphy Hall with the journalism school, and the campus radio station KUOM was in Eddy Hall.

A generation earlier, Dinkytown was also a literary place. In a memoir of the 1930s and 1940s, poet and novelist Frederick Manfred celebrated Dinkytown's evolving community and its several bookstores:

The biggest and the best was the Minnesota Bookstore where students could buy textbooks and where the general public could buy trade books. Bobby Clark was a clerk there and she and I became good friends. Her husband, John Clark, taught Chaucer in the English Department. The other bookstores featured second-hand and rare books. Julius Butwin ran such a store next to the Crane Stationery, and it was from him I got Skeat's Etymological Dictionary of the English Language, *a book that helped me discover the importance of my Frisian-Saxon ancestry, helped me understand how I could read Chaucer with some ease.*

12

FOLK AND MASS CULTURE

THE CASE OF TEVYE

Julius Butwin and his wife, Frances, introduced the English-speaking world to important books and, in the process, shared their own ancestry with others. Bookhunters, at 1411 Fourth Street Southeast, one block north of Perine's, was in the business of helping people find books in the days before the Internet allowed anyone to locate out-of-print or hard-to-find books for themselves. "My parents loved books," recalled their daughter, Miriam Butwin, a longtime Marcy-Holmes resident. Her parents had come from eastern Europe, Frances from Poland and Julius from Russia, and in a conversation in Bookhunters with Bob Simon of Crown Publishing, they were offered an opportunity to

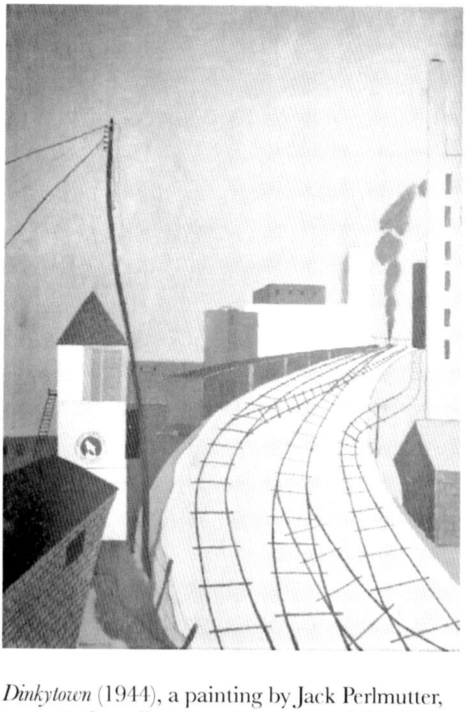

Dinkytown (1944), a painting by Jack Perlmutter, suggests the railroad yard was once visible from Dinkytown. It's the cover of a memoir by his nephew, David Butwin, *A Minnesota Kid* (2012). *Courtesy of David Butwin.*

translate Sholom Aleichem's original Yiddish stories. "My mother always remembered this incident as the source of their project and that my father called out to her: 'Hey, Frances, would you like to join me translating Sholom Aleichem?' So—they did it."

The first book, a collection titled *The Old Country*, was published by Crown in 1946, and "when it met a good critical response, a second volume was done by my mother (my father died in 1945), *Tevye's Daughters*, and later a novel, *Wandering Star*, about a troupe of traveling actors [followed]. Years later, the Tevye stories became *Fiddler on the Roof*—so you could say Fiddler was born in Dinkytown." Miriam Butwin's younger brother has traced the ideas to their mother's childhood in Charleston, South Carolina.

In a review of two books about the history of *Fiddler on the Roof*, Ezra Glinter said that *The Old Country*

> *impressed me as much with its own history as with the material between its covers. Though I didn't learn the details until later, I intuited that* The Old Country *was not just a collection of stories by a turn-of-the-century Yiddish writer; it was, itself, an artifact of midcentury American Jewish life. The book didn't just depict history; it was a piece of it, as well. In the decades since* The Old Country *appeared, and since the 1964 Broadway debut of* Fiddler, *Sholem Aleichem has been thoroughly reevaluated, re-appreciated and re-translated.*

Glinter said he encountered *Fiddler* before he had heard of the author, who, by the way, did not have a fiddler as a major character in his stories. "[I]t is almost impossible today—or at least, very unlikely—to experience Sholom Aleichem unmediated. He comes to us through the lenses of translation and adaptation, each reworking of his material reflecting the moment of its own creation. Even reading him in Yiddish, you can't help but be aware of the later uses of his work. To put it another way, it's hard to get *Fiddler* out of your head." (Even the name, Sholom or Sholem, cannot be encountered unmediated. Because the name comes from a transliteration, it could be correct either way. I've tried to be consistent with the source; the Butwins spelled the name Sholom.)

The Butwins acknowledged the difficulty of translating and selecting representative work from Sholom Aleichem's legacy. "There are twenty-seven stories in the book. I think you'll wish there were more," Frances Butwin wrote in her "Foreword" to *The Old Country*. "There are more. For Jewish literature rejoices in a large body of work by Sholom Aleichem. In all, he wrote some three hundred stories, five novels, many plays, and a number of other works. And we may hope that in time all this work will be translated into English." Frances Butwin said she dropped some archaic language and complex rituals because they would not translate clearly into English. "The work of translating these stories was a delight and a challenge at the same time. Often what was entirely right and simple and flavorsome in Yiddish completely missed fire when translated literally. Some stories just could not be transplanted and had to be abandoned. Sometimes we had to use translators' license with the exact wording."

Yet the original stories depend on language, Frances Butwin wrote in her introduction to *Tevye's Daughters*.

> *Though Sholom Aleichem was a humorist and Tevye is his most famous character, Tevye is not funny. Nearly everything that happens to him and his daughters is tragic. His humor lies in his evaluation of what happens to him, in what he says and the way he says it. In the fact that he misquotes more often than he quotes, and that usually his interpretation of what he is quoting is completely cockeyed, lies his all-pervading charm to the Yiddish reader. No wonder Sholom Aleichem's audiences used to roll in the aisles with laughter. The juxtaposition of a lofty phrase in Hebrew or Aramaic with a homely Yiddish phrase which is supposed to explain it but has no bearing on it whatever—that is the gist of Tevye's humor.*

When the Butwins translated Sholom Aleichem, they had to have the recent Holocaust on their minds and perhaps the anti-Semitism described as pervasive in Minneapolis in contrast to multicultural St. Paul, which had a synagogue almost from its founding.

While the Butwins owned the bookstore in Minneapolis, they lived in St. Paul, where their three children attended public school. Frances, who had been born in Warsaw in 1911, came to the United States with her family in 1922. Julius "was born in 1904 in Volkovysk, a shtetl in the middle of what is now Belarus, then Minsk gubernia of the Tsar's empire. His immediate family came to St. Paul, Minnesota, in 1905," wrote their youngest son, Joseph, who's writing a book about his parents. His mother's Poland

> *was also part of the Tsar's empire. Her parents had themselves only recently arrived in Warsaw from two towns just east of Minsk—Mogilev and Borisov. In Warsaw they were part of what Poles—including Polish Jews—called a "Litvak invasion," part of a vast*

band of recent arrivals considered by some to be dangerous agents of Russian language and literature with a penchant for socialist ideology and godless secularism.

By tradition and experience, then, the Butwins knew something of Sholom Aleichem's world. This Yiddish writer was born Sholom Rabinovitz in 1859 in Pereyaslav, Ukraine, and some of his stories that began in 1894 are framed as correspondence between the dairyman and the author's pseudonym, which came to replace his given name in both his fiction and his life. The Butwins were not the first to translate Sholom Aleichem; his works had been performed in Yiddish film and theater. But the Butwins popularized his work at a time of fear that his culture would disappear.

Even though the original stories may be seen as critical in the world of the 1940s, they became nostalgic. "Taken together," Frances Butwin wrote, "all of these stories are a part of the life, forever vanished, which Sholom Aleichem reproduced so faithfully, with tenderness, with humor and with sharp penetration, but never with malice or bitterness."

The original stories satirized the world of the shetls (small towns) and were translated into the American English of *The Old Country*. When this was later translated into the Broadway musical sensation of *Fiddler on the Roof*, the old-world Yiddish mocking became an amazing universal nostalgia.

Frances Butwin's translation of the Yiddish was, of course, her own interpretation of the specific culture of eastern Europe that by 1946 was destroyed. Prior to the Nazi extermination there had been pogroms by roving bands of Cossacks that resulted in rapes, murders and wanton destruction of Jewish homes. In the immediate aftermath of the Holocaust, Butwin's creative mind was attempting the incomprehensible act of translating a lost world, its culture and language and its immeasurable suffering.

Tevye's quotations, Michael Stern has written, "are used by Tevye as a running commentary on the story itself and often, as weapons in his verbal battle with God. Through his own comparisons with biblical personalities and in the light of his interpretations of classical Jewish sources, the quotations and glosses enable the reader to understand how Tevye sees himself, his family members, and the other persons with whom he deals." They help Tevye, who "suffers grievous misfortunes," to express his bitterness and anger. "When this happens, his Hebrew quotation articulates a standard to which he believes God should adhere, while his Yiddish comment shows how far reality falls short of that ideal."

In *Wonder of Wonders: A Cultural History of Fiddler on the Roof*, Alisa Solomon speculated how far off the rails the stories could have gone if the original artists interested had gained control of the musical. Richard Rodgers and Oscar Hammerstein II—both with German Jewish backgrounds—should have some affinity for the material. But they were busy adapting *Anna and the King of Siam* to become the musical *The King and I*. Perhaps the old country would look like the South Pacific or Oklahoma. Another potential producer was Michael Todd, known for what Solomon called "upscale burlesques." He was the son of a rabbi in a family of Polish immigrants. Solomon's and at least three other books have been written that pick up the evolution of *Fiddler* to Broadway and film by people who took on a serious cultural burden. A successful Broadway production celebrated the fiftieth anniversary of the play in 2016.

Glinter said the play and stories were expected to carry too much weight, even though he said modern acceptance of Jewish culture owed much the stories and the ubiquitous musical. Tevye's tragedies involved both his personal generation gap in which his daughters choose modern over traditional religious ways and the external threats to Jews with pogroms that took people away. The lost world the Butwins conveyed was more than nostalgia; it introduced the pre-Holocaust horrors of anti-Semitism, but the drama seemed to pale in contrast to the Holocaust and Cold War America.

In their translations, the Butwins took us back to a culture and time that could never be completely re-created or understood in 1940s America, and they launched Tevye on a journey that neither he nor they could possibly have imagined.

As a writer for the *Saturday Review* magazine in 1972, David Butwin said he still received letters from people who recalled his father's love of books and the interests he shared with customers. "My father knew books. He was from all I've read and heard a master book hunter, who combed through second hand stores and spent inordinate (to some) time advising customers on what [to] and what not to read."

Julius Butwin died in 1945 just as he and Frances were completing the first translation. He was forty-one, and his children were nine, six and two years old. Son David and daughter Miriam remember hanging around the bookstore, even though it lasted only a few years—it's listed in city directories of 1944 through 1948. "I knew Bridgeman's from my earliest days," David Butwin recalled. "In the 1940s, my parents owned a book shop, Bookhunters, across the street on Fourth near Fifteenth. My sister and I loved rattling around in the store, exploring the dark eerie basement with its tiny biffy, but the highlight of any visit was a stop at Bridgeman's."

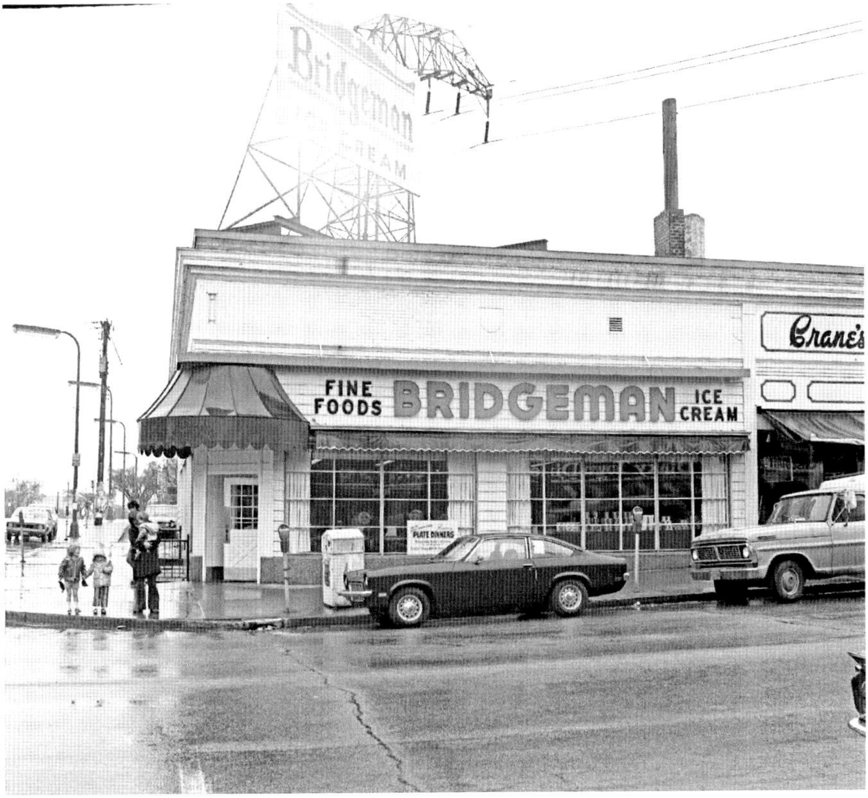

Bridgeman's was a popular ice cream parlor and restaurant through the 1970s. The corner was reused by Purple Onion coffee shop and then a Potbelly sandwich shop. *Photo by Steven Bergerson.*

Faced with raising three children as a single parent, Frances Butwin left the bookstore business, completed a degree in library science from the University of Minnesota in 1953 and worked for about twenty years as a reference librarian for the Minneapolis Public Library. The 1950 city directory lists Varsity Bookstore in the site formerly occupied by Bookhunters.

Their store was one of several bookstores that evoked strong affection from customers. Dinkytown memories collected in recent years often mention bookstores. And the Butwins' store, with its popularization of Yiddish literature, was certainly not the last of Dinkytown businesses to straddle a line between folk and mass culture.

The Butwin translation of Sholom Aleichem's *The Old Country* made the *New York Times* bestseller list in 1946, along with a book by University of Minnesota professor Robert Penn Warren. His *All the King's Men* subsequently won a Pulitzer Prize and was made into two successful films.

13

MANFRED'S MEMORIES

"It was in April of 1937 when I first began living in Dinkytown," wrote poet and novelist Frederick Manfred in a memoir called *Dinkytown*.

Manfred had begun his first job as a reporter for the *Minneapolis Journal* and moved into a boardinghouse at 628 Fourteenth Avenue Southeast, across the street from his brother Floyd, a freshman at the university. Without a car, Manfred caught the Como Harriet streetcar to work. "The lawns had just barely turned green and the lilacs in the backyards were cropping out with thick brown buds amid the crocuses on the sunny side of the garages rustled soft purples," he wrote.

The reporting job provided Manfred with his first full-time salary since graduating in 1934 from Calvin College in Grand Rapids, Michigan, and his recollections provide a window into the social, literary and political life of Dinkytown.

> *On my day off, Thursday, when I wasn't typing what eventually became my first novel,* The Golden Bowl, *I often sauntered south down the street to visit the various stores near the corner of Fourteenth Avenue and Fourth Street: five-and-dime, ice cream palace, Walgreen's Drugstore, the Minnesota Bookstore, Perine's Bookstore, and several hole-in-wall groceries, Chinese laundry, radio repair shop, dry cleaners, a ladies style shop, Varsity Theatre, book-and-stationery shop.*
>
> *Late in the afternoon that corner swarmed with students and occasional professors and housewives. Times were very tough then, yet most students*

> *wore good conventional clothes, sober colors for the men gray and blue, somewhat more lively colors for the ladies yellow and green, with the housewives almost always wearing a shawl pulled tight over their hair only their faces showing. Quips and laughter could be heard all afternoon long. Since everybody was just about in the same plight, almost broke, everybody bore up with a tough-titty smile. We were all in the same foundering boat so we might just as well smile as curse.*
>
> *Thursday evenings I often went to a movie at the Varsity. I somehow always managed to scrape up a quarter for the show. I was quite shy, and didn't date, so the movie was a welcome way to spend an evening. I often looked at the girls and wondered when I'd finally get up enough nerve to ask one of the prettier ones, coeds, if I could take them out. It is interesting to remember that in the two years I lived on that side of the University of Minnesota campus I didn't once run into my future wife, Maryanna Shorba. She lived within a block of where I lived, from 1936 until 1939. ... I thought her a beautiful woman and I've always been sure that had I seen her earlier in Dinkytown I would have surely sought her out.*

Two housemates acquired a two- by ten-foot plank, long enough to reach from a window on the second floor over to a window of the next-door rooming house, where some young women lived.

> *One night the landlady next door living below the two coeds heard what she thought was some suspicious noises directly over her bedroom. She was a huge tall woman with square shoulders and long powerful arms. She burst in on Benny and his friend as they were coupling with two of her female boarders. She let out a roar, pulled the plank over to her side, gave Benny and his buddy each a tremendous kick in the butt, and banished the two girls. Then she sailed over and made a complaint to Mrs. Pappas* [Manfred's landlady] *that she, an abandoned wife, was running a house of ill repute, full of vipers and fornicators and despoilers of virgins, and that she was going to report to the housing authorities at the University of Minnesota.*

Manfred said he wrote the second and third drafts of his first novel at 522 Twelfth Avenue Southeast and the first draft of his novel *This Is the Year*. At this address, too, he received his first box full of rejection notices.

He said he attended meetings of the Farmer Labor Party in an empty store across the street from Varsity Theater.

Listening to the arguments between the radicals and the old-line liberals, between the Reds and the University crowd, livened up many an evening, and taught me something about our society as well as the political climate of the time. There I met several lovely ladies who weren't adverse to having me take them home in my rumbling old blue Dodge. Two of them were delighted to learn that I lived nearby and that most evenings my brother was busy at work (as a way of paying his way through college).

Manfred and his brother moved to 1119 Sixth Street Southeast when his landlady moved. "During those days in 1938, I met through Arthur Naftalin, who was taking journalism at the University, various members of the Jacobin Club; Fred Rarig, Eric Sevareid (then known as Arnie), Sherman Dryer, Richard Scammon, Lee Loevenger, about a dozen of them. Eric also worked with me for a time at the *Journal*. The Jacobins questioned everything and in general tended to be quite liberal." After moving to the Stadium Village area on Oak Street and Washington Avenue, he said he returned periodically to Dinkytown to buy books and go to the Varsity Theater and political meetings.

Early in 1939, I was fired from the Minneapolis Journal. (Eric Sevareid was fired by the same man the year before.) The Journal was in the process of being sold, and the management was cutting back on the help, and the rule was, "last hired first fired." There was also in the firing the hint that I'd been a bit too active in helping establish the Newspaper Guild in the Twin Cities. I lived on Workman's Compensation for a while, was a busboy at a teahouse on Washington Avenue, walked the streets looking for work (of any kind!) and wrote when I had the heart for it.

In 1978, Manfred shared his recollections of Hubert Humphrey, whom he met in a rooming house across the street from Marshall High School in the 1930s. At their first meeting, he and their friends talked about the small towns in South Dakota and Iowa where they had grown up. They occasionally saw each other while Humphrey worked at Brown Drug on Washington Avenue on the other side of campus. Humphrey's family owned a drugstore in South Dakota. Manfred lost his job at the *Journal* while Humphrey was in Louisiana earning his master's degree in political science. Manfred contracted tuberculosis, recuperated in Glen Lake Sanatorium for two years, lived in a rest home, worked on his writing and took a job with *Modern Medicine* as an abstractor. He didn't see Humphrey for four years.

"Then in April, 1943, the phone rang in our home around 9 p.m. I was already in bed with my wife," wrote Manfred. Art Naftalin, who had switched to political science, invited him to meet with friends, including Hubert Humphrey, who was thinking of running for mayor. Humphrey knew that Manfred was a reporter who knew his way around city hall and had union contacts through the Newspaper Guild. Manfred, who also knew his way around the rest of the city, signed on. "So gradually I was the one who rode with Hubert everywhere in his car. I was supposed to be his driver, but he was too impatient to let me drive and I wound up sitting in front with him, listening to him expound on one thing or another. Still Hubert could be a good listener."

Manfred said he encouraged Humphrey to confront a CIO union leader whose support he was seeking. Humphrey responded to the man's question about his views of the Soviet Union: "I doubt that as mayor of Minneapolis I'll be very much concerned with any international dealings with Russia. The really important issue is this: Do you want a good mayor in the office here who will clean up the city, get rid of gambling, prostitution, and all underworld connections?" He also promised "a fair shake to the labor movement."

Manfred also persuaded Humphrey to confront the incumbent in the mayor's office with reporters present. These recollections of the first campaign are a fun read, recounting the old days of threats and offers of bribes and Humphrey's energy, enthusiasm and optimism. "Never did I see him in a down mood," Manfred wrote.

Humphrey lost that first campaign, but two years later, he was elected mayor. Although Manfred doesn't discuss this, Humphrey was the nation's first mayor to establish a city human rights commission to fight racism and anti-Semitism. Then in 1948, he made his famous speech to the Democratic National Convention in Philadelphia advocating civil rights, and the rest, as they say, is history.

While he was living around Dinkytown, Manfred encountered some of the nation's literary lights and their critics, many of whom were on the University of Minnesota faculty. He developed a friendship with Warren, who was finishing the final draft *All the King's Men* when they met. He met poet Allen Tate, also on the faculty, and poet Carl Sandburg and lesser lights like Max Shulman and Thomas Heggen, who were his wife's classmates. Schulman, a humor writer for the *Daily*, created the Dobie Gillis stories and the Dobie film and television series. Heggen wrote *Mister Roberts*, a novel and a play made famous on Broadway and in Hollywood by a previous university student, actor Henry Fonda.

At a Dinkytown reunion in November 2014, Southeast resident Barbara Camm read poetry that connected the university and Dinkytown. One poem, "Today John Berryman Jumped to His Death" by Minnesota poet Joe Paddock, was written on January 7, 1972, when the Pulitzer Prize–winning poet and professor died. Paddock wrote, "A few months back/I sat beside him at the counter/in Gray's Drug Store/his thin hand fluttering/as he struggled/to drink his coffee/eat the buttered center of his toast."

The journalism, English and humanities programs at the university attracted intellectuals who hung out in Dinkytown. The Minneapolis Symphony employed musicians who lived in the area when the orchestra's home was Northrop auditorium on campus.

14

DYLAN, A DOLLAR, A TEN O'CLOCK SCHOLAR

When Bobby Zimmerman moved into a fraternity house in Southeast Minneapolis, he traded his electric guitar in for a Double-O Martin acoustic, browsed record stores to hear new music in the listening booths, changed his name to Bob Dylan and listened to and performed folk music at local coffee houses—all beginning in Dinkytown and the Marcy-Holmes Neighborhood.

"The area around the university was known as Dinkytown, which was kind of like a little village, untypical from the rest of conventional Minneapolis," Dylan wrote in his memoir, *Chronicles, Volume One.* "It was mostly filled with Victorian houses that were being used as student apartments."

Dylan, who lived in the area for about fifteen months beginning in 1959, rented a room above Gray's Drug Store on that corner of Fourteenth Avenue and Fourth Street Southeast for thirty dollars a month.

"Above Gray's, the crash pad was no more than an empty storage room with a sink and a window looking into an alley. No closet or anything. Toilet down the hall. I put a mattress on the floor, bought a used dresser, plugged in a hot plate on top of that—used the outside window ledge as a refrigerator when it got cold," he wrote.

None of the businesses Dylan mentioned remains in Dinkytown, and the last music and guitar store, the Podium, changed ownership and moved to 4151 Minnehaha Avenue South after it was displaced by Venue, a mixed-use apartment building, in 2013.

The Ten O'Clock Scholar, most commonly called just the Scholar, was the best-known center of folk music among the coffee shops near the campus.

Dylan wrote that he made three to five dollars every time he played at the Ten O'Clock Scholar, which he described as "a Beat coffeehouse" near Fifth Street and Fourteenth Avenue Southeast.

Around the same time that Dylan hit town, Paul Nelson and Jon Pankake started the *Little Sandy Review*, a low-budget but national publication devoted to folk music. "We are two people who love folk music very much and want to do all we can to help the good in it grow and the bad to perish." The editors sought feedback for their candid reviews. "By all means, write in and we'll print your letter."

In their second issue, they revealed a favorite: "Until Alan Lomax's first commercial recordings came out some time back, a great portion of the folksong public was unaware that this man, in addition to his innumerable other distinctions, is one of America's finest folksingers. This reviewer has heard no active modern singers other than Pete Seeger (and his genius with audiences) and Jean Ritchie (and the heritage she shares with her music) who can be so commanding and expressive as Lomax."

In his autobiography, however, Dylan called Pankake "a folk music purist enthusiast and sometime literary teacher and film wiseman, who'd been watching me for a while on the scene, made it his business to tell me that what I was doing hadn't escaped him. 'What do you think you're doing? You're singing nothing but Guthrie songs,' he said, jabbing his finger into my chest like he was talking to a poor fool."

Pankake, who lived less than a block from the Scholar, "was part of the folk police, if not the chief commissioner, wasn't impressed with any of the new talent. To him nobody possessed any great mastery—no one could succeed in laying a hand on any of the traditional stuff with any authority."

Dylan acknowledged that Pankake's advice to go beyond Woody Guthrie songs was correct and that Pankake exposed him to rare folk records he would not have heard otherwise.

After acquiring his acoustic guitar, Dylan wrote, "I then went further up the street and dropped into the Ten O'Clock Scholar, a Beat coffeehouse. I was looking for players with kindred pursuits. The first guy I met in Minneapolis like me was sitting around in there. It was John Koerner and he also had an acoustic guitar with him. Koerner was tall and thin with a look of perpetual amusement on his face. We hit it off right away."

The two began performing together and separately. "Now that I crossed the divide, I was head over heels in singing nothing but Guthrie songs—at house parties, in the coffeehouses, street singing, with Koerner, not with Koerner—if I had a shower I would have sung in there, too," Dylan wrote.

Koerner also performed as part of a local trio, whose other members were Dave Ray and Tony Glover. The group, which could have been called Koerner and/or Ray and/or Glover because they worked together and separately, performed more blues than folk music with "Spider" John Koerner on guitar and vocals, Dave "Snaker" Ray on guitar and vocals and Tony "Little Sun" Glover on harmonica. They took nicknames so they could identify with southern African American blues singers, who also had nicknames.

Upon receiving the Minnesota Music Academy's Hall of Fame award in 1985, Koerner said, "We never would have become what we became if we hadn't been hanging around Twin Cities, especially the Bohemian sections of Dinkytown and the West Bank. If anyone knows where some two-bit musicians like ourselves can get some work, leave a message at the 400 bar down at Cedar-Riverside."

The award was presented by Bonnie Raitt, who had approached them to help with her first album for Warner Brothers in January 1971. Pianist Willie Murphy, another university-area entertainer, accompanied her with his band, Willie and the Bees, and produced the album on which she sings Koerner's "I Ain't Blue." Murphy had collaborated with Koerner on "Running, Jumping, Standing Still," originally recorded for Electra and reissued on Red House Records of Minneapolis.

Music wasn't the only appeal of the Scholar. Erik Fraser Storlie and his friends were

> *habitués of Minneapolis' first coffeehouse, which we dubbed the "Squalor." It sat near campus in Dinkytown, several blocks of two- and three-story apartments and storefronts—drug store, ice cream shop, Ivy League clothing store, and even a used bookstore run by the disheveled and bearded eccentric Melvin McCosh. McCosh had already sold me my own copy of Allen Ginsberg's Howl. Sometimes we stayed into the evening listening to music by local wannabes.*
>
> *Splotchy oils hung above the tables along the side walls and, to my amazement, near the door, a black-and-white close-up of a woman's breast, the areola revealing pores, gooseflesh, and tiny hairs. Whenever I walked in, I surveyed it doing my best to show a purely artistic interest.*
>
> *We were getting to know some black people, especially an easygoing young guy everybody called Striker. It felt strange. West High had no blacks. I wanted to ask him how it felt, hanging out with whites. But asking would upset an understanding that getting to know each other was no big deal.*

What was a big deal, Storlie wrote,

> *was to be welcomed into rooms swirling with drink and talk, rooms filled with people who read poetry, and knew philosophy, who had been to Greenwich Village and North Beach, had even published books. Striker might be there. And there'd be folk music too—John Koerner, Dave Ray, Tony Glover, Harry Weber, Bob Dylan, Hugh Brown. Half my friends were now folk musicians, listening to Leadbelly and spinning Folkways records.*

In their book of walking tours, *Walking Twin Cities*, Holly Day and Sherman Wick called Bob Dylan the ghost of Dinkytown. Since arriving from Hibbing on the Iron Range in northern Minnesota, his

> *shadow is omnipresent, thanks to the unbelievable success he attained almost immediately after leaving for New York City in January 1961. The Dinkytown folk scene of this period has a different version of Dylan than the conquering hero myth that has accrued over ensuing years. Dylan is remembered for being booed off the stage at the tiny 10 O'Clock Scholar during its folk heyday and for purloining rare folk records from contemporaries in the small scene.*
>
> *Whether Dylan's success was due entirely to talent and ambition or to the desire of his record company, the media, and a growing youth culture to anoint a rough-hewn poet for their generation is debatable. Regardless, Dylan is an international icon who began his career in Dinkytown, and his shadow is cast on everyone and everything in this little neighborhood.*

Some have said that "Positively Fourth Street" was obviously based on Fourth Street that ran past his room in Dinkytown. Of course, this contention is easily disputed in favor of the less friendly Fourth Street in New York City, where he also spent time.

Memories of the Scholar also vary, with some calling it sleazy and others having fond memories of it. A man who grew up in Minnetonka said he came to Dinkytown as a high school student to hear the man he thought wrote "The Garden Song" ("Inch by inch, row by row, going to make this garden grow") and performed it regularly at the Scholar. A Minneapolis neighbor of mine was also a high school student when he often took a bus from his suburban Brooklyn Center home to Dinkytown to hear folk music at the Scholar and other coffee shops on the West Bank and near Oak and Washington. Neither of them remembers Bob Dylan performing there.

Others will claim they heard Dylan regularly, sometimes remembering more performances than he actually did.

Blame Dylan for some of the exaggeration. Ron Rosenbaum, who interviewed Dylan for *Playboy* magazine in 1978, introduced his article by admitting that his readers already know how Dylan

> *created emotional roadmaps for an entire generation. How, in the midst of increasingly frenzied rock-'n'-roll touring, Dylan continued to surround the details of his personal life with mystery and wise-guy obfuscation, mystery that deepened ominously after his near-fatal motorcycle accident in 1966. And how, after a long period of bucolic retreat devoted to fatherhood, family and country music, he suddenly returned to the stage with big nationwide tours* [in 1974 and 1976].

Introducing his interview in *Playboy* in 1966, Nat Hentoff said many of Dylan's friends failed to foresee his success.

> *Some found its flat Midwestern tones gratingly mesmeric; others agreed with a Missouri folk singer who had likened the Dylan sound to that of "a dog with his leg caught in barbed wire." All agreed, however, that his songs were strangely personal and often disturbing, a pungent mixture of loneliness and defiance laced with traces of Guthrie, echoes of the Negro blues singers and more than a suggestion of country-and-western; but essentially Dylan was developing his own penetratingly distinctive style. Yet the voice was so harsh and the songs so bitterly scornful of conformity, race prejudice and the mythology of the Cold War that most of his friends couldn't conceive of Dylan making it big even though folk music was already on the rise.*

In the interview, though, Dylan denied he was a folk singer. "And folk music is a word I can't use," Dylan said.

> *Folk music is a bunch of fat people. I have to think of all this as traditional music. Traditional music is based on hexagrams. It comes about from legends, Bibles, plagues, and it revolves around vegetables and death. There's nobody that's going to kill traditional music. All these songs about roses growing out of people's brains and lovers who are really geese and swans that turn into angels—they're not going to die. It's all those paranoid people who think that someone's going to come and take away their toilet paper—they're going to die.*

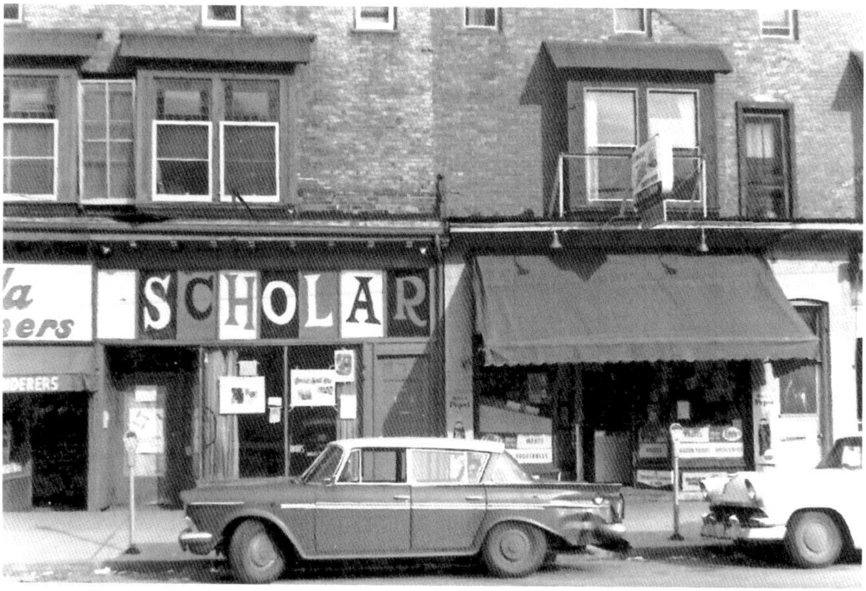

This page: The Ten O'Clock Scholar in 1965 and its demolition in 1967 after a fire. *Photos courtesy Al Milgrom.*

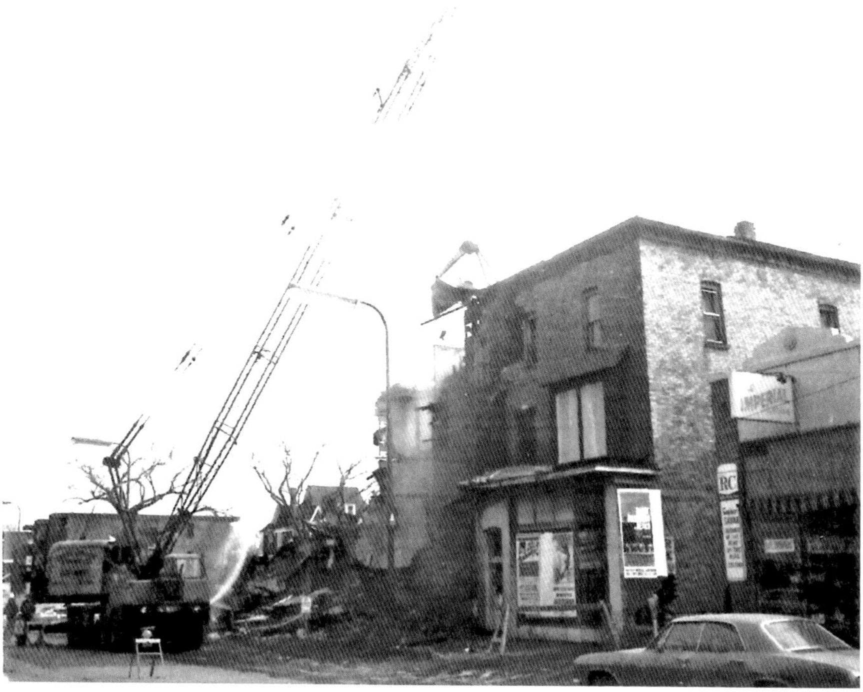

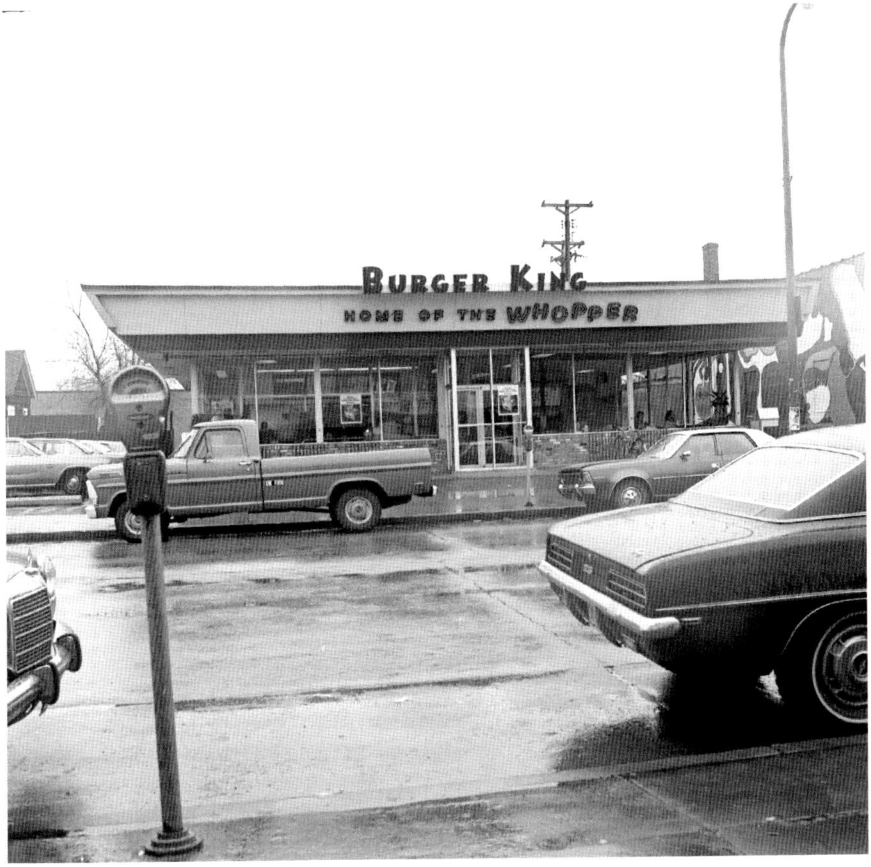

A Burger King and surface parking replaced the building that housed the Ten O'Clock Scholar and other businesses. *Photo by Steven Bergerson, housed by University Archives, University of Minnesota.*

Dylan acknowledged that Dinkytown poet Dave Whittaker introduced him to Woody Guthrie's *Bound for Glory*, a book that strongly influenced him. He decided then to meet Guthrie, who was in a long-term care home in New Jersey. When he left Minneapolis, Dylan was not only out to play to larger audiences and to meet other artists, but more importantly, he was going to meet and spend time with Woody Guthrie whose songs he performed and loved.

In the *New Yorker* in 1964, Hentoff cites Nelson and Pankake on the outcome of that trip.

> *The editors, who were students at the university then, have since noted in their publication: "We recall Bob as a soft-spoken, rather unprepossessing*

> *youngster…well-groomed and neat in the standard campus costume of slacks, sweater, white oxford sneakers, poplin raincoat, and dark glasses."…"In a mere half year," they have recalled in the* Little Sandy Review, *"he had learned to churn up exciting, bluesy, hard-driving harmonica-and-guitar music, and had absorbed during his visits with Guthrie not only the great Okie musician's unpredictable syntax but his very vocal color, diction, and inflection. Dylan's performance that spring evening of a selection of Guthrie…songs was hectic and shaky, but it contained all the elements of the now-perfected performing style that has made him the most original newcomer to folk music."*

Their reaction belied Dylan's *Chronicles* comment about Pankake's distain for newcomers. The manager of the Scholar reportedly stopped Dylan's gig at least once because people were leaving. Whatever the differences, Dylan also performed at the Purple Onion in St. Paul. (There is a Purple Onion coffee shop in Dinkytown in 2016, but it has no connection to Dylan's stay in Dinkytown.)

Dylan's efforts at college education are similarly contradictory. Everyone agrees that he flunked out. When I took a course on the history of American music, the professor confessed that Dylan had failed his music history course. Thus he encouraged us to do other kinds of work, such as a music composition or audio recording, if academic research didn't appeal. He seemed embarrassed to admit that "the greatest folk singer of our time" failed his music course, even though Dylan may have never attended class.

Dylan has said, however, that he never attended classes. But Hentoff gives him credit for at last making an effort:

> *In "My Life in a Stolen Moment," Dylan has summarized his college career dourly: "I sat in science class an' flunked out for refusin' to watch a rabbit die. I got expelled from English class for using four-letter words in a paper describing the English teacher. I also failed out of communication class for callin' up every day and sayin' I couldn't come.…I was kept around for kicks at a fraternity house. They let me live there, an' I did until they wanted me to join."*

These memories seem slightly off key from those recalled in *Chronicles.* Nonetheless, with or without Dylan, the Scholar retains an important place in Dinkytown lore. The simple storefront belied its significance. A fire that started in the adjacent store that neighborhood residents called the "dirty grocery" caused significant damage to the half block of buildings that included apartments and stores. A demolition permit was taken out in March 1967 to level what remained of the buildings from 414 to 430 Fourteenth Avenue Southeast. They were replaced by a Burger King fast-food restaurant—a site that today houses a Subway, Pizza Hut and TCF Bank, and their surface parking lot.

At a Dinkytown reunion on November 23, 2014, nearly 150 current and former Southeast Minneapolis residents heard a folk music set by singer-guitarist Pop Wagner and another set by Willie Murphy playing an energetic keyboard. Videographer Ossian Or, the emcee for the evening, was among several who remembered the Varsity when it was a theater. "I remember when this was a photography studio for many years after the theater closed," he said. "I worked on film and video here. I realize that the person who occupied this as a photo studio for so many years served as a place holder" until Jason McLean created the current space that attracts acts from all over the world to its stage.

Many Dinkytown musicians moved to West Bank venues, especially after the Scholar closed. Journalist Cyn Collins interviewed many of them and created a compilation CD for her book *West Bank Boogie.*

Jerry Rau remained a prominent fixture on Dinkytown sidewalks for decades with his guitar and original folk songs. Many of these local musicians have public online selections through YouTube.

15

POSTWAR SOCIAL CHANGE

The university faced major changes as a result of World War II, Steve Bergerson found in his research.

> *Total enrollment at the University dropped from 21,688 in 1940 to 12,633 in 1943, but the University campus was still filled to overflowing with people enlisted in the war training programs. The University was training Navy, Army and Air Force personnel in specialized fields. There were accelerated nursing courses and Japanese and European language courses. Many fraternity houses were converted to housing for enlisted men or into offices for transferring and clearing men coming to and leaving the campus. University Avenue was blockaded and drill was conducted on the street. Training was accelerated and the average soldier stayed about four weeks.*

A flood of students returned after the war, creating overcrowding that was compounded by the number of professors killed during the war or on military leave, Bergerson wrote. The GI Bill encouraged large numbers of veterans to attend college. "The number of men enrolled at the University increased from 2,805 in the fall of 1944 to 20,358 in the fall of 1946. Total registration after the war was nearly double the pre-war registration and twice as many students were crammed into the same number of classrooms."

Students increased in age, stimulating changes in the campus climate. Older men and women didn't view the fraternities and sororities as necessary as their

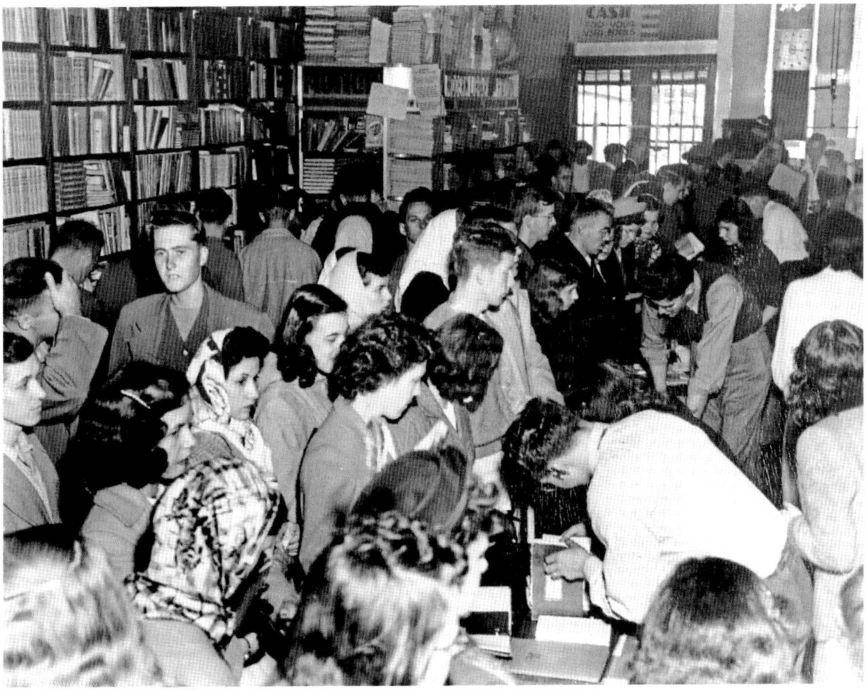

University services were taxed by the influx of students after World War II. Here they are shopping for books at Perine's. *Photo courtesy special collections, Minneapolis Central, Hennepin County Library.*

parents had. "These older, more experienced, war veterans were well aware of the important position the United States held as a world power and were involved as never before in the controversial issues arising from the war and United States foreign and domestic policy," Bergerson wrote. "Dinkytown became a small, self-sufficient town providing everything for the students and the community. In addition to three bookstores, and two groceries, there were dry cleaners, a Laundromat, a hardware store, family restaurants, a theatre, barbers, plumbers, electricians, tailors, drug stores, and a baker." As the campus expanded, housing, already in short supply, gave way to athletic fields.

When leaders of Preserve Historic Dinkytown solicited personal experiences that would support historic designation, two representatives of that World War II generation who responded to requests for Dinkytown memories were former vice president Walter F. Mondale and David W. Noble, professor emeritus of American studies at the University of Minnesota. Both men said their personal experiences in Dinkytown provided vital lessons of integration and social change.

Noble said it would be impossible to overstate the importance of Dinkytown in building community among students and faculty. "Dinkytown became an important part of my academic life in the 1960s," wrote Noble, who received his doctorate in 1952 from the University of Wisconsin with help from the GI Bill and began teaching history and American studies in Minnesota the same year.

> *At that moment I was not aware that I was participating in a major cultural revolution. In retrospect I see World War II calling into question a powerful pattern of segregation that existed in the 1930s. At the end of 1944 I was discharged as a disabled veteran.*
>
> *There was a pattern of segregation that protected the purity of white Protestants from all people of color as well as from white Catholics and Jews.*

Although these groups were not integrated into the campus when he arrived, he watched the process of integration of these groups, along with women, in Dinkytown.

> *As that pattern of segregation broke down so did patterns of racial, religious, and gender segregation. By the 1960s the Minnesota History Department was moving toward an integrated faculty, and American Studies was moving toward a vision of a United States integrated with the rest of the world. By 1960 I found students challenging the segregation of the faculty from students….Dinkytown became a very important place where one could challenge the segregation of faculty from students. Here I was reminded that I was a student as well as a teacher. I was reminded that students had many important things to teach me….Dinkytown also became important to me because its integrated culture at the edge of the campus was challenging the academic tradition that segregated mind and body.*
>
> *I participated in this desegregation movement by chatting with students in Dinkytown. Dinkytown, therefore, is, for me, the place in the 1960s where students and faculty came together to discern ways to break down continuing patterns of segregation, including academic segregation. The students were teaching us that popular culture, especially popular music, was an important part of life. For the students, academics should stop segregating high culture from popular culture. They should stop segregation of classical music from popular music. Soon professors across the country were creating courses on popular culture with an emphasis on popular music. Dinkytown integrationists played their part well in this change.*

In his testimonial published in the *Star Tribune* the morning before the city council voted on historic designation, Mondale reflected on Dinkytown's significance.

> *Throughout its 125-year history, Dinkytown has been a training ground, a laboratory, an entrepreneurial incubator, a "hometown away from home" and "a university of the streets" for students, businesspeople, faculty, alumni, bohemians, neighborhood residents and visitors from all over the world.*
>
> *Dinkytown's strong sense of place is built upon a familiar landscape of buildings and streets that bind generations of engaged Minnesotans who have benefited from this local proliferation of vision and energy.*
>
> *From the 1950s to the 1970s, with its proximity to the university, its affordable spaces and quirky culture, Dinkytown was fertile ground for new creative movements in dance, theater, poetry, publishing and music. The transformative political and social movements of those times took root in challenging conversations at my old friend, Melvin McCosh's bookstore, at the Ten O'Clock Scholar coffeehouse, at the Bridgeman's and Gray's Drug lunch counters. The bus carrying civil-rights activists to Mississippi picked up in Dinkytown in 1964. And Bob Dylan's ringing anthems were positively rooted on Fourth Street.*

Mondale said the Red Barn protest to defend a small business community was as important as the civil rights and antiwar protests germinated there. Minneapolis should "protect the physical structures and scale of Dinkytown from the kind of redevelopment that would utterly erase the memory of a seminal time and place."

Mondale said his connections with Dinkytown have only deepened with time.

> *I am reminded that the visions of social justice tested in Dinkytown and the university community were carried forward by the likes of Hubert Humphrey, Don and Arvonne Fraser, Bob Dylan and, if I may say so, by myself. I am now deep into my 80s, but those memories of what this remarkable little community has meant to all of us remain a deep influence in my life. Dinkytown always has been life sized—indeed dinky—and I am very afraid that if we destroy the small-scale buildings themselves, it will erase those memories and the meaning and, therefore, the history could be seriously impaired.*

Fraternities, sororities and Dinkytown provided opportunities for students to establish their independence from both their parents and the sometimes protective university officials. Historians Stanford Lehmberg and Ann M. Pflaum interviewed former students who associated with intellectuals and artists in Dinkytown in addition to their social lives in fraternities and sororities. Dinkytown became an integral part of students' lives, one of them said. "We never bothered with downtown. We had everything we needed right here," she said. Dinkytown changed in the 1990s with Gray's Drug closing in 1998 and Al's Breakfast still going strong.

16

MILGROM, FILM AND A RED BARN

Three historical events—a Dinkytown film and the convergence of two Save Dinkytown movements—overlapped in April 2015 at the St. Anthony Theater on Main Street across the river from downtown Minneapolis and fifteen blocks from Dinkytown.

Al Milgrom, who at ninety-two was the personification of the Twin Cities film community and creator of numerous film festivals, introduced the first feature-length film of his own at the annual Minneapolis St. Paul International Film Festival. His *The Dinkytown Uprising* was one among two hundred films from sixty different countries introduced at the festival.

Milgrom's documentary tells the story of a month-long protest in 1970 that involved a cast of thousands, to protest the demolition of five small businesses and the construction of a fast-food restaurant called the Red Barn. With his film opening, he participated in yet another discussion about tearing down buildings in Dinkytown. In 2015, however, there were no street demonstrations or confrontations with the police like the ones from forty-five years earlier that were depicted in Milgrom's film.

Milgrom had also spent fifty years introducing Minnesotans to films they would not otherwise see, and at the 2015 film festival, he showed them the history they've forgotten. "When I'm talking to kids in Dinkytown," said Milgrom, "they have no idea what went on—right there on the sidewalks they walk on, on their way to the U." Since then, Milgrom has been showing it at film festivals across North America and raising money in 2016 to bring it out on DVD.

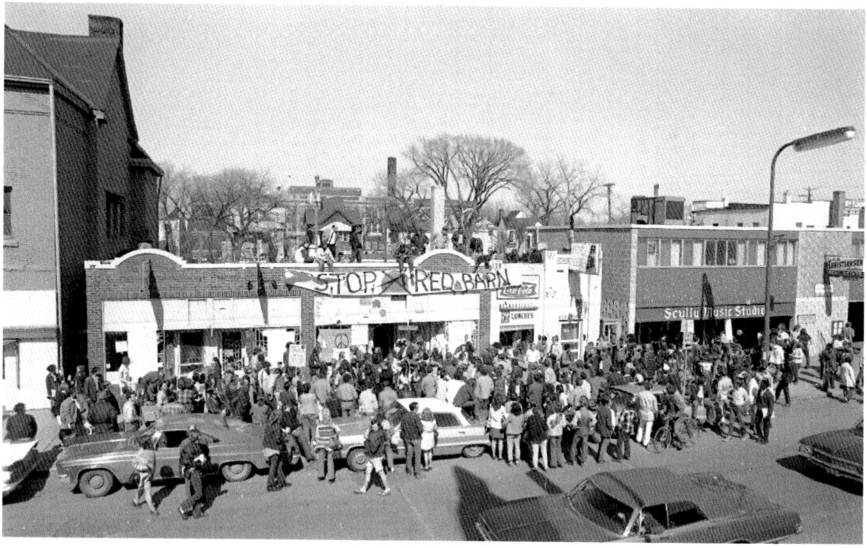

Protesters in 1970 occupied vacant buildings after five businesses had been evicted to make way for a Red Barn fast-food franchise. *Photo by Cheryl Walsh Bellville.*

"The whole idea was there was a '70s generation of activists, idealists—some went so far as to call themselves revolutionaries—who aren't here anymore," Milgrom said. "This was the baby boomer generation that was liberal politically. They ended up out of step with the conservative turn of the United States, even today."

The Dinkytown Uprising was literally forty-five years in the making, beginning when Milgrom filmed the takeover of two Dinktytown buildings on April 1, 1970, by protestors who wanted to prevent their demolition to make way for a Red Barn fast-food franchise. Five small businesses, including a shoe-repair shop and Lou's Diner, had been evicted from the buildings.

Milgrom and his 16mm Éclair movie camera stayed with the protestors for more than a month, filming their activities, interviewing participants about their ideals and goals and witnessing as police in riot gear forcefully evicted them in the dark at 4:00 a.m. on May 6, 1970, and bulldozers took down the buildings.

Later the same day, he followed demonstrators to a Red Barn restaurant near Oak and Washington on the other side of campus, where some protestors were arrested when police forcefully cleared the sidewalk in front of the building.

Within a day, protestors also created a park and planted a "peace garden" on the cleared site. Some roasted wieners over an open fire, and others put up antiwar messages and a blue-and-red poster proclaiming, "Dinkytown Occupation Forces."

Milgrom's contemporary interviews intersect with interviews made over the years as people reminisced, explained their behavior and reflected on how the Red Barn protests affected their lives.

In the film, Dr. David Pence, a Mankato physician, chuckled as he watched a video of himself forty years earlier calling through a megaphone for revolution. "We saw that restraining orders and petitions weren't going to work," Pence said. "We were in a time of trying to build a new community of 'love and peace' against a community of 'militarism and money.'" Pence added that he no longer talks or thinks in those terms. And, he noted, the actions supporting small businesses were not revolutionary.

His sister, Ellen Pence, joined the Red Barn and antiwar activities to follow her elder brother. Unlike him, she continued to work for social justice causes until her death from cancer in 2012. Facing death after her diagnosis, she said that she meditated on her life, "and I always come back to this time." The civil rights movement, the antiwar movement and the women's movement brought great social change, she said. "Very few people can say that in their life major social change happened, and I got to be involved in it."

Milgrom evokes such poignant feelings from some whom he interviewed and sparked some from the audience, especially among people who lived through the events.

He interviewed the late professor Allan Spear of Minneapolis, who served twenty-seven years in the Minnesota Senate before he died in 2008. "In those days, it didn't take much to get me up on a box and to put a microphone in my hand," Spear said, adding that he had not yet been elected to political office at the time of the protests. "Red Barn was seen as a big corporation. …We said the Red Barn was doing to Dinkytown what the United States military was doing in Vietnam.…It sounds far-fetched. It was far-fetched."

News reports kept local anger alive in May 1970. President Nixon announced the U.S. invasion of Cambodia on the same day that a local court issued an order evicting the Red Barn protestors for trespassing. Their forced removal came a day after National Guardsmen killed four antiwar protestors at Kent State University in Ohio. A photograph of Ellen Pence's arrest at the Red Barn on Oak Street appeared in *Time* magazine in a collage of national photos of antiwar protests. In the photo, she appears to be choking because of a police officer's baton on her neck.

Local social change also played a role. Milgrom reports that Dinkytown was once a few blocks of "ma-and-pa shops, small businesses and bookstores." During the late 1960s, Spear added, Dinkytown had become more counterculture than the small business district it once was. Nonetheless, several protestors discussed how Dinkytown felt personal, like a small town a block away from the large university campus.

During the takeover, the protestors—some of whom were university and high school students—cooked their own food in the closed diner, published their own newsletter and created a "hotel" for staying on site, where one of Milgrom's subjects admitted to losing his virginity. The film *Easy Rider* was listed on the marquee of the Varsity Theater across the street; some protesters were admitted free.

In 1970, Red Barn, a chain that folded in the 1980s, would have faced competition in Dinkytown from Burger King, which went out of business in Dinkytown in the late 1990s, and McDonald's, which has been in Dinkytown since 1960. Bob Lafferty, who owned five Twin Cities Red Barn franchises, met occasionally with protesters, and Milgrom shows some tense but friendly banter between them.

With speakers on a megaphone in the background, Milgrom caught some of the personal exchanges. "You need fast food on a campus," Lafferty said. "I think we do a good job." Protest leader David Pence said people work at Red Barn for only $1.60 an hour. One guy said he probably couldn't work at Red Barn with his long hair, and Lafferty said he'd require him to tuck it under his hat. Lafferty also offered to contribute to the creation of a central plaza and parking—perennial issues at the time—in Dinkytown.

Over the years, Milgrom interviewed several key players to see how they had changed. By the 1980s, Milgrom had fifty cans of Red Barn film in his basement when he began transferring film to large videotape for initial editing and finally to digital video for computer editing with the help of fellow director and editor Daniel Geiger, who has edited films for the Coen brothers and other Hollywood producers.

Milgrom has a long list of projects for which he's already shot hours of video. He debuted a twenty-seven-minute documentary, *John Berryman Rediscovered*, at a conference on Berryman in November 2014. Milgrom said he wants to help Minnesota remember Barryman, who was an internationally known Pulitzer Prize–winning poet and professor when he jumped to his death from the Washington Avenue Bridge on campus.

Milgrom, who had taught in the University of Minnesota humanities program with Berryman, said he hopes to turn the Berryman project into a full-length film. "The idea is to capture lost memory," Milgrom said. "The whole idea is of time and memory. I'm picturing the old-timers to get their stories."

He has begun recording monthly meetings of Vinkl, a small group of old-timers who sit in a corner of a Northeast Minneapolis bar and schmooze in Yiddish. "I'm a first-generation American," Milgrom said. "I grew up in Pine City, where my parents spoke Yiddish in the house. I remember all the spoken language. I don't read it." His parents came from the Ukraine and Russia in 1918; his father had been drafted to serve in the czar's army in 1914.

In 2010, he exhibited *The Bramble Experience*, a 16mm documentary about the northern Minnesota Russian community on public television, and it is accessible on YouTube. In the 1960s, Milgrom worked on documentaries on rural poverty and Native Americans.

Milgrom entered the University of Minnesota in 1940, studying chemistry and journalism. Since then, he has worked as a journalist in Minneapolis and a teacher at the university.

"I had artistic ambitions. I got very interested in photography right off the bat," he said. "Even at my advanced age, I'm still trying to figure out who I am."

But most of Milgrom's career has been in exhibiting film. He founded the University Film Society in 1962 and led it for fifty years through many expansions and name changes to exhibit non-Hollywood films that might not otherwise make it to the Twin Cities. He became interested when foreign films came to the United States in the 1940s and in the French New Wave filmmakers in the late 1950s. "One of my motives for the film society was because all these new films were not shown here," he said. "You had to go to San Francisco or New York to see New Wave films. So I formed the film society with some other film buffs."

His own filmmaking grew from this interest. "Many of these filmmakers took film as another form of authorship. That appealed to me. Picking up a camera and getting into film along with photography was a strong motivator." But a fire destroyed all the negatives he made as a student.

The University Film Society eventually expanded its tent to cover the Twin Cities. Milgrom began numerous film festivals, including in 1983 the Rivertown Film Festival, which has become the Minneapolis–St. Paul International Film Festival (MSPIFF). Along the way, he has introduced thematic programs, including a Jewish Film Festival, and he emphasized Polish films, for which he received a medal from the Ministry of Culture in Poland.

Milgrom's legacy continues with the annual Minneapolis–St. Paul International Film Festival. The thirty-fifth festival opened in April 2016 and showcased more than 250 new feature-length, short narrative and documentary films from more than sixty countries. The festival added new venues beyond the St. Anthony Main theater: the Uptown in Minneapolis and the McNally Smith College of Music and Metropolitan State University's new theater in St. Paul. "The largest premier film event in the region and one of the longest running film festivals in the country, MSPIFF is a catalyst for artistic discovery and an essential spring exhibition," the festival's website claims.

17

RED BARN AND PEOPLE'S PARK

"Dinkytown, S.E., is in trouble. It faces extinction," wrote Al Olson in the *Minneapolis Argus* on March 12, 1970. "Extinction by the efforts of a growing, creeping, insidious, cancerous monster called 'commercialism' which has been slowly but surely eating away at Dinkytown to satisfy its ravenous appetite. This time the commercialism is in the guise of the Red Barn franchise."

Olson reported that Robert G. Lafferty, vice-president of Red Barn in the Twin Cities, met with Southeast residents on March 6 and told them that better communication between the city and neighborhood groups would have reduced the opposition to his new business, adding that Dinkytown did not have too many restaurants and denying that another fast-food chain would increase traffic. "The new hamburger assembly line will eliminate five long-established businesses" on Fourth Street Southeast: the Christian Science Reading Room, Lou's Diner, the Co-Ed Beauty Salon, Balfour Jewelers and Solland's Shoe Store, which was twenty-one years old. "They were given notice by registered mail that they must leave by April 1. Plans have been drawn, building permits have been taken out, but no demolition permit has yet been let."

Neighbors had circulated a petition criticizing lack of consultation with the neighborhood, contending that Red Barn buildings are eyesores, saying a drive-in would aggravate traffic problems, claiming an abundance of eating establishments already in the neighborhood and arguing that services from the individually owned businesses will be lost "despite their proven value to the community." The petition included a pledge to boycott the Red Barn on Oak Street, Olson wrote.

"We have a Red Barn on the other side of the campus," Lafferty is quoted as saying in the *Tribune*, "and it has had good acceptance. I don't see why there should be any fuss about this one."

On April Fool's Day, he discovered that there was a fuss. About seventy people moved into the buildings. Molly Ivins, then a reporter for the *Minneapolis Tribune*, wrote about the event:

> *The "occupation" is being continued by university students, high school students, dropouts, street people, middle-aged, middle-class people, artists, community organizers and one Teamster.*
>
> *Some of the people in the occupation forces are there because to the Red Barn symbolizes every tawdry, tasteless bit of uglification ever put up in America.*
>
> *Others are there because to them Red Barn symbolizes every big corporation that has ever changed people's lives without so much as a by-your-leave.*
>
> *Still others are there because the whole thing's a groove, y'know? Like, it's what's happening.*
>
> *And a few, either very young or very old, are there because they hadn't anywhere else to go.*
>
> *Among members of the occupation there are generation gaps, cultural clashes, political differences, class conflicts and plain old personal antipathies.*
>
> *But out of this, the occupiers are trying to create a community: an egalitarian, libertarian community in which there are no leaders, no policemen, and no coercion.*
>
> *Within a week an astonishing complex little society had developed in those five buildings.* [Note: Only two buildings, five businesses.] *Quarters for eating, sleeping, recreation and education had been set up. A decision-making process had developed. Rules had been established. A folklore had spring up.*
>
> *"During the first few days we were here," recalled Jim Bruggeman, a community member, "we were really paranoid about the police. We thought they were coming to get us any minute and we set up a 24-hour guard.*
>
> *"On the second night a cop tip-toed into the People's Hotel (there are two hotels; the luxury establishment has rug on the floor) and woke up one of our guys.*
>
> *"'I just thought I'd tell you,' says this cop, 'that the guard you've got outside to watch for the pigs had fallen asleep. And the cop tip-toed out again."*

Occupiers had been surprised at their relations with the police, some of whom stopped in for coffee and to visit. One supplied signs that said when they were open or closed. Ellen Pence was quoted as saying she would lie on the sidewalk to prevent a bulldozer from demolishing a building.

Protesters established rules. No one under sixteen was allowed during school hours. No dope, booze or weapons were allowed, but they admittedly had some difficulty enforcing the rule on pot. They called the kitchen the People Feeder, and it was open twenty-four hours. Occupiers swept the streets on the entire block over the course of the occupation. Student architects drew up alternative plans for the use of the building, and the Varsity Theater, College Inn and the library opened to provide water and bathrooms.

The city's comprehensive plan for Dinkytown of 1960–64 criticized the fast-food places that were there already. Neighborhood and civic organizations from a variety of backgrounds, including the League of Women Voters, emerged to oppose the Red Barn. An architect called the Red Barn buildings "visual pollution."

Southeast Minneapolis Planning and Coordinating Committee housing committee chairman Rodney French said he was not aware of another time when so many persons in the community were so united on an issue. "He said residents opposed other restaurants in the area, such as McDonald's, Burger King and Bridgeman's, but he said this time the opposition is more united."

French said Red Barn officials referred to a "little old lady" with a dance hall that is causing a lot of trouble. That reference must have been to Loyce Houlton, founder of the Minnesota Dance Theatre next door, who opposed the Red Barn. "When my dance company goes to New York," she said, "we don't go in the name of the company, we go in the name of Dinkytown."

A few days later "protesters, led by a band playing a dirge and man dressed in black, marched from the proposed site to the existing Red Barn restaurant at Oak Street near Washington Avenue to protest the plans." Some "yippie" protesters, not connected to the main protest, stood in front of the Oak Street Red Barn and handed out cow dung in hamburger buns.

Participation in the Red Barn protests might have been boosted by the fact that the University of Minnesota, in response to protests over the invasion of Cambodia, allowed students to "strike" from certain classes in order to participate in social justice or antiwar activities. As noted earlier, the protesters created a peace garden on the site of the demolished buildings. The site was maintained for months but eventually fell into disrepair.

After the Red Barn protests, Houlton's Minnesota Dance Theatre performed her original *The Killing of Susie Cream Cheese* to express solidarity

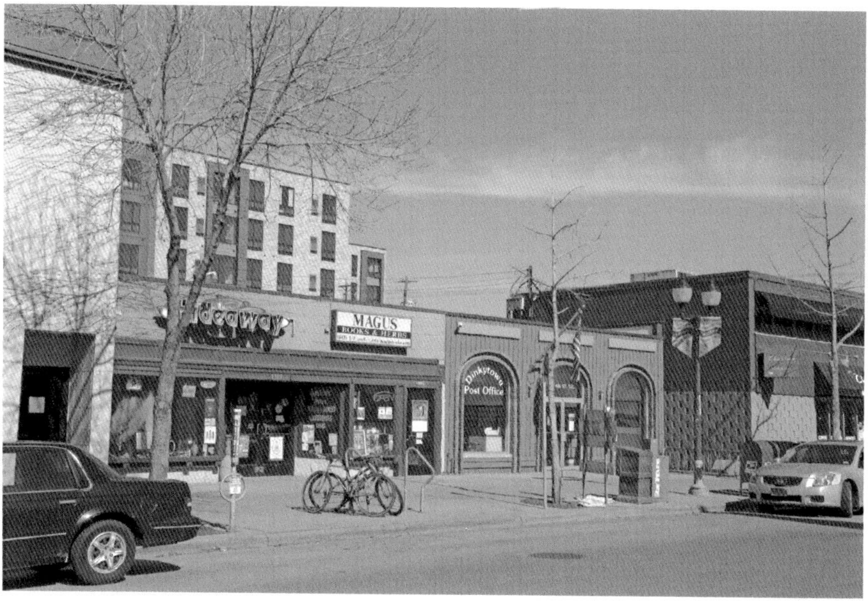

Small-scale buildings replaced those removed in 1970 to build a Red Barn fast-food franchise that was never built. *Photo by Bill Huntzicker.*

with the Red Barn and antiwar protestors outdoors at the People's Park created by the demonstrators. The temporary park was next door to the MDT's first building, which Houlton had opened for meetings of the Red Barn protesters.

Two one-story buildings at 1307–9 Fourth Street have replaced the ones demolished for the Red Barn. They have housed a men's clothing store and Dream Haven Comics before the current tenants: Hideaway, which sells hookah pipes and related supplies, and Magus Books, for people exploring the relationship between themselves and the universe. The other building houses the Dinkytown Branch of the U.S. Postal Service.

If police and protesters exchanged playful banter over the Red Barn in 1970, they had recovered from the playfulness two years later, when police-student confrontations became violent. And university officials, unlike in 1970, were determined that the university would try to continue business as usual.

18

ONE DAY IN MAY 1972

THE WAR COMES HOME

One of the strangest and most violent days in Dinkytown's history was arguably May 10, 1972—midweek of the largest antiwar demonstrations at the University of Minnesota. It was also a day that changed Ted Palmer's life, even though he tried to avoid becoming involved in the conflicts that day.

"I have a pretty good memory," Palmer said. "Things that are really significant you remember like it was yesterday. Outside of the day I was born, this was probably the most exciting day of my life."

As a student, he was sitting at a desk next to an open window on the University Avenue Southeast side of Folwell Hall when the trouble began for him.

He recalled that day during an interview in March 2016,

> *I'm in the language lab listening to corrections of my English paper on a headset. All of a sudden I started weeping; I didn't know why. But I looked down, and I saw a teargas canister rolling under my desk. Police had thrown it, and the gas was coming up in my cubicle. I really didn't know what was going on. I got the heck out of there, ran down the stairs and out on the public sidewalk. I wanted to go west because my car was parked there beyond Dinkytown. But there were all these students running to the east. I got out and ran in the opposite direction they were running.*

He didn't quite realize he was running into the police. "Three minutes earlier I was an innocent bystander. Now I'm charging the police head down like I was playing football," he said. "When I realized I was in the midst of the police, I turned around and ran after the students. I was pretty fit, ran track, worked in Glacier Park, jogged. I could outrun the police; then I ran, caught up with a group of students, and they continued."

Until then, Palmer thought he had avoided entering the fray. "I was a quiet, mild-mannered student," he said, adding that he had been in army ROTC at Cretin High School in St. Paul. In high school, Palmer said, he was required to wear a uniform, and he often walked through the Macalester College campus in St. Paul. "I remember hitchhiking home and being spit on by students. They thought I was a hawk, pro-Vietnam, and everything. I got spit on as a high school kid."

Now he was in his second year at the university taking general liberal arts courses, including astronomy, geology, psychology and creative writing.

"It seemed there were police everywhere. You were safer if you stayed in a group." Students, maybe one hundred of them, were staying in a group. "There was one guy [who] had a bullhorn, shouting at the police and getting them all riled up, calling them names and taunting them. Others were trying to shout him down, to shut him up. I'd say the overall tenor of the students was that they didn't want to get arrested."

Police were behind students pressing them toward Fourth Street Southeast and then toward the intersection with Fourteenth Avenue Southeast, he said.

"Shoppers were coming and going. Shopkeepers were closing doors and locking doors. Students running into shops for safety." A sidewalk sale was underway, and some storeowners took students inside and locked the doors. Some shoppers came outside, saw the situation and couldn't get back into the locked stores behind them, he said.

A helicopter flew from downtown apparently along the railroad tracks, he said, because it had stirred up the pigeons who lived along the tracks. Men in the helicopter dropped tear gas on the intersection, but the gas also drifted to nearby Marshall-University High School and a Montessori school, which had to evacuate the children. In the intersection below, however, pigeon parts fell onto the street demonstrators because pigeons had been sucked into the helicopter rotors. Some drivers used their wipers to clear their windshields.

Palmer's car was beyond Koehler's Garage on the right as he and the protesters headed back toward campus, but Koehler's was the police staging area.

"Whew, that was a close one," he thought as the police stopped at the campus entrance at the Pillsbury Gate. But his moment of relief was short.

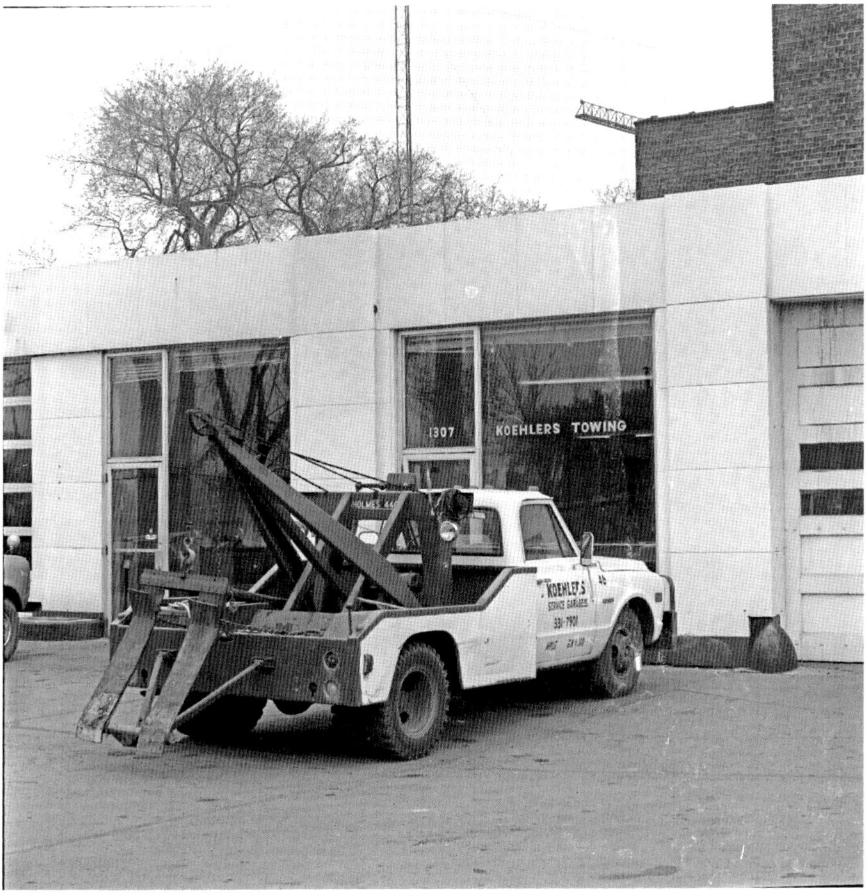

Koehler's Garage, 1307 University Avenue Southeast, served as the staging area for Minneapolis police during campus demonstrations. *Photo by Steven Bergerson.*

There was a guy taking pictures of the police. Two policemen broke ranks and chased the photographer onto the Knoll but they got called back. I was on the edge of the crowd and a policeman saw me by myself and said something to the effect that "at least we can get this guy." I somehow climbed on top of the wall [the east side of the gate], *probably six feet tall. It was a tall wall, and I had my hiking boot*[s] *on. I got on top of the wall; they couldn't reach me. They were hitting my feet with their nightsticks. So I'm here and start running on top of the wall from east to west and they're swinging with their clubs.*

I've got a crowd looking at me from the campus, jeering at the police. The two officers get called back into formation and the crowd disperses. I sit on the ball on the pillar at the gate. I'm sitting on the ball that's hidden by tree branches. My heart is pounding. I'm thinking this is going to make a great story. What I remember was that I'm free and all I have to do is get down off this thing, go home, have dinner and go to bed. I'm also wondering how to get down.

From where he was, Palmer could see both a new group of students coming from the campus and police with gas masks and nightsticks waiting for them. So he quietly warned students about the waiting police so no students were there when the police tried to attack in riot gear and formation.

Sitting on top of the ball on the east side of the Pillsbury Gate, Palmer was trying to stay out of sight of the police, who appeared to have lost track of him. He was hidden by some branches.

I don't want them to see me. A sparrow landed on a branch next to me. I thought someone threw a rock at the police, and I moved and the police saw me. They seemed thrilled. They must have thought, "Here's this guy who ran at us." Obviously, I'm no longer an innocent bystander.

One squad formed semicircle around the pillar. One pulls out [his] *service revolver* [and] *says, "Come on down or I'll shoot you down." I'm feinting great difficulty coming down. Students, one with a camera, are watching.*

In ROTC, Palmer said, he learned that if you're captured by an enemy, the best time to escape is within the first five to ten seconds. "But I realize that's not going to happen." Palmer tried to stay within sight of student witnesses.

When one cop was on his knee with his gun pointed at me, two others are tapping the ground with their night sticks, and the semicircle shielded them from view of the students and traffic. I just knew I was going to get a clubbing if I got down there. I didn't want them to grab my boot.

So I swung around ran east along the top of the wall, jumped down backward with my hands in the air so they and the witnesses can see that I'm not resisting arrest. Now they've got me.

Two squads with me in middle go marching off toward Koehler's Garage. I put my hands in my pockets and made fists so I'd be less likely to be handcuffed and so I didn't pose a threat to them or anything like that. On this march, I did a half step to get into step with them. One officer was impressed and said I must be one of them, but another called me a "shithead" and one hit me in the jaw with a nightstick.

They took him into Koehler's Garage and asked him to sign a confession. He refused and asked to call a lawyer or his mother. Two or three officers then pulled his arms behind him and placed two nightsticks under his arms in such a way that they lifted him off the ground, causing extreme pain and making him feel they could dislocate his shoulders. So he signed a confession. Palmer said he can't even remember all the charges against him, except resisting arrest. They then put him in a paddy wagon to go to jail.

"They stop a city bus and pull a black guy off the bus and put him in the paddy wagon with me. Was he irate! They come and beat him up right in front of me. They definitely roughed him up. After they left, he was crying and I hugged him." Palmer said he had no idea what the man was accused of doing.

"In jail that night," Palmer said, "I think there were thirty-three of us or so. They kept moving us around and splitting us into smaller groups so we ended with groups that had nothing to do with us—so they didn't allow any camaraderie in jail."

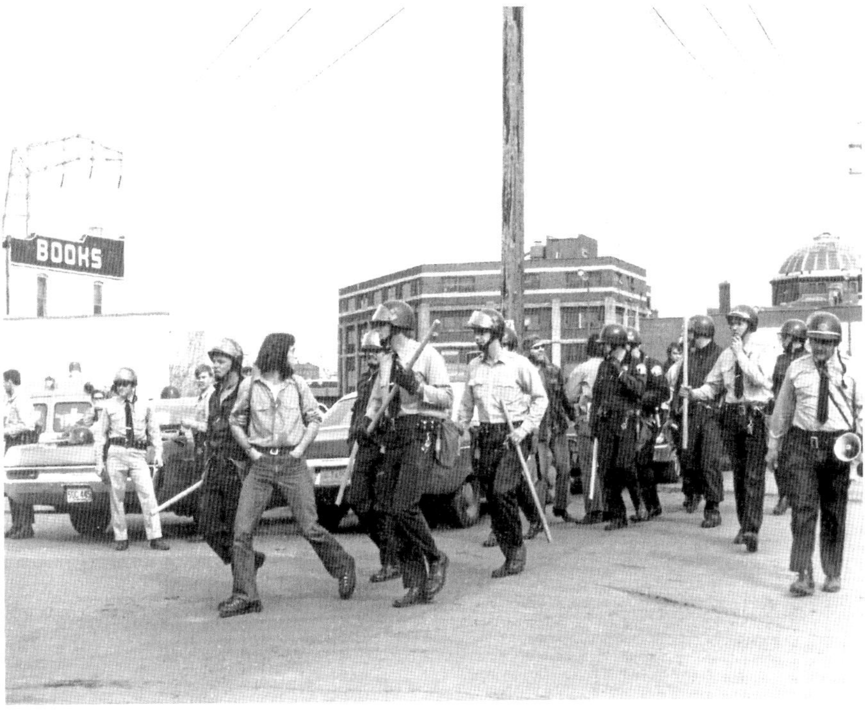

Police arrested Ted Palmer on May 10, 1972, and marched him to Koehler's, where they forced him to sign a confession. *Photo courtesy Ted Palmer.*

Palmer's mother got him released to her custody, and she called his dad's cousin William Colby, who would soon become director of the CIA. "My mom's question was: 'Is Teddy going to have a record?' His response: 'Rosemary, your whole family has a record'" because of the investigations required for his CIA work.

Palmer does not know who took the photograph of police marching him to Koehler's Garage. The photographer slipped him a roll of film, saying he might need it for his trial.

In November, when his case finally went to trial, the judge dismissed the charges for insufficient evidence; besides, he had witnesses and photographs. Sitting in the judge's chambers with his Canadian girlfriend he met while working at Glacier Park, Palmer told the judge they planned to go camping in Mexico. The judge looked them in the eyes and said, "Young man and young woman, life is not a camping trip." Palmer took that as a challenge. He set out to make his life a camping trip. They took off in an old postal truck as a camper and traveled throughout Mexico. It was five years before he returned to college and twenty-eight years before he moved back to Minnesota.

As a graduate student and writer for the University of Minnesota News Service, I worked to see everything I could during this most turbulent week in university history. I know of other people traumatized by the misbehavior of a few members of the Minneapolis Police Department during the first week of May 1972, but few want to discuss it for publication. "They're probably all retired by now," said one man about the police, "but I'll bet they still carry guns, and I don't know how they still feel about what happened."

Palmer got gassed twice in one day—once in his office and once at the intersection of Fourth Street Southeast and Fourteenth Avenue Southeast—and that same intersection was clogged twice in the same day by demonstrators and police.

19

EIGHT DAYS IN MAY 1972

The spring demonstrations that led to Palmer's arrest and the arrests of dozens of other people in May began the previous month in Dinkytown when protesters demonstrated against an air force recruiting station on Fourth Street. About forty members of the Students for a Democratic Society (SDS) took over the recruiting station while about three hundred people gathered to watch, according to the Commission of Inquiry into the campus violence headed by Professor John Darley. "Police re-routed noon-hour traffic around the block on Fourth Street SE; a small number of Minneapolis policemen marched down the sidewalk to the front of the station, ringed the station and evicted the SDS members inside. No one was hurt; no arrests were made."

A larger group of about 150 marched to the Morrill Hall administration building to speak to university president Malcolm Moos. Instead, a student affairs officer met them at the door to the president's office. No uniformed officers were present, but plainclothes campus policemen and members of the Office of Student Affairs (OSA) monitored the situation, in which some damage was done. No one was arrested. A group called Committee of Concerned Asian Scholars set up a camp on campus to protest the escalating war.

The groups had teach-ins on April 19 and April 20 with mixed success; about 500 people attended a rally in front of Morrill Hall on April 20, and about 190 students from several Minnesota campuses boarded buses to attend the national antiwar rally in Washington on Saturday, April 22.

The following chronology depends on my memory and the chronology of the Darley Commission, of which I was a member.

President Nixon started the chain of events on Monday night by announcing the mining of harbors and rivers of Vietnam and intensified bombing near the Chinese border. About 150 students protested in front of the new Federal Building in downtown Minneapolis and the governor's mansion in St. Paul on Monday evening after the speech.

George Romney, Nixon's secretary of housing, was scheduled to appear at a dedication ceremony for the new Cedar-Riverside housing development on Tuesday, May 9. Neighborhood residents who opposed the federally subsidized high-rise housing development on the West Bank had already planned to protest Romney's appearance. The antiwar protest began on the steps of Northrop Auditorium, and about five hundred opponents of the war marched to the West Bank site where Romney was scheduled to appear. The two groups of protesters were met by Minneapolis police in full riot gear. Protesters pulled down a fence and police fought them. Romney did not appear but spoke to a smaller group off site.

The commission reported that several police broke ranks to beat demonstrators with nightsticks that afternoon. As a writer for the University News Service, I tried to see everything I could of antiwar activities that week. I had never seen anything like this day, having grown up in small-town Montana, where I knew many of the local policemen and sheriffs and their deputies. I had usually been skeptical of press reports about "police brutality" in minority neighborhoods of the big cities. The commission here found that police used Mace and beat people with their batons and that demonstrators threw rocks, marshmallows and eggs at the police. I did not see anyone throw any of those things, and I did not see the confrontation at the housing site—my interest involved activities on or nearer the campus. But I did see police attack people for no apparent reason.

I saw two officers holding a young man bent over the trunk of a parked car by the hair to repeatedly bang his head against the trunk lid. A young woman tried to grab one of the officer's arms, and she was knocked to the ground by a jab in the head with a nightstick.

At one point, police were keeping the street clear by threatening anyone who stepped off the curb. I looked down to write something in my reporter's notebook when I felt two hands on my shoulder. I looked up into the face of this helmeted, uniformed officer who said, "Which side are you on, son?" I stuttered, "P-p-p-press." He then gently guided me with a hand on each shoulder and backed me out of the way while they continued clubbing demonstrators. An estimated thirteen people were arrested. Later, students and others met in the Newman Center to plan activities for the next day.

When an even larger crowd of between 1,000 to 1,500 gathered at noon on Wednesday on the steps of Northrop Auditorium, antiwar activist Marv Davidov told the crowd they should congratulate law-and-order mayor Charles Stenvig and his police for stimulating a higher turnout for the protest.

A smaller group of the protesters marched from Northrop to the air force recruiting station in Dinkytown. Two police officers were present and let a few people into the second-story office to see that no one was there. The air force apparently did not wish a rerun of the event a month earlier when protesters threw recruiting literature out the second-story window to the sidewalk below. This time, the office was evacuated, and any records that could be burned had been removed.

As protesters marched to the recruiting station, Minneapolis police gathered at Koehler's Garage, their base of operations, that was also a city impound lot. I walked through the area when the demonstrators were walking toward the recruiting station. Many officers were swinging their nightsticks like baseball bats and joking about upcoming fights. Anyone who saw them could tell a fight was coming. The recruiting station was half a block away but out of sight of the garage.

With no one at the recruiting station, protesters decided to march on the Armory at Seventeenth Avenue Southeast and University Avenue on campus. As protesters marched from the recruiting station to the Armory, they clogged traffic at Fourteenth Avenue and Fourth Street Southeast. A car stopped in the mêlée was vandalized with damage under the hood and a broken windshield.

At the Armory, some protesters tore down a fence and threw rocks at the building. Perhaps as a prank, some fraternity members pushed a junk car into the street. And then a fire started near it, so television news presented a scene that made University Avenue outside the Armory look like a war zone.

People were throwing rocks at the building, someone tore a screen off a window and another person tried to pry a door open. People were trying to break into the building and a small fire was started near the building. Eugene Eidenberg, acting vice-president for administration, said he feared for the safety of the people working inside, most of whom were not in military service.

He then called the police to come to the campus to restore order. But order was not what came with the Minneapolis police. Police cleared University Avenue; arrested some people, none of whom had done the property damage; and began to push the protesters along Church Street through campus toward Washington Avenue in the middle of the campus.

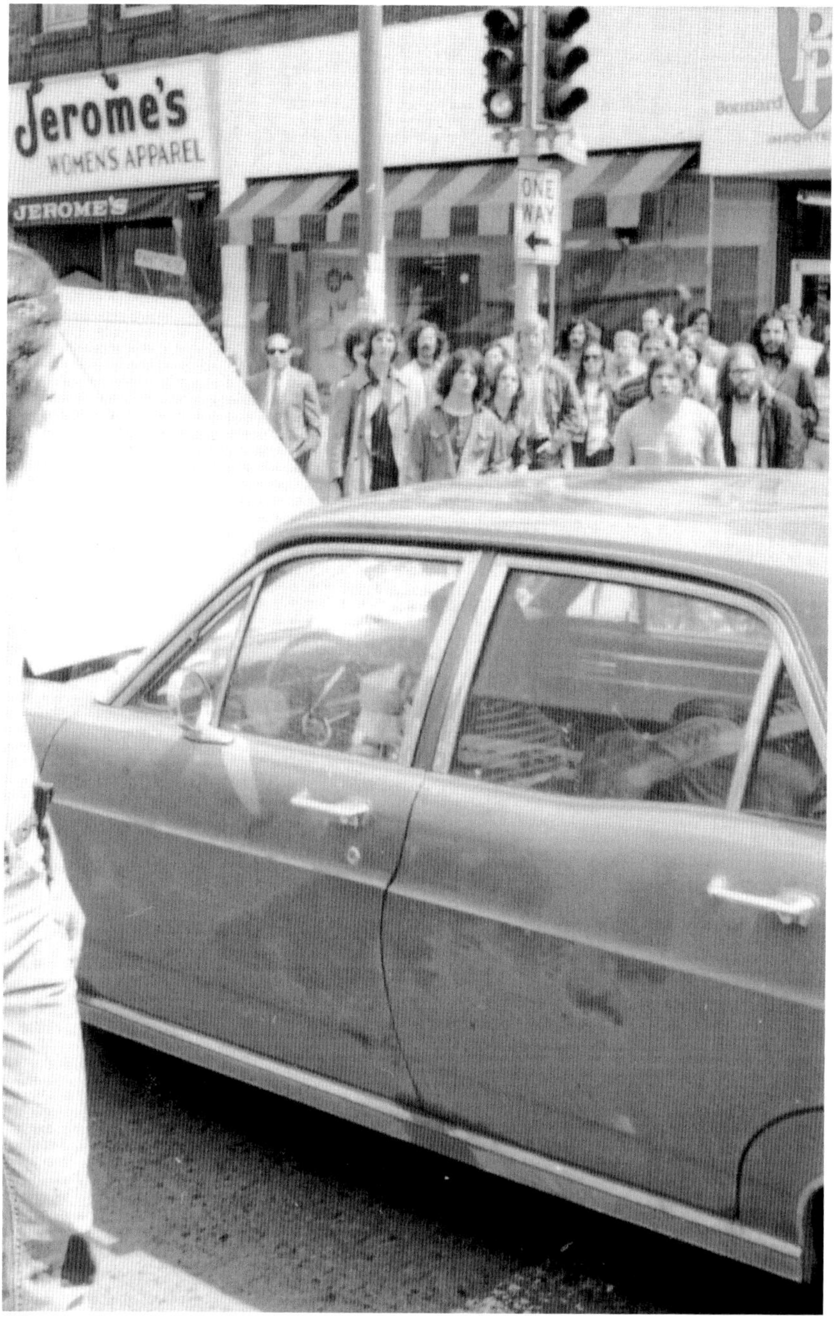

Antiwar protestors vandalized a car trying to get through the intersection of Fourth Street and Fourteenth Avenue Southeast. *Photo courtesy University Archives, University of Minnesota, Twin Cities.*

Administrators, including Eidenberg, tried to get Mayor Stenvig to confine his officers to the area around the Armory and let the university deal with protesters on campus. The mayor would not communicate with them. Some protesters who had gathered at Oak and Washington were also pushed west down Washington toward the center of campus.

Reaching Washington Avenue, protesters tore down the chain-link fence dividing the lanes of traffic, and someone brought some snow fence from a nearby construction site to use as a barricade. Protesters began running toward the campus mall, and police chased after them. Some protestors ran past Ford Hall and turned on to the mall in front of Ford Hall. A few got into a tug of war over the fence with some police officers.

After walking with protesters and a network news reporter from the Armory to Washington Avenue Southeast, I went into Ford Hall, where I could watch both the mall events and Washington Avenue from a corner office. At about 3:00 p.m. police donned gas masks, chased protesters, began throwing tear gas and followed them onto the mall. A student sunbathing and reading a book just happened to be sitting in the wrong place. Protesters ran past him; police followed and several of them beat him with nightsticks.

Tear gas began to permeate the building, even though people closed all the doors and windows. Some older faculty members were getting sick from the gas, and the air on the mall was filling with a fog of gas. The *Minneapolis Tribune* reported that the police used teargas, chemical Mace and a Pepper Fogger gas machine to disperse crowds as large as one thousand people. More than thirty people were treated for injuries at local hospitals.

Mayor Stenvig called Governor Wendell Anderson for support from the Minnesota National Guard. Malcolm Moos, who had been out of town since Tuesday morning, returned and met with leaders from the Guard and regents chairman Elmer L. Andersen at the president's house, which by then was at Marshall and East River Road in St. Paul.

In his autobiography, Andersen discussed the meeting and the decision to allow the Guard on campus. "I was never more proud of a university president than I was of Moos at that meeting," Andersen wrote. "He said, 'If the governor wishes and would feel more comfortable to have the National Guard here, and they'll take their instructions from you and you from us, we can live with that. But they cannot come on campus armed.' The Guard officer said, 'There's no way they go anywhere without being armed. Our National Guard is always armed.' Quietly, Moos said, 'I have to tell you, they won't come on this campus armed. We're not going to have armed soldiers coming after our students. What do you want the

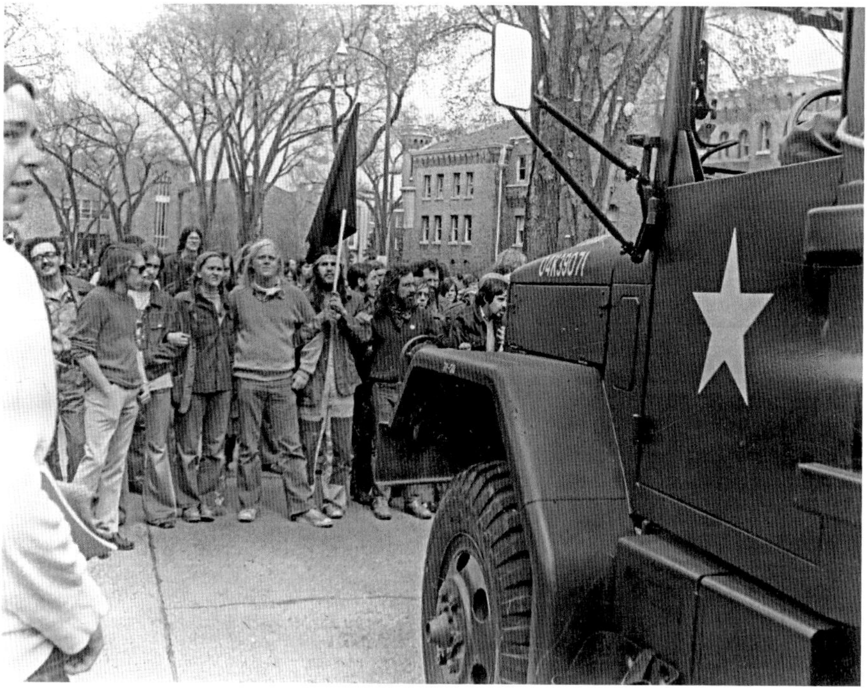

On May 11, 1972, the National Guard was trying to calm tension on campus and in Dinkytown. *Photo from University Archives, University of Minnesota, Twin Cities.*

students to do in response, get armed too?' It was a tense exchange, but Moos prevailed. The National Guard came to campus but as a quiet presence, not a threat." Andersen continued:

> *Our violent eruption occurred while the Guard was present, but it was a clash between students and the Minneapolis police—not the Guard. Former police officer Charlie Stenvig was mayor of Minneapolis in 1972, and he directed the Minneapolis police to take a hard line against the protesters who had barricaded Washington Avenue near Coffman Union. A scuffle was the result, leading to several dozen injuries. Though the injuries were not life-threatening, the ugly incident showed how volatile the campus mood was. Only a handful of students were actively engaged in protests. But if those students had been mishandled in any way, literally thousands stood ready to come to their rescue. The day the police began to rough up student protesters, a crowd immediately gathered.*

Andersen's recollection differs somewhat from what some administrators told me about that night. I was told that administrators welcomed the

Guard as a moderating influence to check the violence of the Minneapolis police. Nonetheless, walking home through Dinkytown late the following night was chilling; the only vehicle on the street was a National Guard jeep with soldiers watching the neighborhood. (I appreciated how Moos handled gun issues. My News Service office was in the basement of Morrill Hall, the administration building. I sent him a memo once suggesting that guards on armored cars need not have their guns drawn when they carry money in and out of our building; he quickly changed the behavior.)

For two days the mall felt refreshingly whole with the fence gone and traffic blocked on the street that divided the campus. The atmosphere was almost like a fair. At night students built a small campfire in the intersection of Church and Washington and sang folk songs. But the rallies grew each day. As many as four thousand gathered on Thursday.

Police removed the barricade early Friday, and the crowd reached around five thousand by Friday afternoon. Former U.S. senator Eugene McCarthy spoke to the protestors in front of Coffman Union on Thursday, and Moos joined the students in the street on Friday. I was on the roof of Ford Hall later on Friday afternoon. The street was blocked from the Washington Avenue Bridge to Oak Street—a distance of about seven blocks.

Beyond the protestors at Oak Street were blue and brown buses and uniforms as far as you could see. A helicopter was flying overhead. On the street below, Reverend Vincent Hawkinson, Alderman John Cairns and others negotiated with a police representative and protestors about the street that had become increasingly symbolic as the week progressed. Many of us present feared that someone could be killed.

Late Friday afternoon, however, Minneapolis police captain Bruce Lindberg reportedly told the protesters they could have the street, that it was not worth getting someone killed. By daybreak the next day police and city bulldozers removed the barricade with a few people, apparently high school students, left at the site.

Throughout the week, protesters demanded that the university shut down for the rest of the term to work against the war; however, the regents met normally on Friday, and classes continued in buildings away from the mall. Provocateurs made efforts to escalate violence, including distributing aluminum pipes and encouraging demonstrators to use them on police. An undercover campus policeman and a protestor confiscated these before anyone used them.

On Saturday, about two thousand people marched from the Northrop plaza to the capitol in St. Paul, where as many as fifteen thosuand people gathered to hear speakers denounce the war.

On the following Monday, demonstrators took over Johnston Hall, an administrative building. I followed an official from the Office of Student Affairs as he told people to leave their offices because protesters were taking control of the buildings. The process evacuated the building without a confrontation, but looking at people's reaction as they were forced from their own offices quashed my idea that a building takeover was a benign form of demonstration.

Later, I sat on the stairs in the lobby of the building as protesters made speeches and discussed other ways to strongly express their views. At some point, the leaders realized some press people were present so we were asked to leave. Soon they received word that presidential candidate George Wallace had been shot while campaigning in Maryland. That event seemed to take the fun out of politics, and the sit-in ended.

Twenty-five years after these events, *Minnesota Daily* reporter Alan Bjerga revisited some of the people and events for a series in the student-run newspaper on May 12, 13 and 14, 1997 (online at mndaily.com). He found that the confrontations left many wounds in the university as an institution and among the people involved. Eidenberg, for example, wondered how the week could have been handled so people would not have been hurt. Bjerga found that the public supported the police over the demonstrators, as they had when the events were in the news. The key players, between both demonstrators and police, had not changed their views either. Police officers continued doing their jobs. Davidov, who died in 2012 at the age of eighty, had moved on to fight nuclear power and the FBI's abuse of civil liberties. Bjerga's reporting provided a thoughtful overview of the eight days, and like many of us, he asked what the events accomplished.

20

DINKYTOWN, MEMORIES AND CHANGE IN 2013

In early 2013, the Opus Development Company proposed a multistory, mixed-use apartment house to displace several businesses, including the House of Hanson grocery. The plan sparked controversy, stimulating some people to share their memories and some to organize to create a historic district to stop further development. The interviews in this section were mostly conducted at that time.

Unlike some other developers, Opus and architect David Graham met repeatedly with neighborhood representatives to make the Venue building consistent with the neighborhood's design guidelines.

Change was not new to Dinkytown, however. Even when Dylan lived there, Dinkytown was not the village it was ten years earlier when Minneapolis's major department store, Dayton's, had a Dinkytown branch, and neighborhood children attended John Marshall High School in the next block.

"I remember much more of a little village, a self-sustaining village, than it is now," said Walter Johnson, who graduated from John Marshall High School in 1946. "There was a grocery store, a butcher shop, a candy store, a dry cleaner, gift shops, a bakery—Gordon's bakery, different generations ran it. When I was in high school, I'd buy a roll there for lunch. The bakery was there for fifty years. We bought all our bread there. There was a very nice jewelry store. I did all of my Christmas shopping in Dinkytown, usually on December 23."

Marcia Pankake, a resident of the Como Neighborhood, also recalls doing her Christmas shopping in Dinkytown—as a student in the 1960s. "Small businesses are what add to desirability of Dinkytown, and they are the reason

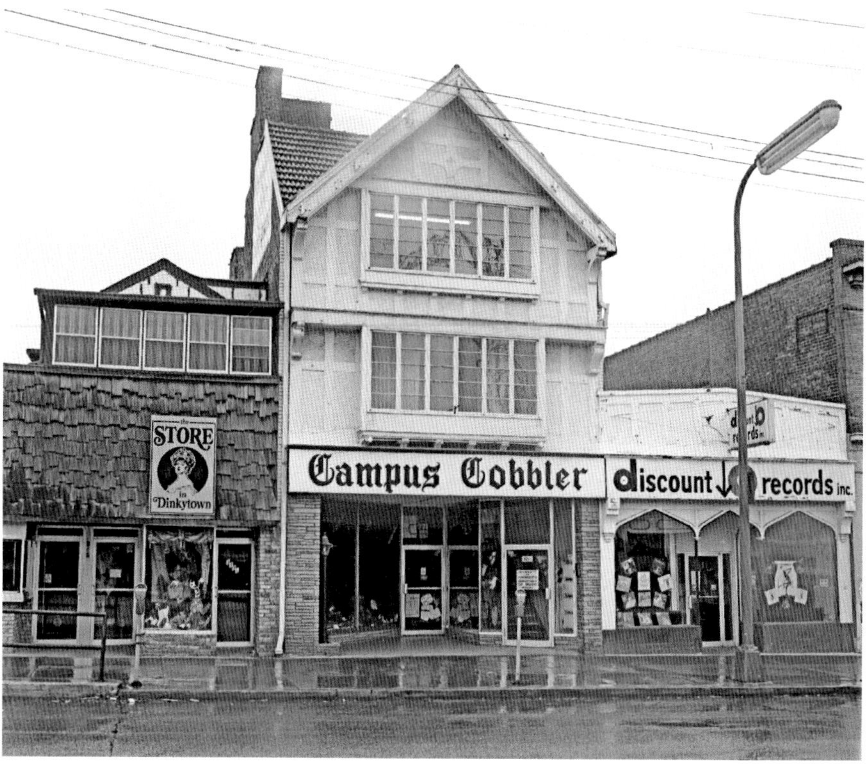

Once a professor's home, this building was Dayton's University Store, its first branch away from downtown Minneapolis and St. Paul. *Photo by Steven Bergerson.*

for going there," Pankake said in 2013. "The Podium draws people from all around. The Needle Doctor used to draw hi-fi enthusiasts, and there were stores for new books and textbooks, three used bookstores, barbershops, an ice cream store and the bakery."

Jeff Molde, who owned Podium for fourteen years, said he worried about area's future. In the 1960s, the Podium sold sheet music, guitars, records and even tobacco products. It was in the old Victorian home that housed Casablanca hair salon on Fifth Street Southeast, which was also demolished for the Opus development.

"There's a nice vibe in Dinkytown," Molde said. "It'd be easy to mess that up."

Within a few days, a Save the Podium Facebook page collected more than one hundred "likes," including one from Bob Dylan and another from Bob Dylan & the Band with the comment, "We wish you all the best!"

The city plan had classified Dinkytown as an activity center—like Stadium Village and Uptown—a dense, busy, active business area.

"The unique character of Dinkytown is in some ways intangible," said Haila R. Maze, a city planner whose responsibilities include Dinkytown. "It's an urban small-scale commercial space that has managed to survive over the years. Having survived is a major accomplishment."

Maze said Dinkytown is a human-scale, eclectic mix of businesses with some local unique businesses. "I hope that there are ways to do infill development that can change it but keep what people value about it," she said in an interview. "We should keep being a place where something is interesting and happening, but we don't want it to be so successful that big players come and squash it."

Dinkytown is threatened because of its success; some small businesses have succeeded, and new developers seem to find it lucrative. Many other neighborhoods would like to have developers lining up to buy their land, she said.

"Dinkytown is a brand that students know," Maze said. "If a building or development is close enough, the owners will market it as a Dinkytown apartment."

Opus developer Matt Rauenhorst said, "We will continue to work with all the stakeholders, including the neighborhood and the city. We will ask the Book House and the Podium if they are interested in being part of our project." Neither of those businesses moved into the new building. The Podium was purchased by and merged with another music store in South Minneapolis, and the Book House moved around the corner to the second floor of Dinkydale.

His project did not touch the popular Kafé 421 or Al's Breakfast, which are not adjacent.

Ironically, change seems to be the one constant in Dinkytown.

The House of Hanson, the Book House and the Podium were torn down for the Venue mixed-use, multistory apartment building with commercial businesses on the street level. The project also filled in Dinkytown's largest parking lot and took out a Victorian house with a hair salon in it and a cinderblock pizza place. The space behind them had included Dinkytown's largest parking lot, a hair salon and a pizza place.

Across Fifth Street Southeast from them, the University Technology Enterprise Center, called UTEC, was torn down to make room for another multistory mixed-use apartment building. UTEC's building was Marshall-University High School until 1982, when the city closed several schools. Marshall High School opened in 1924 and merged with University High School to become Marshall-University High School in 1968. University High had been in Peik Hall until 1968 just inside

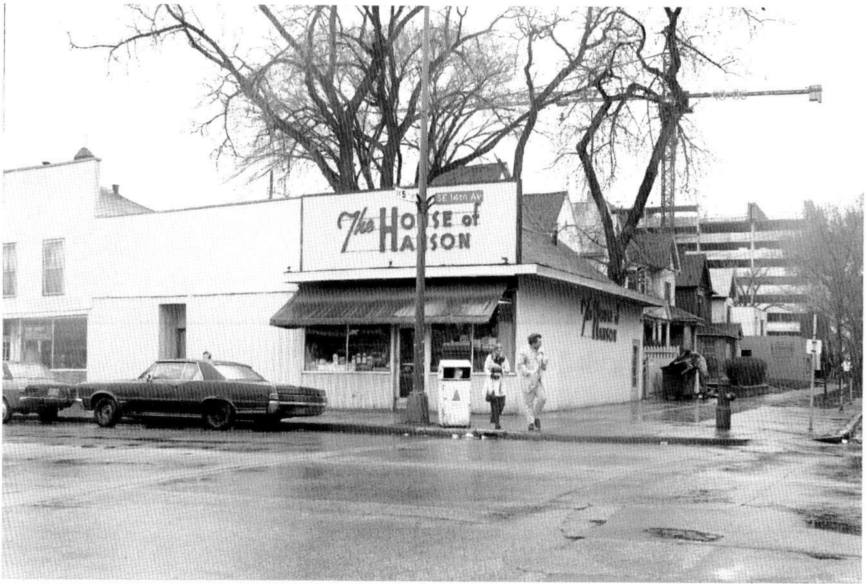

The House of Hanson, a family-run grocery on the corner of Fifth Street and Fourteenth Avenue Southeast, actually was a house with store and soda fountain attached. *Photo by Steven Bergerson.*

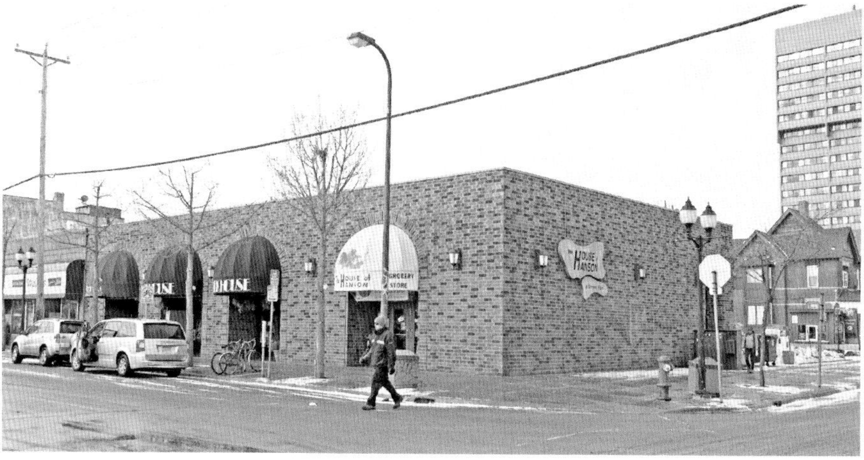

In the 1970s, Bob Hanson moved the home once attached to his store and built this brick structure that also housed other businesses. *Photo by Bill Huntzicker.*

Opposite: The House of Hanson, demolished in 2013, was replaced by the Venue, a mixed-use apartment building with a clothing store and a Starbucks (shown unfinished across the intersection). *Photo by Bill Huntzicker.*

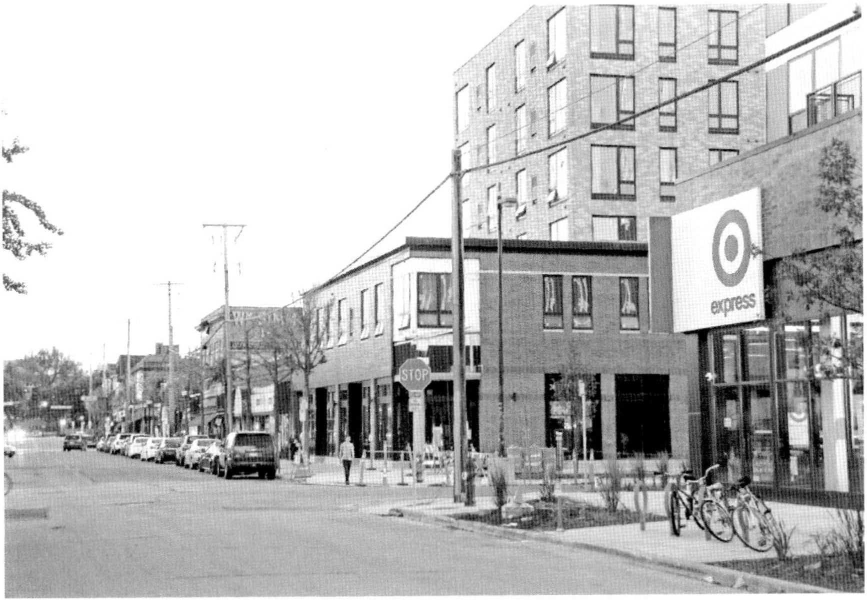

the campus gate, and it remains in the teacher-preparation programs in education.

Walter Johnson, who is now professor emeritus of physics at the University of Minnesota, graduated from Marshall and, except for a year at General Electric in Schenectady, New York, has spent his entire life in the Marcy-Holmes Neighborhood.

He remembers the House of Hanson as an ice cream parlor and Rose Hanson, who ran it. "The only one I remember running it was the mother. I went in there, but not very often."

Mary Kay O'Hearn, who was in Johnson's high school class, recalled that Hanson made her own ice cream. "They'd always try new things, and one of them was licorice ice cream," she said.

Henry Oscar Hanson founded the store on October 3, 1932, back when thirty-five cents was a good day's profit and a quart of ice cream sold for twenty-five cents, said Hanson's granddaughter Laurel Bauer, who owned the business and the building when they closed.

After Hanson died, Rose Hanson ran the store. "Many people, including high school students from Marshall, called her Ma," Bauer said. The House of Hanson was first a café and then an ice cream parlor and a soda fountain with groceries.

Hanson's son Robert Hanson bought the business from his mother after twenty years of working for wages. He closed the soda fountain in the 1960s.

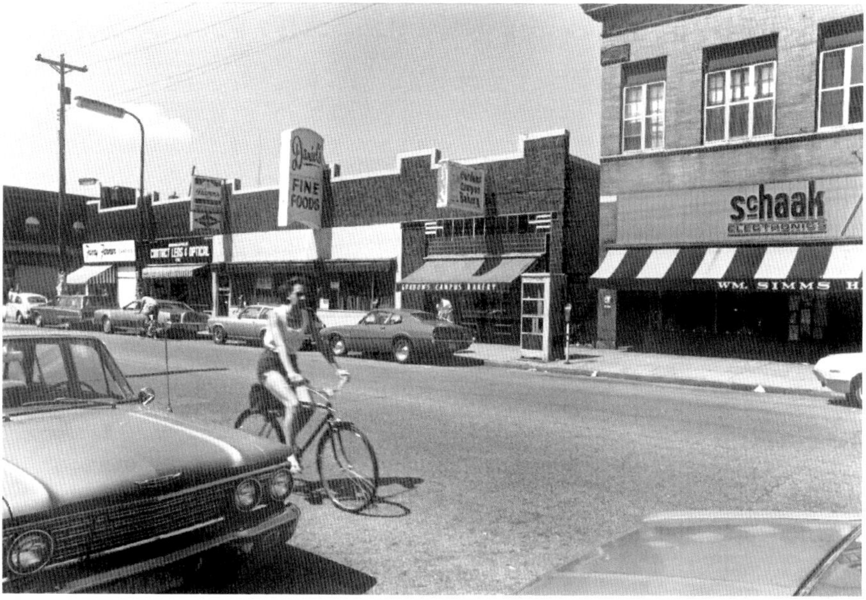

The buildings look the same in the 400 block of Fourteenth Avenue Southeast, but none of these 1974 businesses remained by the end of the century. *Photo by Linda Gammell; courtesy special collections, Hennepin County Library.*

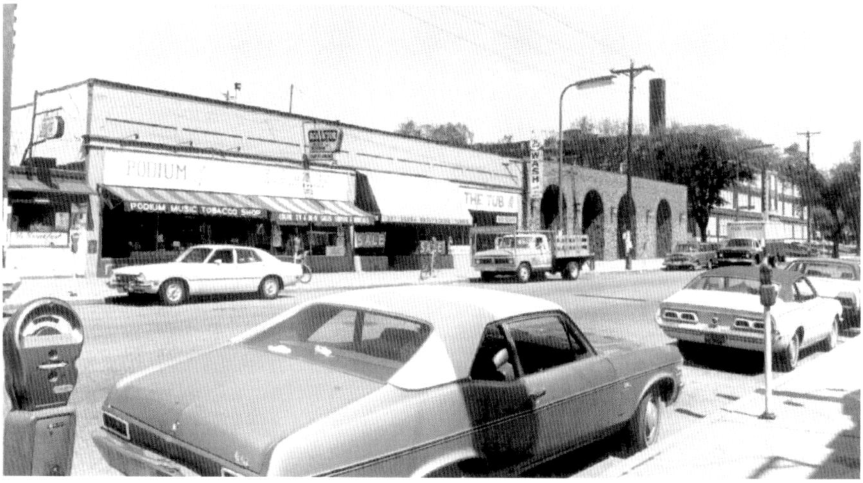

These one-story buildings display a former city goal of low-impact buildings in Dinkytown. *Photo by Linda Gammell, 1974; courtesy special collections, Hennepin County Library.*

"I bought the store from him. None of us got nothin' for nothin'," Bauer said jokingly. The original House of Hanson was attached to the family's home behind the store. In the 1970s, the Hansons moved the home, and the grown Hanson children owned three homes on Seventh Avenue Southeast.

Their last store was built about 1973. "This is not a historical building," she said. When it opened, it housed the House of Hanson, House of T-Shirts, House of Waterbeds and India House stores. The Podium and the Book House moved in later and were the only tenants besides House of Hanson when the building closed.

At one time, Dinkytown had three grocery stores, Bauer said. In those days, every corner had a store before people got into their cars to drive to Cub Foods. "The perception of the convenience store is that it is overpriced," she said, "but the prices of some items compete with Cub."

Bauer said CVS Pharmacy in Sydney Place, another new mixed-use development at the corner of Fifteenth Avenue Southeast and Fourth Street Southeast, took 30 percent of her business.

As the new Marshall building was under construction across the street, Bauer anticipated 20,000 square feet of retail there to compete with her store with only 1,100 square feet. Unknown at the time, the anchor tenant turned out to be Target Express, the Minnesota company's experiment with a smaller focused mission than the typical suburban big-box Target store.

The closing of UTEC with close to ninety businesses meant the loss of one thousand people a day "that we don't see any more," Bauer said, and the city then doubled the taxes on the three land parcels that composed her Dinkytown parking lot. "I didn't go looking for this situation," Bauer said. "It presented itself, and it's just the right time for my family" to leave the business.

Kristen Eide-Tollefson, who owned the Book House in Bauer's building, was not happy to go, and her staff started a successful blog of supporters. Three managers and a staff of six to nine dedicated booksellers have been working ten to twelve hours a day, she said. They want to keep the business going.

The group organized as Preserve Historic Dinkytown to lead the effort to create Dinkytown as a historic district and to collect people's stories and artifacts. They continued at preservehistoricdinkytown.org.

"I have spent the last three years investing heavily in preparing the store to be run by a new generation because I want the store to stay here, so the university has access to the kinds of books the Book House provides and the services the Book House provides," Eide-Tollefson said.

She founded the business with her former husband; they both had been booksellers specializing in academic books for libraries. For a time, their partners were also Lynn and Rob Wozniak, who lived in the neighborhood. Their son John Wozniak attended nearby Marcy elementary school and founded the rock group called the Marcy Playground. For a time, Eide-Tollefson's stepson Jim Cummings Jr. ran a second used bookstore in the same block as the Book House.

"We've made good business decisions," Eide-Tollefson said. "We're the last surviving bookstore in the area as a result." She said she started a mail-order business in 1994 and an online business in 2008, and her staff reorganized the store with clearer display space to make it more inviting and easier to find things. About 50 percent of her business was online through her own website, and those of book distributors Amazon.com, ABE Books and Alibris. Her website is bookhouseindinkytown.com.

Like the opponents of Red Barn forty years earlier, Eide-Tollefson said new buildings and chain stores will "change the ecology of Dinkytown" with higher rents.

Developers said the rents will have to be at the market rate, or they won't sell.

Hanson's building was only one story because the site was zoned C-1 for commercial use to keep the business area low density. I remember talking with Bob Hanson when his building was new in the 1970s. He said then he wanted to do a bigger building but that the city wouldn't let him.

In the twenty-first century, however, the city put a greater priority on density to attract new residents to the inner city. To build for more height and density, though, Opus needed the city to rezone the site C-3A, the same as the Sydney Hall site on the opposite corner across from Dinkytown. Other zoning categories and variances allowed the construction of higher multiuse developments, including the Marshall building and 1301 University Avenue Southeast that houses the Purple Onion coffee shop and café.

The first Purple Onion in Dinkytown opened in 1993 at Fourth Street and Fourteenth Avenue Southeast, where Bridgeman's had closed, and it became the anchor tenant of the new building at 1301 University Avenue East. Owner Pat Weinberg's website said, "the Purple Onion bridges a gap between the vibrance of the University of Minnesota campus and the bustling energy of Dinkytown."

Rezoning and variances were required for nearly a dozen developments under construction or on the drawing board at the same time in the Marcy-Holmes Neighborhood within blocks of Dinkytown and the riverfront. These requirements provide an opportunity for groups like the Dinkytown Business Association and the Marcy-Holmes Neighborhood Association to influence the city council on the developments.

But the planning process can't solve every issue, such as the problem with small-scale businesses that don't have deep pockets. "When new space comes in, the per-square-foot rent will be higher. The new spaces are less likely to be affordable to small-scale businesses," Maze said. Some places, like Grand Avenue in St. Paul and Uptown in Minneapolis, have managed to preserve some local character while welcoming new developments.

To protect the less dense traditional areas, the Marcy-Holmes Neighborhood Association had proposed more intensive development along Fifteenth Avenue Southeast going north from Dinkytown, but developers had not assembled the necessary contiguous parcels for high-rises there.

Planning can help with issues—such as parking, traffic flow and public safety—that are bigger than any one project. Some planning tools, Maze said, can be used to preserve the character and feel of a place.

Neighborhood negotiations with developers might not be enough to preserve Dinkytown. The developers of Sydney Place said they'd welcome back the tenants of the old buildings before the renovation of DinkyDome and the addition of its new apartment building.

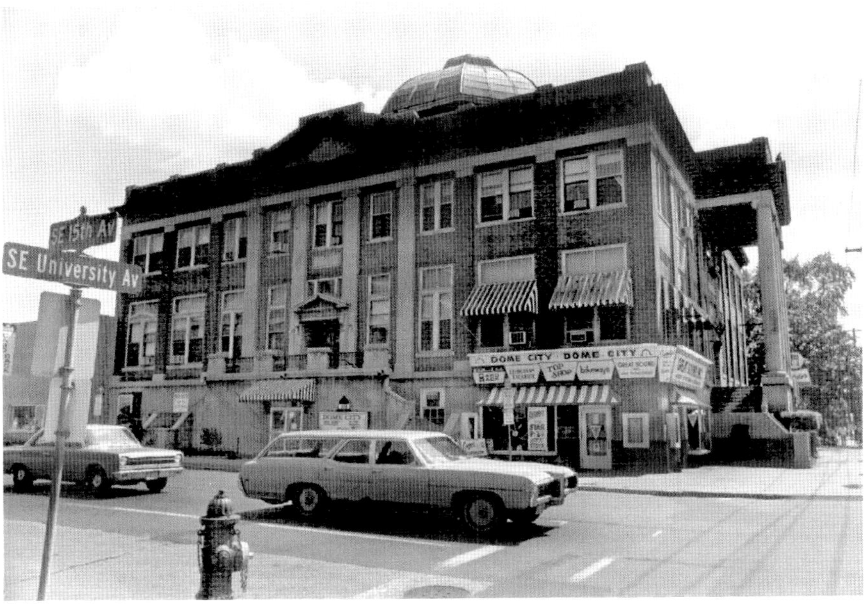

The former Minnesota Bible College became a business mall and later part of a mixed-use apartment complex. *Photo by Linda Gammell, 1974; courtesy special collections, Hennepin County Public Library.*

Skott Johnson, president of the Dinkytown Business Association at the time, also said increasing rent changed the nature of the place. Johnson, who was DBA president for about eighteen years, remained so long because he said he had the time to attend lots of meetings and because he enjoyed "making the rounds"—his daily walks to visit with other business owners.

"Part of the charm of Dinkytown is that the owners are on site. People know you," Johnson said. "Dave, the barber, who died last summer, knew everybody. He worked here sixty-four years. I think that's a good feeling. You don't see that in Downtown or Uptown anywhere." Johnson's own business, Autographics, did custom printing and had sometimes been a one-man operation. The low rent allowed such small businesses to remain, but new buildings will bring higher prices. "My building isn't much to look at, but it's cheap rent," he said. Rent in some of Dinkytown's older buildings is as little as $1,500 to $2,000 a month while new storefronts in DinkyDome are looking at $10,000 a month, Skott Johnson said.

With the increasing rent, local businesses could be replaced by chain stores, like CVS and Target, which can afford the higher costs. "But the chains are not all bad," Skott Johnson said. "We have McDonalds, Subway, who have been excellent, excellent neighbors who have been involved. There are others who say you have to talk to a manager in New York or Australia if you want them to pay dues or participate in an event. We're also worried about the character of the area," he said. "It looks like a dinky town."

Skott Johnson expressed concern that new buildings may not be as durable as the ones being torn down. The University of Minnesota is building a new "super dorm" at Seventeenth and University Avenues Southeast that's "absolutely beautiful brick and stone." This building covers the site of the former Newman Center.

"Our new buildings are not much to look at by comparison. The university is building for a hundred years; these buildings are going up for fifteen to twenty years for a return on investment," he said.

Dinkytown has some older stone and brick buildings, such as Dinkydale, which houses several businesses.

He named many businesses and owners who have been around for years, and he praised Loring Café owner Jason McLean for preserving the exterior integrity of the Gray's Drug Store and the Varsity Theater. "We're concerned about the look, and we're concerned about the welfare of existing businesses."

Many people praise McLean's imaginative reuse of Gray's as a restaurant, but his changes would not meet historic preservation standards.

Some relate the welfare of business to parking. Parking has been a perennial issue in Dinkytown. Some businesses say there's a severe parking shortage while others say that less parking acknowledges the growth of pedestrian and bicycle traffic.

"I'm worried about the lack of parking that this might end up producing," long-term resident Walter Johnson said. "I don't see where customers for the little shops that are now in Dinkytown are going to park. There's a point to the idea of making the place more pedestrian and bicycle friendly," he said, "but I don't think most people ride bicycles all year-round. It always has been a bicycle place. I certainly used it that way for many years." Many people from outside the area drive to Dinkytown for dining at Kafé 421 and the Shuang Cheng restaurant in Dinkydale. "We had a friend visiting from Florida and the one thing he wanted to do was go to that Chinese restaurant. I don't know how he heard about it," Walter Johnson said. "It grieves me terribly that Kafé 421 [at 421 Fourteenth Avenue Southeast] isn't going to have parking because it's a nice restaurant. There are some groups of people who go through Dinkytown who aren't young. I'm also interested in parking for the church at Thirteenth and University [Avenues Southeast]."

Most of Skott Johnson's Autographics business came from other Dinkytown stores and University departments. Johnson closed the business, retired and left Dinkytown at the end of 2013.

Brett Naylor, who owns the building that housed Autographics and several businesses east of the Varsity Theater, has told tenants that he could sell their aging building if the opportunity arises. Naylor developed the apartment building at 1301 University Avenue Southeast that houses the Purple Onion coffeehouse and café.

The name of the apartment building is simply 1301 University, and it occupies the site that was once a Pure Oil service station, Koehler's Garage and a city impound lot. After those businesses closed in the mid-1970s, a Pizza Hut moved into a major remake of the building with space for video games and other family activities of the day.

"1301 University provides an upscale student living experience with superlative convenience," proclaims its website. "Literally steps away from the landmarks of Dinkytown and directly across the street from University of Minnesota campus, 1301 University holds 92 contemporary units, ranging from studio to four-bedroom layouts, all housed in a handsome, collegiately-inspired façade. The ground floor is proudly occupied by The Purple Onion Cafe, a Dinkytown institution." The site described the location as "in the University/Dinkytown entertainment district, steps from trendsetting restaurants, coffee houses, theatres, & lively night spots," with "spectacular views of the Minneapolis skyline."

Many newcomers and old-timers have ideas about what Dinkytown should become. Resident Walter Johnson said:

> *It would be hard to say what to keep. I think there is a community. I think the business people have a community there, but those kinds of things come and go—develop and disappear—I don't think anything like that is permanent. As far as I'm concerned, I'd rather see more of a general shopping area than what it* [is] *now. I think it's patterned; it's changed by the changing clientele. There aren't as many families that live close to it, and there are more students. And the students don't do a butcher shop or a bakery.*
>
> *We certainly use the Post Office and Autographics. We use Fast Eddie's* [shoe repair in Dinkydale] *so there are some things we use in Dinkytown, but we're not doing our shopping there anymore. There was a dry cleaner I used that was run by a man and his wife—they were really old. They were sort of like grandparents to me.*

They were next to Perine's bookstore, which was on the ground floor of the building that houses Annie's Parlor and Kitty Cat Klub.

O'Hearn also recalls an earlier Dinkytown that included Dayton's University Store. "Dayton's had two restaurants—the Tent upstairs and the Dungeon downstairs—and they were both nice restaurants. I think a Grandpa Dayton wanted that store to be there. That was there a long time. Very nice."

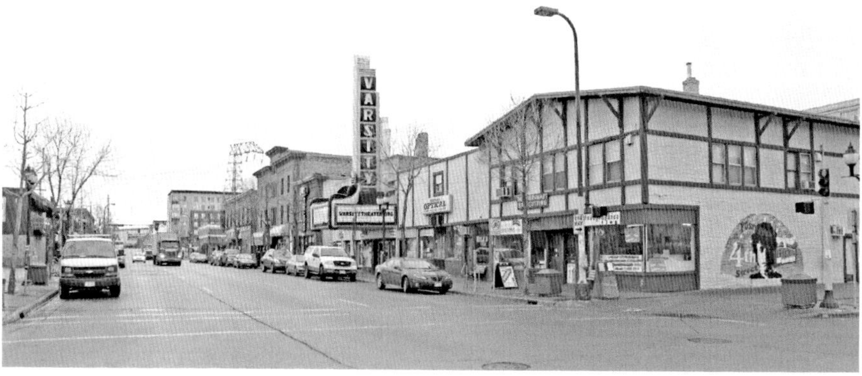

Fourth Street Southeast has Varsity Theater and Dinkydale with Loring Café on the far corner. Two storefronts house bicycle shops. *Photo by Bill Huntzicker.*

Dayton's University Store opened in 1927 and closed in June 1950. The Dayton-Hudson corporation, which had created the very successful chain of Target discount stores, sold its Dayton and other major department stores and changed the corporation's name to Target in 2000. A Target Express, the first of Target's downsized and special-market stores from the large retail chain, became the first anchor business for the Marshall building.

Mrs. Smith's Tea Room was cater-corner from the St. Lawrence rectory at Fifth Street and Twelfth Avenue. "I was there many times. They had very good chicken pot pie," said O'Hearn, who attended St. Lawrence Elementary School next to the high school. Another restaurant, Mrs. Bryan's Tea Room, was nearby at 1005 University Avenue Southeast.

Astrid Swain also recalled having teahouses in the neighborhood. She and her husband walked to church on Sunday at University Lutheran Church of Hope and then to a teahouse at Fifth Street and Thirteenth Avenue Southeast. "The lady who owned it always wore a long dress and was always dressed up, so on Sundays we went there quite often."

Astrid Swain was born in Sweden; grew up near Hibbing, Minnesota; and moved to Minneapolis as a young woman. An aunt to Tom Swain, she married Bill Swain in 1948 and lived about two blocks from Dinkytown for sixty-seven years. She doesn't remember it as being very different from other Minneapolis neighborhoods. Her husband, Howard Swain (friends called him Bill), worked for the family business in Dinkytown and remained a truck driver long after his father closed it. "He loved to drive. We traveled a lot. We were in every single state, except one way out East."

O'Hearn said that many of her high school and college friends found jobs in the restaurants and retail stores in Dinkytown. She misses the Bridge Café, which was where CVS stands today, where she went with friends after school, and she recalls Bridgeman's on the corner where Potbelly currently rents, Simms Hardware at 411 Fourteenth Avenue, Schaak Electronics nearby and the Dinky Town Dime next to Gray's Drug.

Schafer Brothers had a grocery store and meat market at 405 Fourteenth Avenue Southeast; Ortie's Corn Shop sold popcorn near the Varsity Theater. A photography studio and a camera and record shop were also in that block.

Marcia Pankake, who came to the University of Minnesota in 1960, misses the music scene and bookstores. "I'm sorry there're so few bookstores now," she said, recalling McCosh's, Perine's, Minnesota Co-op, Co-op Junior and at least three other used bookstores. The Book House was the only one left in 2016.

"The flavor of Dinkytown is an effervescence in the air; you have that by having specific things, like a grocery store," she said. "Little small businesses

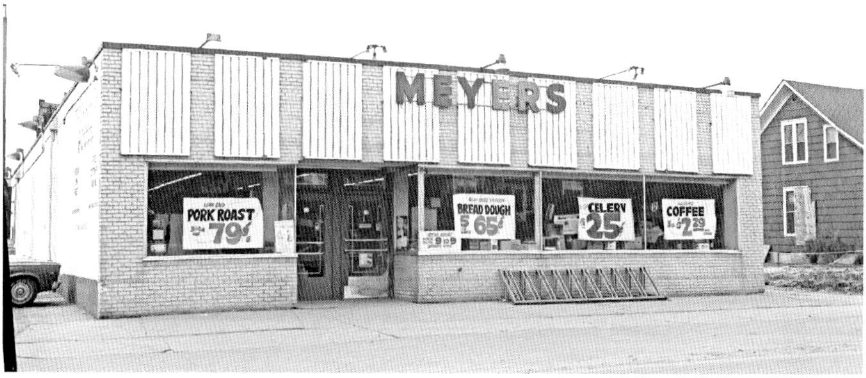

Meyer's Grocery as seen in 1973. The building houses a liquor store in 2016. *Photo by Steven Bergerson; accessible through University Archives, University of Minnesota, Twin Cities.*

are what add to desirability of Dinkytown—the purpose for going there. The Podium drew people from all around—people who live in a few miles will stay for things besides the Podium. People used to drive to Dinkytown to see the Needle Doctor, Jerry Raskin. Now he is somewhere else that you need a car to go to. Apartment residents will be transients if they're aiming at students, and they may not be as good for business."

"Meyer's was a terrific grocery store," she said about the store where the Dinkytown Wine and Spirits is in 2016 at 1412 Fifth Street Southeast. Meyer's had a butcher shop and free delivery. She shopped on her way home from the university, and by the time she walked home, the groceries would arrive about the same time she did.

New development could be the seed of renewal, said Tom Dale, aka Tom the Tailor, whose leather shop started above Gray's Drug in 1971. Later, he worked out of his home in the Southeast Como Neighborhood until his death in October 2013. "Unfortunately, they're bringing down more history in the process," Dale had said. "The Book House along with the Podium and Al's Breakfast are beloved by the community."

The "most storied and legendary" places should be preserved, Dale said, "but I just think Dinkytown has been looking for ways to exist ever since students got cars and moved off campus. The funny thing is that part of me wants to go back to Dinkytown. I dream that I found a spot that I could afford and go back there, but I still have the customers I had in Dinkytown." Dale continued:

> *Being upstairs of the drugstore was like being at the Vatican. Everyone knew where it was. You could just say you were in Dinkytown above Gray's Drug, and you didn't need to give directions. It was a landmark, an institutional destination. Making the property more desirable may force many more businesses to close, but maybe there's more opportunities for different types of business. I tend to look at the glass as half full, especially when things are inevitable.*

Keeping Varsity Theater, Vescio's restaurant and Al's Breakfast would be important, Dale said. "Fast Eddie's is a really good shoe repair, often listed as the best in the city. There is a place called Magus Books [on spirituality] downstairs next to the Post Office. In spite of all the gentrification in Dinkytown, there are still one-of-a-kind businesses tucked away there." Stores like Everyday People with used clothing prospered for a while despite the high rent.

Al's Breakfast, the narrow fourteen-stool, award-winning diner, makes everyone's list of Dinkytown treasures. Al's was created by filling in an alley between two buildings. It is part of the Simms Hardware/Schaak Electronics building that houses the Espresso Royale Caffe next door, which caters to a diverse clientele. Dan Zielske, part owner of the Espresso Royale, said his building changed owners in the 2013 turmoil over new development. The Schaak family sold the building to the company that owns Green Mill restaurants.

"I'm not necessarily one of those Dinkytowners that harken back to the days of Bob Dylan and wax ridiculously that Dinkytown won't come back again," Zielske said, but he admitted missing the record stores and office supply stores that have gone. He laments of the loss of so many coffee shops.

"I went to high school in Roseville, and we'd ride our bikes here. We'd be occupied all day in Dinkytown. We'd ride bikes, visit the stores, take in a movie at the Varsity and lunch at Annie's. That was in the early '80s and late '70s," Zielske said. "There have been a lot of changes since I started [the business] in here in 1988."

"I love Dinkytown," Eide-Tollefson said, "and I'm as concerned about Dinkytown as I am for my own business, which I've been in for thirty-six years. The Podium has been here much longer."

Star Tribune columnist James Lileks shared some memories of Dinkytown and commented on the proposed development. "If they knock down some history and displace some good, quirky stores, they'd be smart to rent the ground floor to cluttered bookstores and guitar shops," Lileks wrote. "If they're typical, they'll rent it to The Interchangeable Pretentious Sandwich Company or some such chain."

But, he concluded, "if they lay one finger on Al's Breakfast, I'll be at the barricades. There's progress, and then there's madness."

21

DINKIEST PLACE, BIGGEST REPUTATION

When Governor Wendell Anderson, a former Gopher hockey star, introduced the new University of Minnesota president C. Peter Magrath around the athletic department in 1974, he started the day with breakfast at Al's in Dinkytown. Although they spent the day meeting with athletics managers and other student, faculty and administrative leaders, the governor said the university president should start the day at Al's as he did as a student athlete. Their visit to athletic fields included a run to work off some of the calories.

One summer morning in 2013, Tom McDonald, an attorney specializing in international law and former ambassador to Zimbabwe, returned to Al's. "This place got me through law school," said McDonald, who graduated in 1978. "I try to come here every time I'm in town. I love the food, the atmosphere, the people. I've brought young lawyers when we're here for business meetings." McDonald ate blueberry pancakes and bacon at Al's fourteen-stool counter while a chauffeur waited at the black Lincoln in front. Besides the pancakes, McDonald also recommends huevos rancheros.

Most customers walk, bike or drive like Alan Koppenhaber, who commutes from suburban Coon Rapids to help maintain the phone system at the University of Minnesota. "About eight months ago, I realized that the coffee and doughnuts I was getting from SA daily were not as good and healthy" as a breakfast at Al's, where he gets "two eggs and toast for about the same amount of money."

Like former law students McDonald and Anderson, many people over several generations have returned to Al's Breakfast to relive their college years. (This writer seldom visited Al's as a student, but as an old man, I've become a regular—an addict.)

Jeffrey Hunsberger, who works for the state in St. Paul, has been eating at Al's since he was a teenager growing up in Southeast Minneapolis. "They make good food and they're good people," said Hunsberger, who often stops "to catch breakfast" between his Southwest Minneapolis home and his job in St. Paul.

During homecoming and student orientation seasons, parents often bring their children to introduce them to Al's as a University of Minnesota tradition. "Kids bring parents and parents bring their kids," said co-owner Doug Grina.

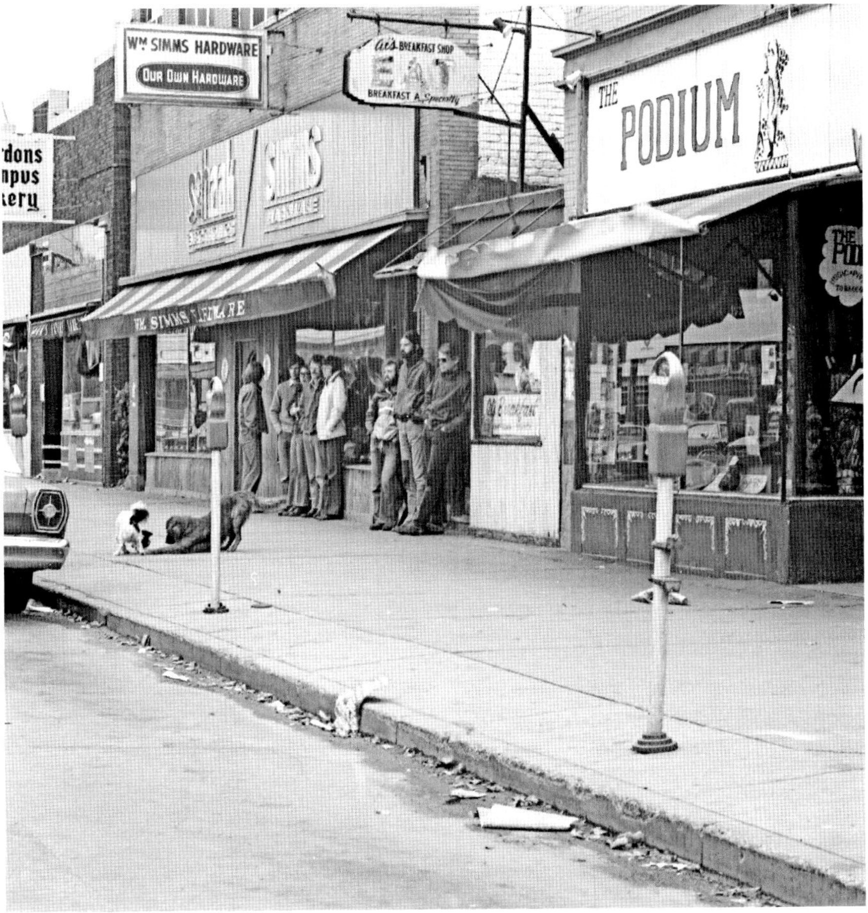

Customers often line up in front of Al's Breakfast to await one of the fourteen stools at the counter. *Photo by Steven Bergerson in the 1970s.*

"We're obviously connected to the university, but we get people from all over the city as well," co-owner Jim Brandes said. "The university students, even when they're not going to school, they eat breakfast. They may be introduced to us through the university and, after they're out, they continue to come here."

"It's very seldom that freshmen and sophomores will step through the doors here," Brandes said, to which Grina added, "Unless their parents bring them."

Al's Breakfast became symbolic in the fights over Dinkytown preservation. Al's Breakfast—located at 413 Fourteenth Avenue Southeast—is the narrowest restaurant in the Twin Cities at about ten feet wide and is perhaps the dinkiest place in Dinkytown, but it has become more significant than its size suggests.

In 2004, co-owners Doug Grina and Jim Brandes donned tuxedos to accept an "America's Classics" award from the James Beard Foundation in New York City. The medal, described as the Academy Award for restaurants, hangs from a ribbon on the wall behind the counter. "Distinguished by their timeless appeal, they serve quality food that reflects the character of their communities," the foundation's website says of classics award winners. "In the spirit of James Beard, who enjoyed a paper cone of fried belly clams as much as a white tablecloth dinner, we encourage you to visit these classics. You are sure to find a warm welcome, and deeply satisfying food."

Grina attributed Al's media fame to a notice in a book by Jane and Michael Stern, travel writers who specialize in restaurants. Since then, Al's has been listed by the *New York Times* as one of the ten best breakfast places and by *USA Today* as one of the ten best pancake houses in the nation. A five-page article in *Gourmet* magazine in 1994 and an oft-rerun visit from the Food Channel's *Diners, Drive-ins and Dives* have helped.

"Al's is Nirvana for those of us who spend our lives in search of a great diner breakfast," Michael Stern said in a 2010 post on his website. "Customers waiting for one of the fourteen stools at the counter stand hovering just above and behind those who are seated and eating. In the narrow space between the counter and the back bar…Al's hash slingers race to and fro with seasoned aplomb."

Publicity goes only so far, though. "It's our regulars that make it for us," Brandes said. "We do get a lot of people who see us on TV, but that's not a driving force for us. If we relied on them, we'd be out of business."

Grina and Brandes remember Al Bergstrom, who founded the business in 1950. Bergstrom, who had cooked at a restaurant across the street, recalled riding his bicycle through an alley that was later blocked when the adjacent hardware store built a storage shed around 1937. "You don't see a lot of sheds that last for sixty years—sixty-three years—as Al's [has]," Grina said.

The property was converted to an eating space and housed different restaurants with nearly annual turnover from 1939 until Al's moved in, said Madelyn Sundberg, a University of Minnesota graduate student doing historic preservation research in 2013. In 1950, Alfred "Al" Bergstrom quit his job as chef at Dutch Treat Café because the business was too large. So he purchased the Hunky Dory hamburger stand across the street and opened Al's Café. "By 1973 Al had cemented the role of Al's Breakfast in the University of Minnesota community and retired after twenty-three years of short-order cooking," Sundberg said. For the first seven years, she said, Al's served three meals a day for seven days a week, saying he cut to breakfast to reduce waste.

When he changed the name to Al's Breakfast in 1958, he added a jab at the growing number of chain businesses in the area by adding "Dinkytown Branch" under the name on the sign. When Bergstrom retired on May 15, 1973, Governor Anderson declared an Al Bergstrom Day, sending his friend a framed official proclamation appreciating Al's "wholesome food and warm hospitality." In the 1980s, university music professor David Baldwin composed a series of works for brass quintets in honor of Al's, and Sundberg listed three fictional stories and one memoir that use Al's as a setting. One customer told me he became a music major after seeing the musical piece performed at an Al's anniversary party.

In 1974, Bergstrom sold the business to his nephew Phil Bergstrom, who formed a partnership with Brandes and another partner. Phil Bergstrom sold his share to Grina in January 1979. In her twentieth year working at Al's, Alison Kirwin planned to begin buying out Brandes in the summer of 2016 as he phased into his retirement.

Bergstrom himself had become a Dinkytown institution standing at the grill in his chef's hat and white apron inside the café's picture window. Brandes and Kirwin often stand there in 2016 without the uniform.

Mary Rose "M.R." Ciatti, who grew up in the Como Neighborhood and lives in adjacent Northeast Minneapolis, started at Al's in 1986, when Grina asked her to substitute for three months, and, she added, "the rest is history." Thirty years later, she began to consider retiring. Besides her friendly service, Ciatti was known for her traffic-directing skills to manage the seating. First, she shouts, "move down to the phone" to keep customers moving into the building, rather than clustering at the door where a gathering could create the illusion of a larger crowd and longer wait.

The phone refers to the pay telephone that used to hang on the wall opposite the entrance. When the phone was removed years ago, Nic Benson,

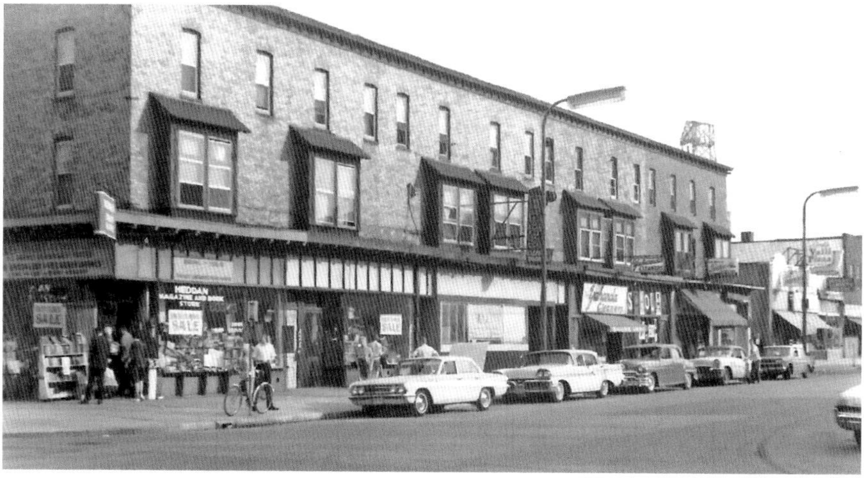

Between the two awnings on the far side of this half block of businesses was the Scholar coffee shop in 1965. *Photo courtesy Al Milgrom.*

a regular customer and photographer, supplied a larger-than-life photo of a pay phone to replace it.

Ciatti also enforced rules about waiting. If you meet friends, you cannot hold a seat for them until they all arrive. When a group assembles, they wait together for the next open seats. If two stools open up that are not next to each other, seated customers will shift, creating a vacancy of two or more stools.

When pressed to guess, Grina estimated that they serve close to one thousand customers a week. Besides menus on the yellow Formica counter, you will find cream and syrup pitchers and sugar and salt and pepper shakers created by local potters.

Behind the counter, shelves contain cups, plastic dinosaurs to entertain children and hundreds of little yellow books that record prepaid breakfasts. Besides Al's, the hardware store building now houses Caffé Espresso Royal and five upstairs apartments. A fire on October 25, 2013, did considerable damage to one of the upstairs apartments, but Caffé Espresso was closed for only a day and a half; Al's didn't close at all.

Right after the second-story window blew out of the building and flames were spewing forth, Grina said, a customer ran into Al's shouting, "Feed me quick! They might close you soon!" The fire department got the fire under control within a few minutes, and Al's service was not interrupted despite the accumulating smoke. The fire, Sundberg said, may indicate how vulnerable the iconic building is and strengthen the argument for historic preservation.

22
DINKYTOWN BECOMES HISTORIC

On July 10, 2015, the Minneapolis City Council officially approved "Local historic designation: Dinkytown Commercial Historic District" with all members present and voting unanimously. The plan, as advocated by Councilmember Jacob Frey, who represented the area, designated the smaller of two proposed boundaries in the city's Dinkytown study. The smaller district highlights the streetcar era from 1899 to 1929 (the longer proposed period would have run through the 1970s).

And it left many issues, including height of new additions and new construction, to be resolved through future negotiation over guidelines. Here are the conditions: After limiting the district to the twenty-three resources listed in "the proposed boundary for 1899–1929 period of significance" and establishing interim rules while the guidelines are established, the resolution required the planning staff to work with Frey and the Zoning and Planning Committee to create guidelines that "1) allow for maximum flexibility in retaining the eclectic nature of the district; 2) will not give deference or historic designation to under-utilized space such as surface parking lots; 3) value the façade facing the streetscape with less value given to the backside of the buildings; and 4) will not limit height and the evolving character of the district."

The local guidelines, of course, were the sticking point in the controversy over historic designation. Property owners did not want to support historic designation until they knew what guidelines would control their ability to change their properties. They expressed satisfaction that the façades of

From The Steps of Northrop Memorial Demonstrators Marched To The Air Force Recruiting Office in Dinkytown

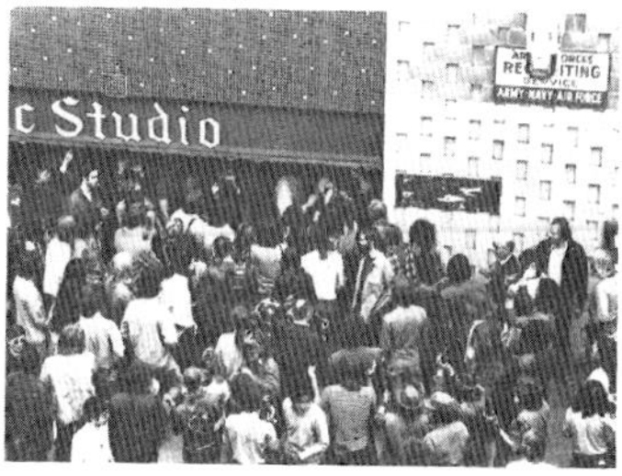

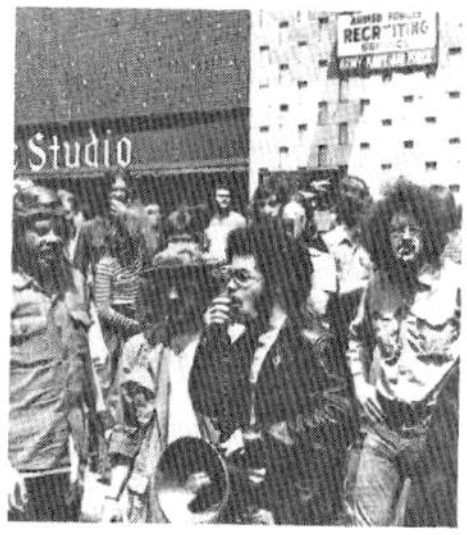

This page is from a student pamphlet recalling a day of antiwar protest, May 10, 1972, with students marching to the air force recruiting station in Dinkytown. *Photo courtesy Ted Palmer.*

buildings were favored over the buildings themselves, and preservationists expressed their happiness over getting the designation.

The dilemma has been to preserve the eclectic and "funky" nature of Dinkytown despite the continuing pressures for new development and increasing density in the city. Principal city planner Haila Maze, who coordinated the process over several years, has said maintaining the scale and massing of the one- to four-story buildings would help.

Frey, however, attacked the idea of including the "horrible looking structure" at 1315 Fourth Street Southeast, which the city council has approved for demolition, and the McDonald's at the corner of Fourth Street and Fifteenth Avenue Southeast. Both were built in the 1950s and 1960s and are at the ends of the historic site on Fourth Street Southeast. The "horrible looking structure" was built in 1955 of perforated cinderblocks with a second floor added in 1964, leaving a drive-through entry to a parking lot behind the building. The building was the site of the air force recruiting center, a repeated target of antiwar demonstrators.

At the meeting, Frey said he did not want to preserve surface parking lots, noting that the 1315 address and the land behind it will be open for development. At time of council action, it was for sale by developer Kelly Doran, who proposed first an apartment building and later a hotel on the site. Doran apparently abandoned the hotel project after the council rejected the demolition permit for the adjacent brick building and started the preservation study.

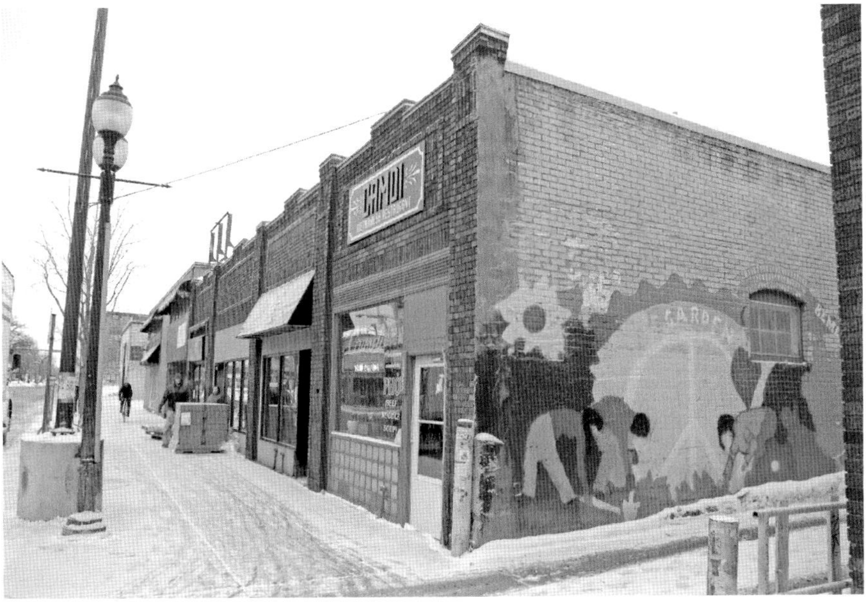

The city council stopped demolition of this building pending a review for possible historic preservation. The mural celebrates the short-lived peace garden of 1970. *Photo by Bill Huntzicker.*

At the Zoning and Planning Committee, Frey said the larger district that included memories of the 1950s through the 1970s was just too large and eclectic without a defining theme, leaving the process to people's memories. "It depends on the individual," Frey said, "and it coincides to a time in their lives when they were dating someone hot, smoking and staying up late. That's not history. That's college."

At the later city council meeting, however, Frey indirectly addressed criticism that he had been dismissive of the longer period proposed by preservation activists. "I want to point out that the counter culture movement, the civil rights movement, the antiwar movement are incredibly important, and the information gathered [about this history] contributed to the ultimate designation of the street car era," he said.

"It is now time to focus on the future of our great local and regional commercial destination," said the news release on behalf of Mike Mulrooney, president of the DBA and owner of Blarney Pub & Grill. "The partial designation of some areas of Dinkytown as historic, speaks to the nature of our commercial corridor as having a longstanding connection with the University of Minnesota, its eclectic makeup, its independent small businesses and its patrons that have added to the fabric of our community."

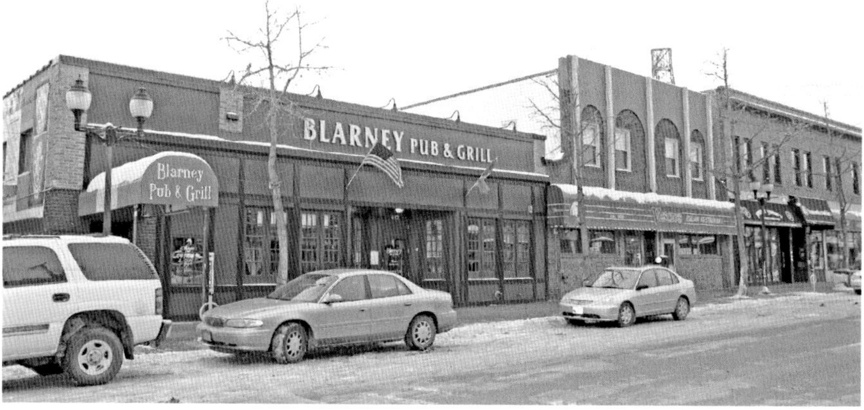

Blarney Pub & Grill is in the building once occupied by Valli Pizza on a site that was once Swain Fuel & Transfer. *Photo by Bill Huntzicker.*

As with earlier debates over city planning, the two-year debate over the designation for Dinkytown broke into factions—the business owners, the landowners/landlords and the residents of the surrounding Marcy-Holmes Neighborhood. Each group reflected its divergent interests from the others as the conflict grew. After the city council's action, however, each side declared victory in ways that indicated that the conflicts could continue as preservation guidelines are negotiated.

Conflicts over the scale and mass of the buildings are likely to continue, as city planners work with stakeholders to implement preservation guidelines. Similarly, building owners may face more scrutiny as they change their structures, and permits to demolish buildings—even aging ones—may be harder to obtain. At the same time, the council excluded from protection buildings from the 1950s and 1960s, perhaps arbitrarily choosing some buildings as more historic than others.

The historic preservation debate—begun by advocates seeking to halt the advance of new midrise, mixed-use housing into the core of the business district—brought to the fore the varied ways of viewing Dinkytown. And the parties involved found historic roots, precedents and constituents to support their positions.

Before the preservation debate, however, the city's long-range plan had designated Dinkytown an "activity center," a commercial area that should anticipate high-density development that encourages a busy street life both day and night. Activity centers theoretically encourage pedestrian over automobile traffic and a wide range of commercial, office, entertainment, educational and residential uses. The plan discourages automobile-based businesses like surface parking lots and drive-through services in activity centers. At the same time, developments should encourage climate-sensitive designs and improve public spaces.

City policies, thus, set up a debate between developers anticipating bigger new buildings and those seeking to halt the demolition of lower-intensity buildings that had given Dinkytown its traditional character. One thing that became clear after the historic designation was that the devil in the details would be discovered in the future, possibly over many years as building owners seek to change or demolish their buildings.

The major themes of Dinkytown history involve the streetcar era, its orientation to the university, its unique commercial center and the continuing change and continuity of the area, said principal city planner Haila Maze in summarizing her 595-page report to the Heritage Preservation Commission (HPC) on June 9, 2015. Her study started with Dinkytown's four-block boundary, then removed noncontributing properties and included part of the lower-level railroad trench that runs diagonally through the district. Dinkytown was always a commuting hub for students, and Fourteenth Avenue Southeast was always the original commercial corridor, even though "some of the earliest buildings no longer exist," Maze said.

Michael Koop, of the heritage preservation department of the Minnesota Historical Society, criticized the idea of stretching a historic district over the longer period from 1899 through 1972 and added that 1972 was too recent for historic designation. Koop said his department, often called SHPO (for State Historic Preservation Office), is required by state and city laws to review and comment on projects, but its recommendations are not binding. He said he regarded the city's plan as a draft, and he praised the research by the city and Dinkytown advocates who have been documenting the area's cultural significance. But, he said, he did not want to keep reviewing future drafts of the proposal as it's updated.

He criticized listing the railroad bridges built in the 1990s, but Maze said the bridges were rebuilt on the original sites—an unusual layout of a small commercial district intersected by major railroads. One bridge that held a busy urban intersection at Fourth Street and Fifteenth Avenue Southeast had to be rebuilt after it fell down in 1975, causing cars waiting at a stoplight to slide into a slow-moving train. Fortunately, no one was hurt.

While agreeing that Dinkytown should continue to grow and change, the Minneapolis Heritage Preservation Commission unanimously

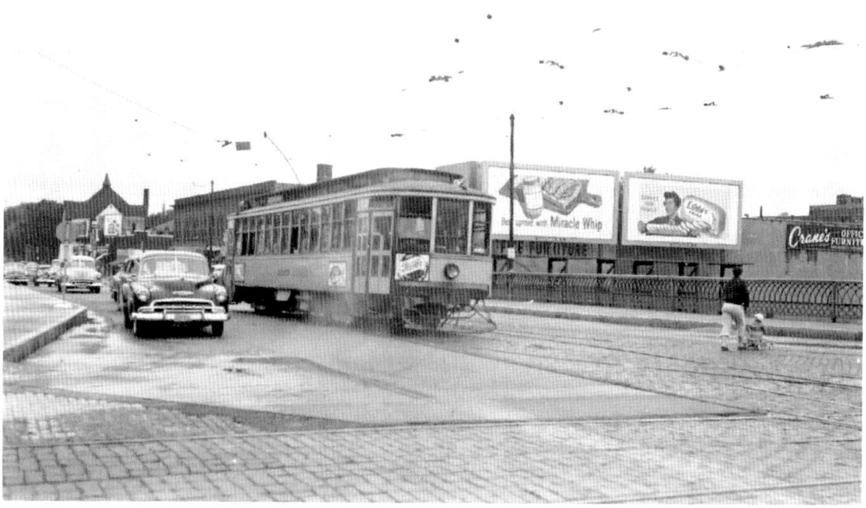

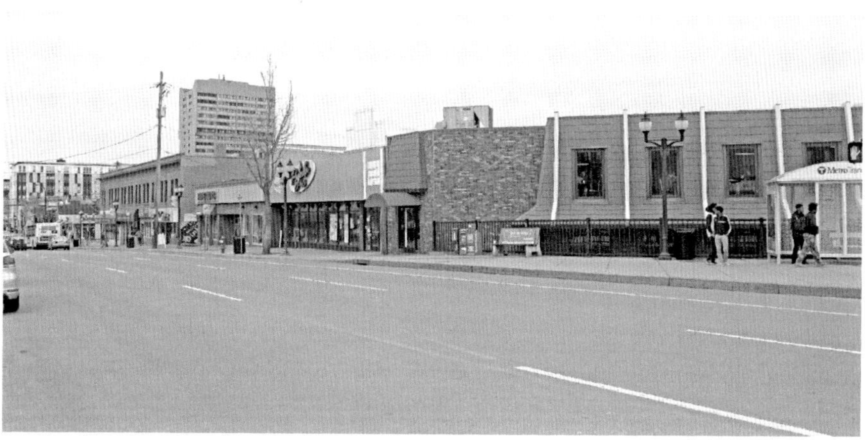

This page: The older bridge holding up the intersection of Fourth Street Southeast and Fifteenth Avenue Southeast collapsed in 1975. McDonald's has only the second floor visible from the street. *Older photo courtesy University Archives, University of Minnesota; newer one by Bill Huntzicker.*

recommended a month before the city council action that most of the four-block business district be designated for historic preservation. The HPC decision came after hearing about two hours of testimony, some of it impassioned on both sides. About twenty people testified, raising first principles, such as the balance between free enterprise and urban planning, and then questions like what is history, what can be preserved and what is Dinkytown.

Guidelines should be collaborative and flexible, said Jack Byers, manager of long-range planning for Minneapolis Community Planning and

Economic Development. "As individual structures we do not see the bridges that are there now as historic," Byers said. "As part of the cultural landscape, though, Dinkytown would not be what it is without bridges over the railroad. The grade separation was done in the first decade of the twentieth century. The city felt so strongly that they built diagonal bridges."

Bridges usually connect two points, but these bridges do more than that. The bridge at Fourth Street Southeast and Fifteenth Avenue Southeast "connects points A and B and holds a city intersection as well." Byers compared Dinkytown to the St. Anthony Falls and the Warehouse districts that have changed and evolved near downtown Minneapolis.

Kristen Eide-Tollefson characterized the situation as "delicate," as she hoped for preservation guidelines that business owners can support. "I am a Dinkytown business owner and project coordinator for Preserve Historic Dinkytown. I'm very anxious to see these interests held together. The city's small-area plan for Dinkytown has a market analysis that shows that its history and its quirky character are its appeal."

Mulrooney said his Dinkytown Business Alliance opposed historic designation without seeing the preservation guidelines. The university is the biggest engine of change, he said, and it will continue to make Dinkytown unique and eclectic without preservation. "The streetcar era is gone, and there isn't much left to even know it was there. Vietnam protests happened everywhere and not just in Dinkytown. The trench is a bike path, and it will remain a bike path."

After city council approval, Preserve Historic Dinkytown declared, "This is a momentous day!...Although the boundaries approved are those from the streetcar era 1899–1929, there was acknowledgment of the seminal period of the '50s through early '70s—the era that was the proving ground for the cultural, social, and political movements that are still informing what is happening today."

23

OWNERSHIP HAS ITS PRIVILEGES

In December 2013, eleven Dinkytown property owners—that's nearly all of them—organized to attack the proposed small-area plan and any design guidelines or historic designation for their four-block business district.

At the same time, they said that expanding the planning district and rezoning it to C3A, "the highest density mixed-use district—is essential for this area." C3A makes possible the six-story apartment buildings with commercial street-level space—two of which were then under construction in the four blocks of Dinkytown and several others being built nearby.

Despite eight months of open meetings by the small-area planning group, a letter signed by individuals organized as the Dinkytown Property Owners Group accused Minneapolis city planners and the Dinkytown Business Association of neglecting their property interests in planning for Dinkytown.

"To be clear, it is important to point out that the Owners Group is a completely separate entity, with differing viewpoints and perspectives, than the Dinkytown Business Association," the letter said. "We are concerned that the process thus far is not benefitting from the input of property owners in the district."

The plan addresses four major categories: heritage preservation, economic development, transportation and parking and land use and design. The owners' letter opposed any historic preservation or design principles.

"Property Owners oppose any designation of Dinkytown as a local or national historic district, part of the Minnesota Main Street Program or as a Conservation District," the letter said. "While our group agrees that there may be certain properties that warrant historic recognition, the Property Owners also believe that any such designation should be made with precision so that it applies only to properties truly worth saving, and that any attempt to place a designation on the entire area would be a mistake."

The Owners Group said they are "keenly aware of the evolution" of Dinkytown with the changes in tenants and frequent building renovations and redevelopment. A historic district would "hinder this natural evolution" of Dinkytown and its unique character. Historic designation "would significantly diminish the value of existing properties, stifle renovations needed for tenant expansions or routine re-tenanting, and prevent the occurrence of responsible future redevelopment of older buildings," the group said.

The Dinkytown property owners also challenged the idea that Dinkytown's uniqueness was historic. "A historic designation could have a very negative impact on the ability of Dinkytown business to retain its unique flavor." For example, Jason McLean's redevelopment of the Loring Pasta Bar and Varsity Theater—recently recognized as having among the most creative restrooms in the nation—would not have been possible with historic guidelines, the group said.

Historic designation would stop "creative, innovative and artistic designs for Dinkytown properties," and historic district tax credits would not pay for the hassle and expense of saving smaller the properties, they said.

The owners' group opposed not only historic guidelines but also any design criteria because "creating criteria of one-size-fits-all does not fit with Dinkytown eclectic history." Instead, Dinkytown must adapt to "a changing mix of tenants" and "ever changing market conditions." Customers and the market should determine the area's changing needs.

A public parking facility close to or in Dinkytown is the "ultimate fix" for the parking problem, the group said. Short of that, the group proposed a portal or link to the university's existing ramp on Fourth Street Southeast with more advertising of it, a new parking ramp over the railroad trench with access from different levels and a link to the bike path and walkway below and additional on-street parking with meters along curbs on the bridges.

Since Skott Johnson's retirement and the fight over preservation, the Dinkytown Business Association has become the Dinkytown Business Alliance to separate itself from the earlier DBA that property owners said was moving too fast toward historic preservation and other issues that had separated the businesses from their landlords.

Dinkytown is a special-service district that can tax itself for special projects, like snow removal and holiday lighting. The four-block district was recently expanded to take in DinkyDome and Marshall Apartments. In an interview, developer Kelly Doran questioned the need for the special-service district assessment that pays for snow removal, banners and Christmas tree lights.

Former DBA president Skott Johnson said the district was created after the state improved Fourth Street Southeast as a state highway. Because Fourth Street was narrower than highway requirements, the state proposed widening the street to leave the sidewalk so narrow people would have to walk single file and the Varsity Theater marquee would stick out into a lane of traffic. The Dinkytown businesses compromised with the state, promising to expeditiously remove snow to avoid impeding traffic.

The Dinkytown banners help foster a sense of community, and the holiday lights improve safety, said Greg Pillsbury, co-owner of Burrito Loco restaurant. Several people said snow removal from the sidewalks was unreliable before the special district.

24

DINKYTOWN CHARACTERS

Everyone who hangs around Dinkytown has some favorite characters they think should be covered in any story about the place. Unfortunately, many of them don't even have last names or names that even the old-timers can remember.

One famous character in the 1920s was William Harrison "Stiffy" Steadman, who came to Minnesota in 1923 to take over the bankrupt restaurant at 313 Fourteenth Avenue, where the Kitty Cat Klub is in 2016. Steven Bergerson found that Stiffy had established himself as a campus tradition within two years. Bergerson wrote, "His sayings were published regularly in the *Minnesota Daily* and he missed only one Gopher game in his entire time in Dinkytown. People remember Stiffy as a little man with horn-rimmed glasses, always wearing knickers, sitting on the home team bench. He believed that he built spirit, and spirit was what the University needed."

Marv Davidov became known as a civil rights and antiwar activist, especially after he helped create the Honeywell Project, which targeted the stockholders of companies that made weapons of war. He encouraged people to buy stock and vote against weapons manufacturing in stockholder meetings. A consummate storyteller, he once sold tickets to public meetings at which he read his FBI file.

Some characters had "the" for their middle names. When the *Minnesota Daily* wanted historical comments on Dinkytown, they often went to Tom the Tailor and Dave the Barber.

Thomas E. Dale, known as Tom the Tailor around Dinkytown, died in September 2013. Leather biker jackets far outnumbered suits and ties inside the chapel while motorcycles—ranging from scooters to rare classics—crowded cars out of the parking lot as about 150 people gathered on September 28, 2013, to remember his life. He specialized in leatherwork in his shop, which was located above Gray's Drug. He was a motorcycle enthusiast and Girl Scout leader. Identifying with fellow baby boomer motorcycle enthusiasts who were gaining weight in their midsections, he created the Zip-r-strip, a leather strip with a zipper on both sides to allow people to expand the waist of a leather jacket. The extenders were sold in Harley-Davidson stores. He was a tailor for more than thirty-four years.

Skott Johnson said Tom Dale used to glue a quarter to the sidewalk and watch from his shop as people tried to pick it up.

Dale was friends with Jerry Rau, a popular singer and guitar player who frequented the sidewalks of Dinkytown in the 1970s. Both were Vietnam vets who opposed the war. Rau often stood on the sidewalks playing his guitar, singing and selling cassette tapes of his original music. Some have described Rau as more important to Dinkytown than Dylan.

Dave Watts, "Dave the Barber," had cut in Dinkytown for fifty years before his death a few years ago. I doubt that he ever did retire. After a partial retirement, he used to have an early morning breakfast at Al's before meeting someone by appointment to give a haircut. Watts was interviewed in Milgrom's film commenting on how impressed he was with the peace garden that protesters quickly planted after begin evicted from the vacated buildings. After forty-two years of cutting hair in Dinkytown, Milo David, who was sometimes a partner with Watts, retired in March 2011.

Another character was not a person but a store. Aunt Bee's Knitting Bag was a niche craft store in Dinkytown that closed in 1975 after ten years in business. Aunt Bee's sold knitting needles, crochet hooks, yarn and other needs for the hobby from the store at 1301 Fourth Street Southeast. Albert and Bertha Johnson, who owned the business, decided to close after receiving a thirty-day eviction notice. Although the landlord offered her a smaller location, she retired rather than moving the business.

Mama D was both a business and a personality. Giovanna D'Agostina, also known as Mama D, died in 2009. In her obituary, the *Star Tribune* reported, "Every March 19, Mama D celebrated the lesser-known holiday of St. Joseph's Day by honoring the patron saint of charity to the poor by serving free meals to the needy at her eldest son Sam's Dinkytown restaurant, Sammy D's, from the 1960s to the early 1980s. The restaurant was later

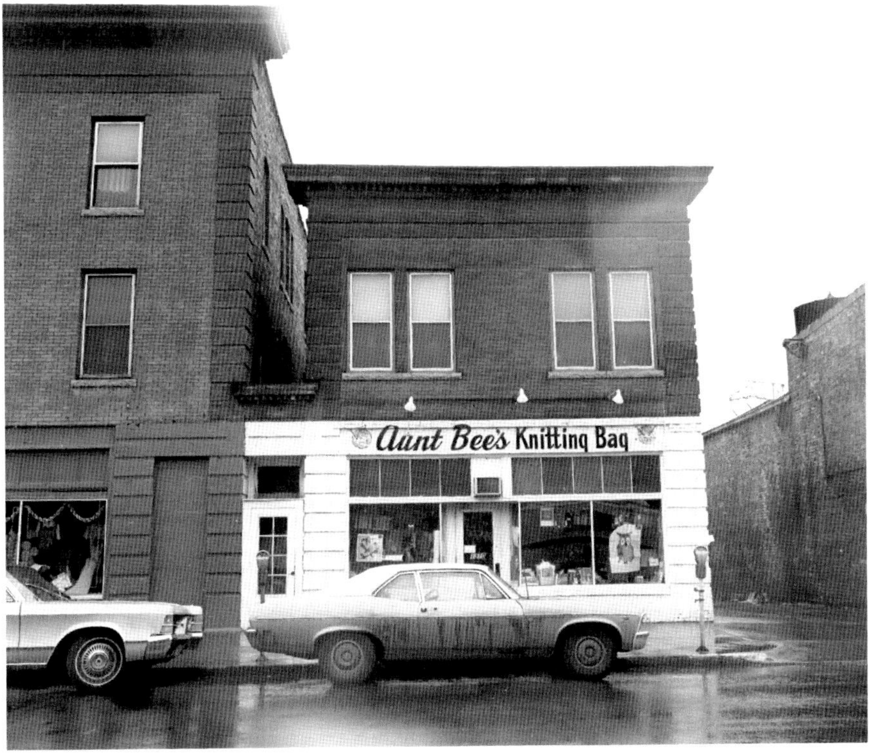

Aunt Bee's Knitting Bag was in the former annex to College Inn, a space occupied by Erik's Bike Shop in 2016. *Photo by Steven Bergerson.*

renamed Mama D's." The newspaper commented, "Mama D, who was 94, 'was everybody's mom,' her son John said. 'She called the hippie generation her kids, and she loved them.'"

She divulged some of her Italian delicacies in three cookbooks, and she cultivated relationships with celebrities, most notably Tony Bennett.

"Sure, you can call me Mama D," she wrote in the opening lines of her memoir. "Listen, everybody calls me that. I don't mind....As I used to say to the hippies from the University of Minnesota in the 1960s: 'Shut up and listen, I want to tell you something.' Then I'd try to make them see that I was on their side and that they didn't need to resort to violence or drugs or dropping out."

Although she grew up in Minneapolis, she was living in Chicago when her son opened a sandwich shop in Dinkytown. She moved home to help him and expanded Sammy D's sandwich into a popular Italian restaurant.

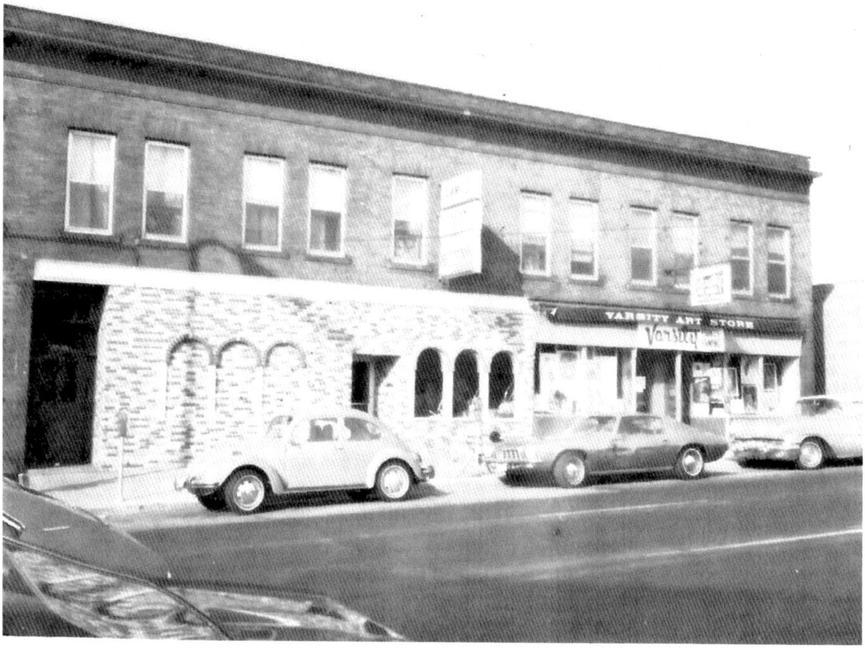

In the 1960s, Sammy D's Italian restaurant added the rock-covered façade. A generation earlier, the store next door housed the Butwins' Bookhunters. *Photo courtesy Al Milgrom.*

She wrote in her memoir:

> *Dinkytown had plenty of restaurants: Vescio's, Bridgeman's, Valli Pizza, the Tokyo, Grays Drugtore, and a McDonald's. The competition was stiff, but we prospered. I like to think my emphasis on treating the customers as friends made part of the difference. I had been apprehensive about working at Sam's sandwich shop because I knew the customers were mostly young people who were better educated than I. My English was not always perfect. But I was in for a very pleasant surprise: the young people accepted me for who I was. The younger generation of the 1960s had a much more egalitarian sense of human relations than their parents or grandparents had.*

She was also full of advice: "I have found over the years that God balances the books in our lives if we have tried hard enough and have reciprocated the good fortunes in our lives by helping others along the way."

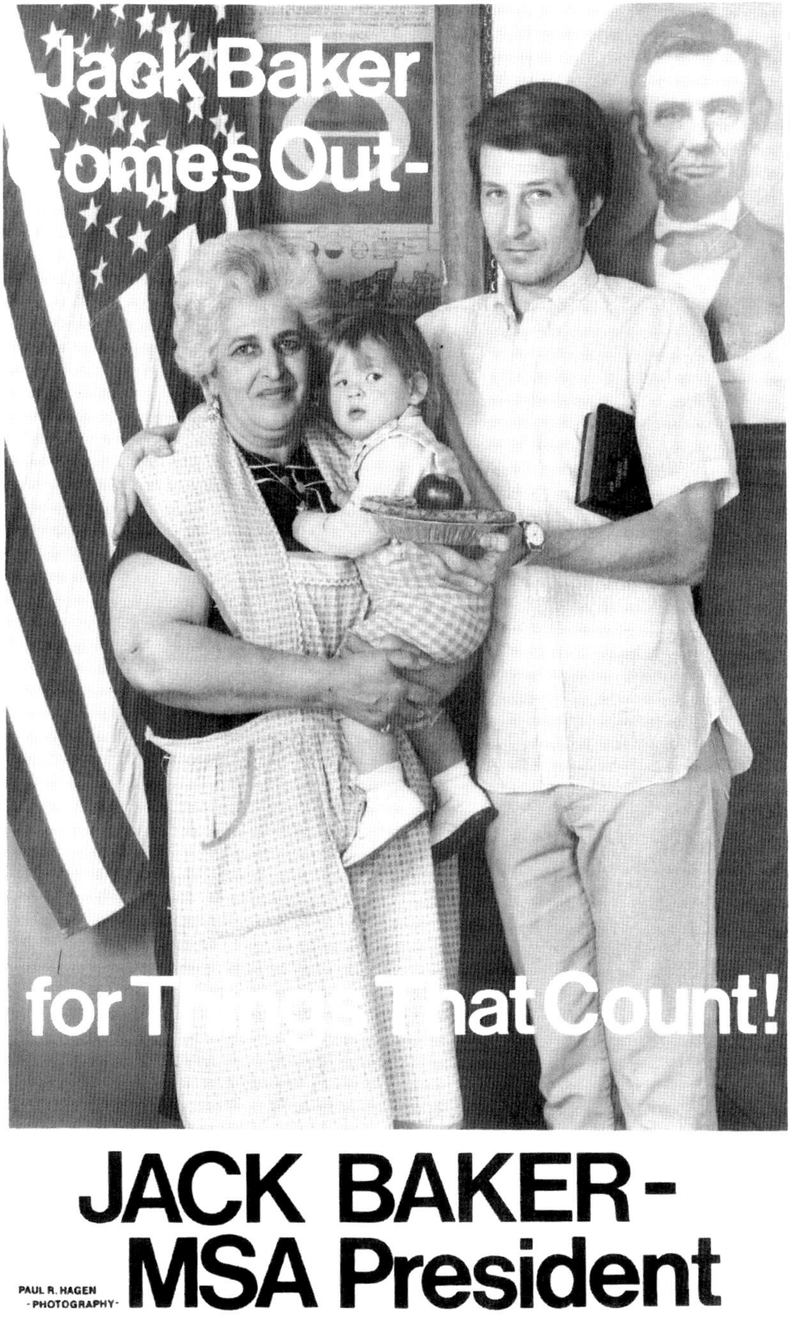

Mama D joined a collection of patriotic icons in this campaign poster for Jack Baker, the first openly gay student body president at the University of Minnesota. *Courtesy Jack Baker.*

When Jack Baker ran for president of the student body at the university in 1970, Mama D was on his poster to represent motherhood in a scene that included the candidate with her, a baby, a flag, an ecology flag, an apple pie and a picture of Lincoln. Baker was one half of the first married gay couple in the nation in the 1970s, when they found it very difficult to get their marriage recognized. Later, when Baker ran for city council, Mama D was on another poster for him emphasizing Dinkytown.

When the College Inn hotel became Dinkydale shopping center, journalists had some other nominations for Dinkytown characters. In the *Southeast Angle* neighborhood newspaper of November 1996, Jillian Myrom wrote, "The College Inn Hotel's awkward name is the first clue to its nature: while many rooms were open for rent on daily, weekly, and monthly bases, other rooms were kept by individuals for years, decades even. The rooms offered the basics, a bed, a sink, a window. Each floor had a communal bathroom, and Jennie's Boarding House on the first floor offered daily meals to hotel occupants and local students." Myrom reported that Donna and Orville Fair bought the hotel in 1946 and managed it until 1961. Summer tenants included a dredging crew working the Mississippi River, and winter residents included members of the Minneapolis Symphony, now the Minnesota Orchestra.

Myrom continued: "While Dinkytown teems with famous locals, some of whom continue their businesses in town—Dave the Barber, Tom the Tailor, Ed the Cleaner, Leroy the Mailman, Ralph the Newsman—the favorite tales of the College Inn Hotel involve lesser known characters who lived as supporting actors in the history of Dinkytown." One tenant, Helen Huntington, came from a wealthy West Coast family, and her rent checks came from a trust fund in California. "There was Maury Bernstein, the accordionist who played a weekly show on a local radio station. When he couldn't make the monthly rent he would leave his accordion as collateral with owners Maris and Linnea Grovendor, who owned the hotel from 1964 to 1971. The Grovendors quickly wised up and realized that without the accordion, Maury would be hard pressed to find the rent."

When the Fairs owned the hotel, rent ranged from eight to twelve dollars a night depending on the room. The Grovendors charged three to four dollars a night, eleven to thirteen dollars a week and thirty dollars a month. Two Dinkytown businessmen seeking more rental space purchased the building in 1971 and converted it from a fifty-two-room hotel into a shopping mall. The Dinkytown Antiquarian Bookstore occupied portions of the second and third floors in the 1990s; the Book House moved into the space in 2013.

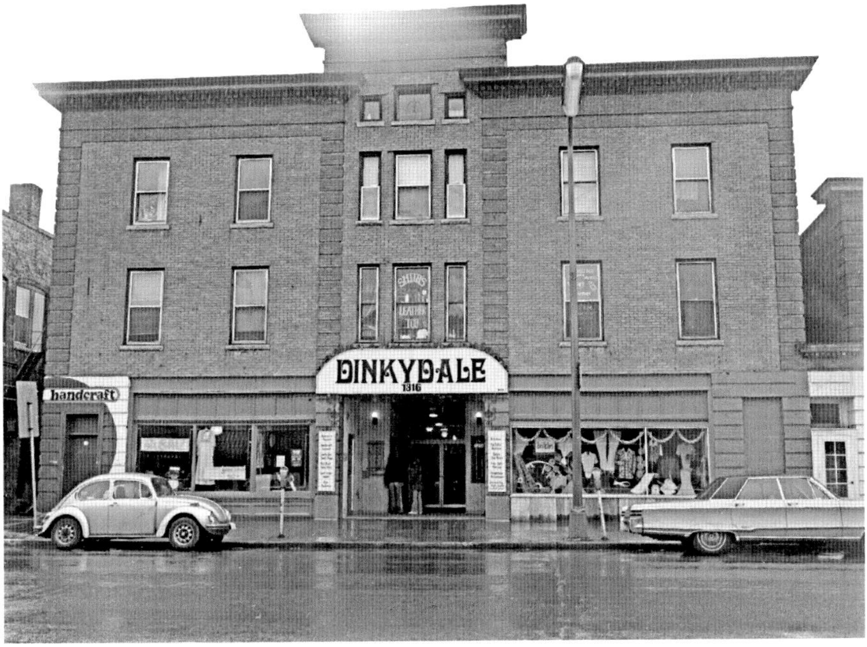

Dinkydale, once the College Inn hotel, has been converted to shops. In 2016, Dinkytown's last remaining bookstore was on the second floor. *Photo by Steven Bergerson.*

In the April 13, 1972 *Minneapolis Star*, Barbara Flanagan praised the developers who converted the College Inn to Dinkydale. "Jerry Manes, owner of the Campus Cobbler shoe store, and Phil Greenberg, who owns Britches, a sportswear shop, looked at Chicago's Old Town, San Francisco's Ghirardelli Square and many other refurbished old buildings before they did the job."

25

SOUTHEAST LIBRARIES

Will Southeast Minneapolis ever get a new community library? While some community residents complain that replacing the library at Dinkytown has been repeatedly delayed, county officials said planning for a new building could begin late in 2013. It didn't.

Then Hennepin County told Marcy-Holmes residents in February 2016 that it was beginning planning for construction in 2018. In early 2015, the county completed a report that summarized, from a series of neighborhood meetings, what area residents wanted to see in a library. The library at 1222 Fourth Street Southeast serves University of Minnesota students and residents of four adjacent neighborhoods: Marcy-Holmes, Como, University and Prospect Park/East River Road.

The current building across the street from Dinkytown's four blocks was widely perceived to be inadequate, even for a library open only three days a week. The building is not accessible for people with disabilities, and it lacks parking and necessary interior space.

A consultant's report said the current building could be rehabilitated for reuse, and some neighborhood residents say they'd like to preserve the building for historic reasons as an example of the late Ralph Rapson's modern architecture.

City and county officials often look at a map and say that because this neighborhood is adjacent to the university, residents have access to the libraries and athletic facilities at the university. This is not true. Residents do not have the same access as students and faculty to university libraries and other facilities. The Southeast Library has periodically been threatened with closure, but a citywide referendum to build a new downtown central library also promised to improve neighborhood libraries, including Southeast.

The Southeast Library serves diverse neighborhoods that include minorities and international students, says Southeast librarian Eric Heideman. "University students use it a lot," Heideman said. "It serves a very diverse group, including many different ethnic groups and cultures. There has been an increase in the number of parents with small children in recent years."

Heideman, who began as a children's librarian in 1998, became head librarian for the building in June 2001. He continues with weekly story time at 10:30 a.m. most Saturdays for families with children ages two and above. He also does story time and other programs scheduled to accommodate elementary schools within walking distance. Heideman takes pride in the science fiction collection—his personal favorite topic. He edits an occasional anthology of science fiction and essays called *Tales of the Unanticipated.* Because of the library's proximity to the university, he carries a collection of history, biography and popular science.

Books, DVDs and CDs from other libraries in the system can be paged for use and checked out at Southeast.

The Southeast Library building, designed by Minneapolis architect Ralph Rapson, opened in 1963 as the university branch of the State Capitol Credit Union, now Affinity Plus. Four years later, around Christmas 1967, the building, an example of modern architecture, became the Southeast Library.

Between 1904 and 1967, the Southeast Library was in the white marble Pillsbury building at 100 University Avenue Southeast on the corner of University and Central across the street from Chute Square. Since the library moved out, the building has housed the Dolly Fiterman Fine Arts Gallery, Phillips philanthropic foundation, the Doctors Diagnostic Laboratories and other offices.

The old marble building of Beaux-Arts design by architect Charles R. Aldrich was built for Minneapolis Public Library by philanthropist and university patron John S. Pillsbury.

"I developed the plan of giving the East Side a library which would be suited to the needs of the whole people," Pillsbury once told a historian. "Some of my friends do not like the site I have chosen, but I believe it is the best situated to serve the needs of the largest number." The Beaux-Arts style had recently been popularized by the 1893 World's Columbian Exposition in Chicago.

26

A TOUR OF DINKYTOWN

We have everything you need in Dinkytown!" So claimed Dinkytown businesses when they advertised their first contest in January 2004 with a folded poster that opened to a stylized relief map.

"Dinkytown Home to 'U'; It's the First Dinkytown Sweepstakes!" the poster said, before asking the reader to "Watch for Information About Winning a Stereo, CD Player, Color TV, plus many other great prizes. Contest Information will be posted in Dinkytown businesses by January 15, 2004."

Of those merchants, these remained in the same location a dozen years later in 2016: Chateau Student Co-op, Kafé 421, Dinkytown Wine & Spirits, Vescio's Italian Restaurant, McDonald's, Annie's Parlour, Loring Pasta Bar, the Refinery, Shuang Cheng Restaurant, Burrito Loco, Fast Eddie's, Varsity Bikes, Erik's Bikes, Gold Country, Camdi Restaurant, Library Bar & Restaurant, U.S. Post Office, U.S. Bank, Espresso Royale Caffé and the Steak Knife.

The following remained in Dinkytown but in different locations from 2004: Pizza Hut, Subway, TCF Bank, the Book House, Erbert's & Gerbert's and Purple Onion.

The artist of this relief map added some symbolism, such as books on top of the bookstores, to indicate the type of businesses in the buildings. And he sanitized the scene by removing any suggestion of the railroad tracks that run under the area.

Major differences between then and now can be seen on this poster. The building on the left across from McDonald's was once the Bridge Café,

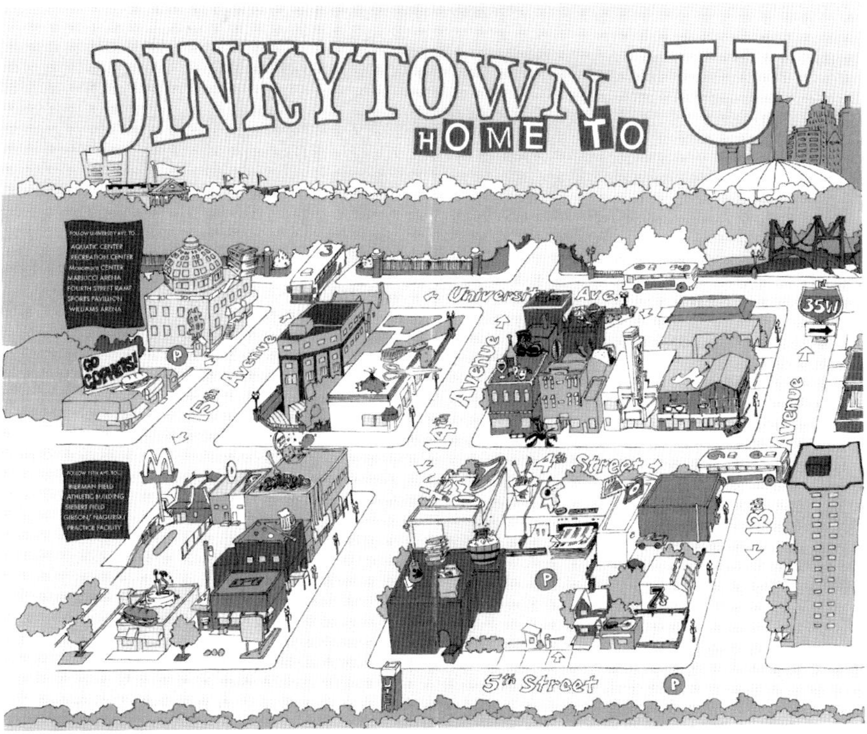

Dinkytown businesses used this poster to promote a contest celebrating their businesses. *Courtesy Skott Johnson, former president of Dinkytown Business Association.*

a classy restaurant with wood booths on the interior. Later it became the Bridge Steak House and then various coffee shops. In 2016, the site holds an apartment building and CVS pharmacy. The sandwich on the roof suggests Erbert's & Gerbert's sandwich shop that reopened in the new Sydney Hall after it was built. A washtub filled with suds sits on the Tub Laundry, a guitar on the Podium and a purple onion sticks out of the roof of what was then the Purple Onion.

On the left of the I-35W highway sign is a low building in red on the original poster. It was a Pizza Hut that replaced Koehler's Garage on that site. In the foreground along Fifth Street Southeast some smaller business buildings and surface parking remained. A chimney suggesting UTEC sticks out of trees in the foreground. Above the horizon on top are suggestions of the taller university buildings on the left and the Minneapolis skyline, with the old Humphrey Metrodome on the right.

Two boxes on the left give directions: the first says, "Follow University Avenue to Aquatic Center, Recreation Center, Mcnamara [*sic*] Center,

Mariucci Arena, Fourth Street Ramp, Sports Pavillion, Williams Arena," and the other says, "Follow 15th Ave. to Bierman Field, Athletic Building, Siebert Field, Gibson/Nagurski Practice Facility."

The emphasis on athletics here foreshadows a major university expansion that could further affect Dinkytown in the future. Over the years, athletic facilities have taken out neighborhood housing and, in recent decades, railroad yards and granaries. The TCF Bank Stadium in 2009 dramatically increased traffic to the university. Before it was built, Dinkytown business leaders feared dramatic increases in traffic. After it was completed, however, some complained how easily traffic moved through without ever seeing Dinkytown.

Police and students confronted one another dramatically around Dinkytown for the first time since the 1970s when social events or parties celebrating athletic contests got out of hand, particularly in 2009 and 2014. The fuel for these protests seemed to be alcohol rather than antiwar anger.

Headquarters for Gopher athletics began a major expansion in 2016 cater-corner from the McDonald's parking lot at Fifteenth Avenue and Fifth Street Southeast. Some sportscasters have even begun using the term Dinkytown to refer to the administration that makes policy or personnel changes in university athletics.

The overview of Dinkytown provided by aerial and architectural photographer Steven Bergerson in 2016 allows us to see the developing contrasts in the four blocks. A growing number of six- to eight-story mixed-use and apartment buildings can be seen surrounding Dinkytown.

Looking at the photo in the lower left is the Dome City on the corner of University and Fifteenth Avenues Southeast that's now a part of the apartment complex that includes Sydney Hall, the attached apartment building on the right in the foreground. The following tour is based on your following along with the aerial photo on page 169.

University Avenue Southeast is on the left and Fourth Street Southeast on the right of the two buildings. The trench—former railroad bed converted to the Dinkytown Greenway—starts on the lower right of the scene and goes diagonally under the intersection of Fourth and Fifteenth and, from there, under the Fourteenth Avenue Southeast Bridge. The railroad bed leaves the scene on the left as it's about to go under the University Avenue Bridge.

Dome City, on corner of University and Fifteenth Avenues Southeast, is the former site of the Minnesota Bible College. Businesses pictured in Linda Gammell's 1974 photo (see page 135) include Bikeways Bicycle Store, Card Rack Gift Store, Dome City Shopping Center, Ethiopian Exquisite

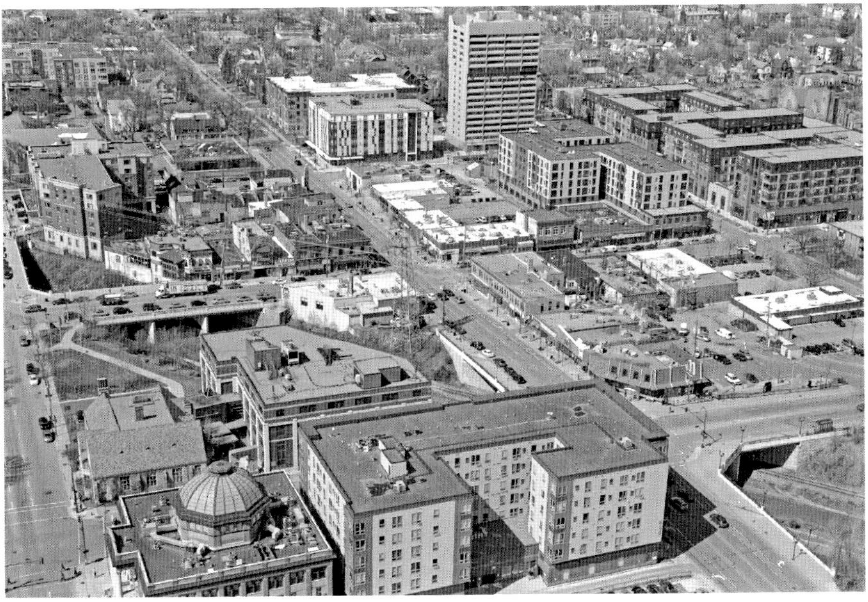

An aerial photograph of Dinkytown in early 2016 by architectural and aerial photographer Steven Bergerson.

Gift Store, Great Sound Audio Electronics Store, Sandy's Restaurant and Top Shop.

Street-level shops remain in the Dome City, but the second floor on which food venders, a coffee shop, a photocopy store and other retailers surrounded a circular atrium with a marble floor under the glass dome has become a common space for tenants of the apartment building.

Across Fifteenth from the Dome is the YMCA building from the 1920s that has become university offices. To the right and connected to that is the Donhowe building that used to be University of Minnesota shops along the railroad tracks. These two buildings have won the university an EPA Energy Star rating awards for energy efficiency.

Continuing along University from the old Y, there is a rectangle of grass where Perine Book Company and H.W. Wilson Company once stood in separate buildings. After the Wilson Company was demolished, a White Castle burger place once stood on that corner of University and Fourteenth Avenues Southeast between the bridge and the Pillsbury Gate entrance to the University of Minnesota campus—just out of sight on the left of the photo above.

Continuing on University across Fourteenth Avenue Southeast the trench where trains used to run below grade is on the right. One track was still used for access to rail-storage tracks in 2016, and a bicycle and pedestrian path and university service vehicle road also used the trench.

Across the tracks on the right is a brown-and-tan brick mixed-use apartment building at 1301 University Avenue Southeast. On the ground level is the current Purple Onion coffeehouse. This was the first midrise, mixed-use apartment building constructed within Dinkytown's four blocks. Across Thirteenth Avenue is the University Baptist Church of which only the roof is visible in the photo on page 169.

The site of the 1301 University building was once Koehler's Garage and with an adjacent service station on the corner. After Koehler's vacated the building, it became a Pizza Hut with a game room containing some of the earliest generation of coin-operated video games.

Returning to the lower right of the photo on page 169, you can follow Fourth Street Southeast through Dinkytown. On the left is Sydney Hall, the mixed-use building with a CVS Pharmacy on the corner of Fifteenth Avenue Southeast and other retail stores along the avenue toward the university.

Cater-corner from CVS is the two-story McDonald's with one entrance on Fourth Street and the other below grade at the parking lot and railroad level. McDonald's and its parking lot are on land once used by Swain's Transfer & Fuel Co. for storing horses, wagons and later trucks for its delivery and shipping business. The parking lot fills the rest of the block to Fifth Street Southeast (just out of view of this scene).

The only store facing Fifth Street in that block is Dinkytown Wine & Spirits in a building that once housed Meyer's grocery. Just beyond it is another surface parking lot in front of a structure that houses a Pizza Hut, Subway and TCF Bank on the site that once housed a Burger King. The building and parking lot replaced a half-block building that housed second-story apartments and street-level businesses, including a bookstore, a dry cleaners, a grocery store and the famous Scholar Coffee shop. To the left of that building, you can see the rear of Blarney's Pub and Vescio's Italian Restaurant.

Blarney's is on the address once used by Swain's, which backed against the space that McDonald's parking lot occupies on Fifteenth Avenue Southeast today. A barbershop once worked in the corner in the back of Blarney's building. Customers approached between the Burger King and what was then Valli Pizza with a basement restaurant called the Dinkytowner.

Coming back along Fourth Street Southeast toward McDonald's in the same building, there are addresses that once served Sammy D's restaurant and Bookhunters bookstore. Nelson's Office Supplies once was in the building that houses Pagoda Restaurant today between Five Guys and McDonald's.

Across Fourth Street is a white triangular building bounded by the railroad, Fourteenth Avenue and Fourth Street Southeast. In the 1960s, it housed Bridgeman's ice cream parlor, McCosh's Bookstore, Crane's Office Supply and Al Johnson's men's clothing. In 2016, it houses three restaurants facing Fourteenth: Potbelly sandwiches, Qdoba Mexican Grill and One Two Three Sushi, whose cartoon logo can be seen on the building above the railroad tracks.

Across Fourteenth Avenue Southeast (above the white building in the photo on page 169) is a building that has been Perine Book Company, an art supply company and a print shop—often at the same time. In 2016, it houses the Kitty Cat Klub on ground level and Annie's Parlour upstairs, which sells burgers, ice cream and beer.

On the right of it is a building that once housed a Bruegger's Bagel and Caribou Coffee on the ground level and a Kinko's copy shop in the basement entrance in the front of the building. All three of those businesses were favorite shops of mine—Kinko's usually late night at the last minute before an academic paper was due, and the other two in the morning on the walk to the campus. This building was constructed in 1984 after fire took out the previous building, which had included a travel agency and the Store, a women's clothing business.

On the right of that building, psychology professor Harlow S. Gale had this three-story Tudor Revival building designed by prominent Minneapolis architect Ernest Kennedy in 1910. His bachelor quarters above the Oak Tree Restaurant became a center for some radical campus thinkers in his day. Gale lived in the upper floors with retail on the street until he sold the building to Dayton's Department Store in 1928.

Continuing to the right on Fourteenth Avenue Southeast, the corner building from 1923 once housed the separate businesses of Dinky Town Dime and Gray's Drug, beginning about 1946. An earlier building constructed in 1902 was the Minneapolis Street Railway Company storage facility and station.

To the right across Fourth Street Southeast are buildings that look in the photo on page 169 like they have white roofs. On the corner is a small walk-in bank that was once a Fanny Farmer candy store. Comparing that block with the photos on page 132, you can see the same buildings in place with different uses today. The only consistent business on that side of Fourteenth Avenue Southeast is Al's Breakfast, which has been there since 1950.

From Fanny Farmer candy store, stores in the 1974 photos are Fanny Farmer, Minneapolis Contact Lens and Optical, Daniels Restaurant, Schaak Electronics/Simms Hardware (sharing the building), Al's Breakfast,

Podium Music Store and Tobacco Shop, an electronics store, Sports World sporting goods, Tub Laundry, the new brick House of Hanson building and Marshall-University High School across the street. Before the photos on pages 132 and 143 were taken, the Podium had been in a house on Fifth Street Southeast, and sometime after this picture, it moved into the newer House of Hanson building demolished in 2013.

St. Lawrence Catholic Church is adjacent to the Marshall on Fifth Street Southeast and, on the right of Marshall, you can see the University Lutheran Church of Hope across Sixth Street Southeast at the edge of the photo.

In the top right of the photo on page 169, Fifth Street Southeast moves between two newer taller buildings—the Venue on the left and the Marshall on the right—on the north edge of Dinkytown. At the end of that block is the Chateau Student Housing Co-op, the tallest building in Dinkytown and the first to break the low-density plan. Ironically, this building is roughly contemporary with the House of Hanson building that was limited by zoning to one story.

On the left of the Chateau is a six-story mixed-use apartment building opened in early 2016 under the same management as the Chateau. Across Fourth Street is the Ralph Rapson–designed library building with only the roof visible in the photo.

Moving west on Fourth Street Southeast is another mixed-use building on the site once occupied by the Wesley Society and later by the Minneapolis Free School and the Heart of the Earth, a Native American survival school.

Looking to the left from the top of the Chateau is a cluster of town houses that is barely visible. These town homes are Pillsbury Housing, which are available to graduate students and young faculty. They are on the site of John S. Pillsbury's mansion, which is where much of our Dinkytown story began.

BIBLIOGRAPHY

The best place to follow Dinkytown developments is the *Minnesota Daily*, where the student journalists are as good as any reporters you'll find anywhere. See also the *Star Tribune* of Minneapolis and MinnPost.com. The Marcy-Holmes.org website will also post dcvelopments occasionally, as will Preserve Historic Dinkytown and the Dinkytown Business Alliance. You can also follow the issues at the "Dinkytown Historic District Designation Study" page of the Minneapolis Community Planning & Economic Development website.

Albrecht, Donald, Andrew S. Dolkart and Seri Worden, eds. *Saving Place: 50 Years of New York City Landmarks*. New York: Museum of the City of New York and Monacelli Press, 2015.

Aleichem, Sholom. *The Old Country*. Translated by Julius and Frances Butwin. New York: Crown, 1946.

———. *Tevye's Daughters*. Translated by Frances Butwin. New York: Crown, 1949.

———. *Wandering Star: A Novel*. Translated by Frances Butwin. New York: Crown, 1952.

Andersen, Elmer L. *A Man's Reach*. Edited by Lori Sturdevant. Minneapolis: University of Minnesota Press, 2000.

Butwin, David. *A Minnesota Kid: In Search of Heroes and Ghosts.* Rockland: Maine Authors Publishing, 2012

Butwin, Joseph. "Tevye on King Street: Charleston and the Translation of Sholem Aleichem." *American Jewish History* 93, no. 2 (2007): 129–58.

Clifford, Geraldine Joncich. "Best Loved…and Besieged: Maris Louise Sanford, 1836–1929." In *Lone Voyagers: Academic Women in Coeducational Institutions, 1870–1937*. New York: Feminist Press of the City University of New York, 1989.

Collins, Cyn. *West Bank Boogie: Forty Years of Music, Mayhem and Memories.* Minneapolis: Triangle Park Creative, 2007.

Cott, Jonathan, ed. *Bob Dylan: The Essential Interviews*. New York: Wenner Books, 2006.

D'Agostino, Giovanna. *I'm Mama D: Shut Up and Listen, I Want to Tell You Something.* Minneapolis, MN: Nodin Press, 1992.

Dauber, Jeremy. *The Worlds of Sholem Aleichem: The Remarkable Life and Afterlife of the Man Who Created Tevye*. New York: Schocken, 2013.

Day, Holly, and Sherman Wick. *Walking Twin Cities*. 2nd ed. Birmingham, AL: Wilderness Press, 2013.

Diers, John W., and Aaron Isaacs. *Twin Cities by Trolley: The Streetcar Era in Minneapolis and St. Paul.* Minneapolis: University of Minnesota Press, 2007.

Dylan, Bob. *Chronicles Volume One.* New York: Simon and Schuster, 2004.

Felien, Ed. *Take the Streets.* Minneapolis, MN: Southside Pride, 2008.

Firkins, Oscar W. *Cyrus Northrop: A Memoir.* Minneapolis: University of Minnesota Press, 1925.

Folwell, William Watts. *William Watts Folwell: The Autobiography and Letters of a Pioneer of Culture*. Edited by Solon J. Buck. Minneapolis: University of Minnesota Press, 1933.

Glinter, Ezra. "Will the Real Sholem Aleichem Please Stand Up?" *Forward*, November 24, 2013. http://forward.com/culture/188007/will-the-real-sholem-aleichem-please-stand-up.

Gray, James G. *Open Wide the Door*. Minneapolis: University of Minnesota Press, 1958.

———. *The University of Minnesota 1851–1951*. Minneapolis: University of Minnesota Press, 1951.

Hiscock, Jennie I. *I Remember*. Whitehall, WI: Whitehall Printing Company, Dan Camp Press, [n.d., library number says 1976].

———. *I Remember Book II.* Brainerd, MN: Bang Printing, 1983.

Hofsommer, Don L. *Minneapolis and the Age of Railways*. Minneapolis: University of Minnesota Press, 2005.

———. *Tootin' Louie: A History of the Minneapolis and St. Louis Railway*. Minneapolis: University of Minnesota Press, 2005.

Johnson, E. Bird, ed. *Forty Years of the University of Minnesota.* Minneapolis, MN: General Alumni Association, 1910.

Kane, Lucile M. *The Waterfall That Built a City: The Falls of St. Anthony in Minneapolis*. St. Paul: Minnesota Historical Society, 1966.

Keillor, Steven J. *Grand Excursion: Antebellum American Discovers the Upper Mississippi*. Afton, MN: Afton Historical Society Press, 2004.

Lawler, John. *The H.W. Wilson Company: Half a Century of Bibliographic Publishing*. Minneapolis: University of Minnesota Press, 1950.

Lehmberg, Stanford, and Ann M. Pflaum. *The University of Minnesota 1945–2000*. Minneapolis: University of Minnesota Press, 2001.

Manfred, Frederick. *Duke's Mixture*. Sioux Falls, SD: Augustana College Center for Western Studies, 1994. Chapter 16, "Dinkytown," has been published as a pamphlet by Dinkytown Antiquarian Bookstore Dinkytown Antiquarian Bookstore.

———. "Hubert Horatio Humphrey a Memoir by Frederick Manfred." *Minnesota History*, Fall 1978: 86–101.

McConnell, Michael, and Jack Baker. *The Wedding Heard 'Round the World: America's First Gay Marriage*. Minneapolis: University of Minnesota Press, 2016.

Petersen, Penny A. *Hiding in Plain Sight: Minneapolis' First Neighborhood*. Minneapolis, MN: Marcy-Holmes Neighborhood Association, n.d.

Roberts, Sam. *Grand Central: How a Train Station Transformed America*. New York: Grand Central Publishing, 2013.

Smith, David C. *City of Parks: The Story of Minneapolis Parks*. Minneapolis, MN: Foundation for Minneapolis Parks, 2008.

Solomon, Alisa. *Wonder of Wonders: A Cultural History of Fiddler on the Roof*. New York: Picador, 2013.

Stern, Michael. "Tevye's Art of Quotation." *Prooftexts: Special Issue on Sholem Aleichem; The Critical Tradition* 6, no. 1 (January 1986): 79–96.

Storlie, Erik Fraser. *Go Deep & Take Plenty of Root*. Minneapolis, MN: self-published, 2013.

Sturdevant, Lori, with George S. Pillsbury. *The Pillsburys of Minnesota*. Minneapolis, MN: Nodin Press, 2011.

Swain, Tom H., with Lori Sturdevant. *Citizen Swain: Tales from a Minnesota Life*. Minneapolis: University of Minnesota Press, 2015.

Archivists Pat Coleman of the Minnesota Historical Society and Cecily Marcus of the Andersen Library at the University of Minnesota said they would welcome recollections, memorabilia and documents related to the area: https://www.lib.umn.edu/about/staff/cecily-marcus; MHS Link: http://www.mnhs.org/collections/donate.php.

ABOUT THE AUTHOR

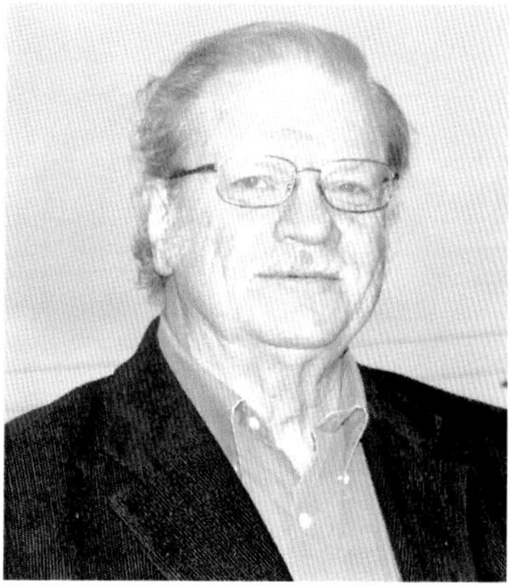

Bill Huntzicker, who grew up on a ranch and in small towns in Montana, has lived in Southeast Minneapolis for nearly fifty years. Huntzicker, who holds a doctorate in American studies from the University of Minnesota, is a writer and teacher of journalism. He's the author of *The Popular Press 1833–1865* (Greenwood Press, 1999) and numerous academic articles on nineteenth-century journalism.

About the Introduction Writer

Steven Bergerson is a graduate of the University of Minnesota who worked with fellow student Pat Flood researching the history of Dinkytown in the 1970s. Steve and Pat's research was donated to the University of Minnesota Archives.